James M. Wilson

Essays and Addresses

an attempt to treat some religious questions in a scientific spirit

James M. Wilson

Essays and Addresses
an attempt to treat some religious questions in a scientific spirit

ISBN/EAN: 9783337266561

Printed in Europe, USA, Canada, Australia, Japan

Cover: Foto ©Lupo / pixelio.de

More available books at **www.hansebooks.com**

ESSAYS AND ADDRESSES

ESSAYS AND ADDRESSES

AN ATTEMPT

TO TREAT SOME RELIGIOUS QUESTIONS

IN A SCIENTIFIC SPIRIT

BY THE

VEN. JAMES M. WILSON, M.A.

LATE HEADMASTER OF CLIFTON COLLEGE;
VICAR OF ROCHDALE; ARCHDEACON OF MANCHESTER

London

MACMILLAN AND CO.

AND NEW YORK

1894

First Edition 1887
Second Edition 1894

PREFACE TO THE SECOND EDITION

IT is a great satisfaction to me to have learned that a cheap edition of this volume has been wanted. It deals exclusively with principles, and is not, I think, out of date ; and in revising it for the press I have not found it necessary to make any alterations.

THE VICARAGE, ROCHDALE,
October 1894.

PREFACE TO THE FIRST EDITION

MOST of the addresses in this volume have been printed before in fugitive shape, and are now reprinted in nearly chronological order, with very slight alterations. It will be found, I think, that they have a certain unity of purpose,—an attempt to state clearly the results of reflection on some questions connected with religion in its present intellectual aspects. Some of these lectures in their pamphlet form interested the few persons into whose hands they found their way, and I hope that they may now be helpful to a wider circle of readers, who are occupied with the same questions.

The Letter to a Bristol Artisan was privately circulated for reasons stated in the opening pages of the letter. But those reasons are not now equally valid, and in deference to some opinions for which I have the highest respect, I have included it in the volume.

With reference to the lecture on Stoicism, I wish to disclaim any first-hand knowledge of Seneca, and all but a slight acquaintance with the other Stoic writers in the original. Those readers who know C. Martha's *Moralistes sous l'Empire Romain* will see that I have used that excellent essay largely.

J. M. WILSON.

CLIFTON COLLEGE,
May 1887.

CONTENTS

WATER

SOME PROPERTIES AND PECULIARITIES OF IT ; A CHAPTER IN NATURAL THEOLOGY [1]

On the many occasions on which I have had the honour to lecture before your society, I have chosen as my subject some branch of astronomy, or physics, or meteorology, and have endeavoured to put before you in a clear and elementary manner the methods and results of scientific investigation. But on the present occasion my aim is somewhat different: I have not only to lay before you some scientific facts, which are, however, probably familiar to many of my audience, but I intend to explain what appears to me to be the true philosophy of these and many similar facts. I think that as I have so often lectured before you on science, you have a sort of right to know from what point of view I regard scientific knowledge ; how it fits in with other knowledge ; and as this is probably the last lecture I shall give here, I may well select this subject for this evening's work.

I may remind you, further, that you are not a scientific but a philosophical society ; and therefore I need make no apology for passing somewhat beyond the bounds

[1] Delivered before the Nottingham Literary and Philosophical Society, 22nd of March 1877, in the Mechanics' Hall, and published at the request of the President. Reprinted from the Second Edition. A. J. Lawrence, Rugby.

usually imposed on science, and travelling into regions
outside.   I am indeed well aware that just at the present
time science is familiar and fashionable, and philosophy
is unfamiliar and out of fashion; but this is not a durable
state of opinion.   It is the intense desire to penetrate
behind mere sequences as revealed by science to the
modus operandi and the Cause and Author of all, that keeps
up, consciously or unconsciously, the eager pursuit of
science.   It is not utility, and not curiosity, and not the
love of mere intellectual exercise, that induces men to
spend toilsome days and nights in researches; it is
the instinct that somehow and somewhen toil will be
rewarded, to our successors if not to ourselves, by a clearer
insight into the mystery of the universe.

My lecture then consists of two distinct parts: the first
part is purely a matter of science and exposition as to the
properties of water, dealing only with facts and verifiable
conclusions; and, as usual, I shall be glad at the close of
the lecture to answer questions or clear up points which I
may have left obscure: the second part is a theory, or
mode of viewing facts, containing inferences from them
which, to my mind, carry with them preponderating weight
of evidence, though from their very nature they are incapable of absolute demonstration.   To offer to answer
questions on this part would be to place myself in a totally
wrong position with reference both to yourselves and my
subject.   No one can speak authoritatively on such matters,
and least of all the present speaker to the present
audience, and I therefore hope it will not be misunderstood if I attempt no reply to any discussion which may
arise on the second part of my lecture.

First, then, as to the facts.   I wish to lay before you
some brief comprehensive sketch of the chief properties of
water, and to show how marvellously these properties fit
into the general economy of the world.   The world may
be looked on, in one aspect, as a vast and wonderful
machine; and one of the most important parts of the
mechanism is *water*.   I want to make you admire more
than ever the perfection of this part of the mechanism of

the world: and to admire one must understand, one must
have a certain degree of familiarity with the mechanism.

First, then, water has the property, in common with
other bodies, of *expansion* with heat. Warm water is
lighter than cold: I think we should be puzzled to explain
the mechanism by which heat effects this result. We are
too familiar with it, perhaps, to have even thought about
it. But consider what the effect of this expansion is, how
necessary, we may say, in order that the world should be
what it is. The surface of the ocean in tropical regions
is warmed by the sun, and being warmed is made light;
it rises to the top and flows away over the surface like oil
over water, to north and south. The great Gulf Stream
and the whole system of oceanic currents is due to this
fact. The expansion of water by heat is a necessary
condition for the existence of these currents, which bring
warmth from the equator to our northern shores, among
others, and in return supply cold currents to the equatorial
regions. This property water shares with other substances.
It may be said to be a law of nature, uniformly true, that
inorganic substances expand when heated.

But experiment shows that in one property of expansion
water is unique, absolutely unique. All other liquids,
without exception, as they get colder contract until they
solidify. Water alone is an exception. As it cools down,
and approaches 40° F., its rate of contraction diminishes,
and at 40° F. it ceases to contract. If it is further cooled
it begins to *expand:* and expands more and more till it
reaches 32° F., and then under ordinary circumstances it
freezes.

What the peculiarity of the mechanism of a drop of
water is that produces this effect we are absolutely unable
even to guess. But such an exception to an otherwise
invariable law must be produced by some very singular
property of the molecules of water and of their relations
to heat.

But we can trace the result of this peculiarity. Consider a lake cooling down as winter approaches. The
surface is cooled, and the surface water is consequently

heavier, and it therefore sinks, and warm water rises to
take its place.   This vertical circulation will go on as long
as the surface water becomes heavier by becoming colder.
It will, therefore, in the single case of water, stop before
the whole of the lake is reduced to the temperature of
freezing : it will stop when both the surface and the rest
of the lake have reached the temperature of 40° F.   Then
the surface water, as it is further cooled by winter, will
become lighter, and will float on the top, and will
ultimately be cooled down, if the winter is severe enough,
to its freezing point, and we shall have a layer of ice over
comparatively warm water.   The use of this, as we find it,
in preservation of animal life in the water, is obvious.

But water not only expands in this unique way before
it freezes, but in the act of freezing it undergoes a sudden
and large further expansion.   It shares this property with
a very few other substances, as iron, bismuth, and anti-
mony.   It is to this property of iron that we owe, it is
said, the possibility of casting it.   As it solidifies it expands
and fills the moulds; whereas a casting in lead would
shrink, and leave vacant places.   The consequence of this
property of water is that ice *floats*.   Hence the surface
only of lakes and the sea freezes, the ice itself serving as a
barrier to protect the warm water below from further cold.
If water did not possess these rare and singular physical
properties that I have described, many lakes and parts of
the sea would in winter time be converted into one mass
of ice, and animal life in them perish.

The expansion of water in freezing plays a considerable
part too in geological action, helping to break up rock and
renew the soil which is constantly removed by rain.

Think next of *evaporation*.   What a wonderful thing it
is that water, a liquid, should dissolve as it were in air,
and take the invisible form of vapour !   Which of us
understands how it is done ?   The vapour rises and interpenetrates the air, and diffuses itself to all heights, and all
distances.

And what is the use of the vapour ?   It is this that
solves the great problem of supplying water to all the dry

land however far above the sea, or far in the interior of
continents. From all water, salt or fresh, vapour rises ;
its lightness, which is extraordinary, makes it a great
motive power in the atmosphere ; on the winds that it
thus helps to cause it is borne over the land, and con-
denses against the colder heights, and so produces rain,
that phenomenon which never fails to excite the admiration of true lovers of nature. When we think of the
mechanism that is necessary to supply a town with water,
its failures, its costliness, let us think also of the mechanism
which supplies all the world with water, with perfectly pure
water, and admire these drops that water the earth, and
form the rivers that run among the hills.

And what a wonderful thing the *liquidity* of water is.
What a singular adjustment there is between the pressure
of the atmosphere, and mean temperature of the air, and
the rate of evaporation. All the properties of water would
be of no use if there were no pressure on it. The water
would rise wholly into vapour ; it would sublime from ice :
and we should know water, as we know iodine, in the
forms of ice and vapour, but in the liquid state only as a
curious result of experiment. It is curious to reflect that
the liquidity of water depends on the mass and size of the
earth, and the quantity of uncombined gases that form
our atmosphere, and our mean distance from the sun.
These elements are adjusted to one another in such
manner as to produce the actual result we see.

Let us now consider some other singular relations of
water to heat. Bodies differ among themselves very much
in the quantity of heat they take to warm them. A pound
of mercury, or a pound of iron, would get hot when placed
over a fire, or in the sun, very much quicker than a pound
of water. In fact, when physicists investigate this property of bodies, they find that water is once more *unique*.
Its specific heat, as this property is called, is far greater
than that of all other bodies, solid or liquid.

The importance of this property is plain. It does not
get heated so quickly by the sun as every other substance
would in its place, but when so heated it carries more

heat, and gives out more heat when it cools. All the machinery of oceanic currents would be valueless but for this additional property of water. How can warm water be transferred from the Gulf of Mexico to the shores of Norway? We should say it must be very hot at starting to retain any heat for so long. But that would be inconsistent with the habitability of the Gulf of Mexico and all the tropics: or it must travel very fast, with a very rapid current, causing much inconvenience and difficulty. But no—the object is otherwise accomplished. Water has the power of absorbing and carrying heat to an unequalled amount, and thus without having its temperature unduly raised in the tropics, and without being conveyed very rapidly, it can be conveyed thousands of miles, and part with its heat all the way, and yet retain no inconsiderable supply of heat at the end.

What philosopher can tell us by what internal mechanism the constitution of water is such that it can so store up heat? But it can do this, and so it equalises the temperature of the earth to a degree which it is difficult exactly to estimate, but which is certainly great. Heat is taken from the tropics and conveyed to the rest of the earth. Water not only constitutes the heating apparatus of the world, in virtue of its commonness and its expansion, but it possesses the one exceptional property which makes it fit to be so used.

There is another relation to heat in which, once more, water is quite *unique*. It takes a certain quantity of heat to melt a solid. A lump of lead in a ladle over a fire gets hotter and hotter until it begins to melt. While it is melting the temperature is stationary, and the heat that is being poured into it is spent in melting it. Ice, like other solids, can only be melted by heat being thus, as it were, poured into it. But of all solids ice requires far the greatest amount of heat to melt it.

The consequences of this peculiarity are plain. The vast accumulations of snow in the winter would all melt in the first days of warm weather, of weather in which the thermometer rises above the freezing point, but for this extraordinary latent heat, as it is called, of water. The floods that would follow in all regions where snow lies through the winter would be such as to destroy everything. The snowfall of months would have to be discharged in a few days or hours.

Another less obvious consequence is, that in extreme cold the very freezing of water gives out heat. As much heat is given out by a pound of water as it freezes as would raise it 140° F. This sounds like a paradox, I fear; but it is true, and this singular property of water greatly mitigates the cold of the Arctic and sub-Arctic regions. The cold is expended on freezing the water instead of in lowering the temperature still further.

And in the other great transformation of water, from the liquid to the vaporous state, it is as exceptional as it is in all the relations already mentioned. All liquids require the expenditure of some heat to evaporate them, but none approaches water in the quantity that it requires. It is surprising to reflect that as much heat is required to evaporate a pound of water as would raise 960 lbs. 1° F., or raise more than 5 lbs. from freezing to boiling. And experiment shows that all this heat is stored up in the vapour, and is all given out again when the vapour is once more converted into water. A little steam turned into a vessel of water will make it boil. One pound of steam will boil 5 lbs. of ice-cold water. And we can trace the use of this extraordinary latent heat of vapour, though we cannot explain it. The sun pours its heat on the water in the tropics, and not only warms it, but evaporates it. A larger quantity of heat is spent on evaporation than on mere warming. With this vast store of heat the vapour is borne away by the winds, and as it is converted into rain by cold, it gives up then, precisely where it is wanted, where it is cold, its store of heat. Every gallon of rain that falls has yielded to the atmosphere that surrounded the place where it was condensed as much heat as would raise 5⅓ gallons from freezing to boiling. This has been a wet winter. Yes; and it has been a very warm winter. As much heat is given out to the county by the fall of

15 inches of rain as would be obtained if all the coal raised in England were burned within the year in the county of Nottingham.

What heating apparatus is comparable to aqueous vapour! it retains its stores of heat, itself not being hot, and discharges them where and when the heat is most needed. If one were set to invent a heating apparatus which should convey heat from one part of the world to another, on condition that the body conveying the heat should itself be cool, how should we think it possible? Yet aqueous vapour is doing it every day of our lives. And what subtle mechanician will tell us how aqueous vapour does all this? What is the mystery of a drop of water?

This is the great agency by which climates are equalised. In the tropics the heat is spent, disappears with the vapour: by the no less wonderful methods before described the vapour flies over the earth; and the identical quantity of heat expended in the tropics reappears along with the gracious rain in distant lands, and wintry climes, and on inland mountains, where water and heat are the two essentials for life and habitability.

Then, again, think of the formation of dew. Under cloudless skies, where rain rarely falls, even there an arrangement exists by which every leaf has its allowance of water night after night. It would take me too long to go into this, or indeed any part of the subject, fully; I can only remind you of it, and suggest it for consideration as one of the wonderful and beneficent properties of water.

There is one more relation of water to heat as singular as all the rest; its power of absorption of radiant heat. If we proposed to make "a trap to catch a sunbeam,"— to use the title of a book I remember,—some contrivance which should catch sunbeams, the idea would seem worthy of the philosophers of Laputa. But aqueous vapour is the very trap we want. This is one of the results of Tyndall's investigations of some years ago, and was quite unexpected. The sun pours down its radiant heat on the earth. The radiant heat passes through our air and the vapour that interpenetrates the air, and strikes the earth and warms it. The vapour then is transparent to the heat that comes from the sun, and lets it through. The warmed earth, in its turn, radiates its heat upwards. At night, when the cold clear air is over the earth, heat is pouring out from all the surface; and the air, apart from vapour, is almost perfectly transparent to this heat. But here a new property of aqueous vapour steps in. Aqueous vapour will not let the heat radiated from the earth pass through. It absorbs it; it serves as a covering, as a light but warm blanket to the earth at night. We can see its effect in general from observing what takes place in the few places on the earth where it is only present in small quantities; there at night the temperature falls greatly, and bitter nights follow scorching days. This would be the rule, be universal, and not the rare exception, but for this singular and beautiful property of water. As this property is perhaps less familiar than the others I have mentioned, I will give some particulars which will show how singular it is. Vapour is perfectly transparent to light or luminous heat rays; it does not occupy more perhaps than $\frac{1}{200}$ of the space occupied by the air; that is, it is present in very small proportion, and yet it stops, according to the researches of Professor Tyndall, more than 100 times as much heat as all the air together,— 20,000 times as much as an equal quantity of air. So opaque is it to heat that no inconsiderable portion of the heat radiated from the earth is stopped within the first 30 or 40 feet: probably not less than half. To mention one more fact in this connection: aqueous vapour is opaque to heat radiated from all kinds of warm, but not very hot, bodies; but to heat radiated from wet bodies it is quite exceptionally opaque. Hence when dew is once formed, the heat that is given up by further radiation is detained close to the surface.

The vapour of water acts, then, in a very extraordinary way. Just as glass lets the heat of the sun through, but will screen you from the heat of the fire, so aqueous vapour

admits and then detains the heat of the sun. The
temperature of our planet is higher, as well as very much
more equable, than it would be but for this singular
property of vapour.

The chemical properties of water would open a vast
field. Its powers of dissolving salts, and of fertilising soil,
are perhaps the most extraordinary; and I will mention
these only. The value of vegetable soil for producing
plants depends of course on the salts that it contains.
The soil must contain potash, and silicic acid, and
ammonia, and phosphates, etc., in order that plants may
grow. Now rain dissolves all these. Why then does not
the rain as it passes through the soil dissolve all these
precious salts out of the soil, and carry them to the rivers
and thence to the sea? Why do the floods on the water
meadows, and the artificial irrigation, not take away all
fertility from the soil? This no one can answer. But
Liebig, I remember, declares that soil can extract these
salts from water that contains them, but that water cannot
dissolve them out of soil. They are held by the soil, and
will not be given up. That great solvent here loses its
power. What has not water done in the past history of
the earth? The records of Geology are mainly the history
of the work of water. But to speak of this would perhaps
be beside the mark to-night.

One more peculiarity, however, I must mention: the
relation of water to light. Whence comes the deep azure
of the sky? Whence come the gorgeous colours of sun-
rise and sunset? a never-failing beauty, and source of
pleasure and admiration and awe. They are all due to
some action, probably reflective and diffractive, which
minute suspended globules of water exercise on the com-
posite light that falls on it.

What miracle of mechanism is concealed in a molecule
of water that shall make it perform these various offices
I have detailed: that shall make the drop expand with
heat, but yet expand again to its freezing point; that shall
make it expand as it freezes, and give up so much heat as
it does so; that shall enable it to evaporate and diffuse

itself over all heights and all distances from the sea, and whether as liquid or vapour have the power of storing up in itself such unequalled quantities of heat: and at the same time be a shield to protect the earth from the loss of heat; and while it does all this, and more than I or any man can say, it brings also the indescribable beauty of summer clouds, and rainbows, and sunsets, and all the pageantry of the sky?

When *men* invent a machine, they invent one that does one, or perhaps two things; but here is a machine, a drop of water, that quietly and unceasingly performs its thousand offices, and we know not how: we can only wonder. But let us wonder with intelligence. An intensely stupid man once said of some marvel which a friend was going to explain, "Don't tell me: I don't like to know: I like to wonder." That is the climax of stupid wonder. Should we wonder less or more if we could magnify a drop to such a size that we could study its mechanism as we can study the parts of a watch?

This is exactly what the greatest physicists of our day are doing: and I do not think it will diminish your wonder and admiration of a drop of water if I give you some of their results. It is not a subject I have studied at first hand, and I am doing little more than quote from Professor Tait's *Recent Advances in Physical Science*, and from papers by Maxwell.

Many eminent workers, such as Bernouilli, and Lesage, and Joule, and Maxwell, and Thomson, and Clausius, and Boltzmann, have endeavoured to find out whether water is the uniform homogeneous substance it appears to our eyes to be, or whether, just as a sandstone consists of grains of sand, so a drop of water, if sufficiently magnified, would be seen to consist of grains, not further divisible. They have come to the conclusion that these grains do really exist. They are called molecules of water, and it is possible within certain not very large limits of error to ascertain their size and their distances apart.

Four methods are used for this purpose, none of which, however, are sufficiently simple for me to venture to attempt to explain them on this occasion. No more interesting subject could be suggested as a subject for a lecture. One is, by the electricity developed by contact of two metals ; another, from the dispersion of light in a prism ; another, by the tension of soap bubbles ; and the last, from the laws of diffusion and friction of gases. But all these various methods concur in fixing the size of a molecule of water as about one-500,000,000th of an inch in diameter. This number is so large that we find a difficulty in deriving any idea from it. A clearer conception can be got by supposing, as Thomson does, a drop of water to be magnified until the grain becomes visible. Let it be magnified until a drop the size of a pea is as large as the earth itself. The molecules then would be about as large as cricket balls. The limits of error are such that it may be pretty confidently asserted that they would be larger than shot, but not so large as footballs.

To express the number of such molecules in a drop almost surpasses the power of figures. It amounts to not far from a million million million millions.

It is these molecules that dart from the surface of water and make vapour. They penetrate among the molecules of air, in incessant motion, like gnats in a swarm dancing in a summer evening ; they fly with a velocity that can be computed, exceeding that of the swiftest cannon-shot, 20 miles a minute, for the distances, almost inconceivably small, that separate molecules, and have their directions altered by collisions thousands of millions of times in a second.

I will not endeavour to impress this further ; and will only make one remark on it. It is the properties not of cubic inches of water, or of drops of water, but of these infinitesimal molecules that we have been studying. It is these whose motions are quickened by heat, so that they take more room and expand ; and it is from some at present inconceivable property of these molecules that at one part of the thermometric scale heat does *not* expand them, but contracts them. It is these that rearrange themselves in exquisite crystalline order as ice ; these that evaporate, and carry with them stores of heat. These molecules are unalterable, permanent. They are incapable of growth or decay or destruction. We can conceive no origin for them but creation. And I say that there is nothing more truly wonderful, nothing that fills the mind of any one who is intelligent enough to grasp what I have described with more of awe, admiration, and reverence, than the constitution and properties of a drop of water and its molecules.

There is neither great nor small in the universe. We call astronomical distances great, because they are large compared with our own bodies; we call the diameter of the molecules of water small, because they are small by the same standard. But if we can conceive a mind that judges by no such standard, there is neither great nor small. The universe and its myriad suns may not be more to such a mind than a drop of water and its myriads of molecules. We judge of time by the duration of our lives, by our faculties; and we call the secular cycles of astronomy long; and the intervals between the collisions of the molecules of vapour short: but each alike is time; and what happens in time and space, whether great or small, is subject to the same mathematical laws.

I have now concluded the first part of my lecture. There are some, perhaps, to whom I have told a thrice-told tale; but to most of you who have heard me I trust I have given some new and interesting information,—information so interesting as almost to be exciting; to fill the mind; to make it desire and crave for some further view of these wondrous properties of water and their origin.

I proceed now to what may be called the philosophy, as distinguished from the science, of these matters.

It is not possible to study questions of Physical Science systematically and thoroughly without introducing the ideas of effect and cause. Our minds are so constituted that we cannot accept such facts as I have enumerated without seeking to colligate them, and ascertain their cause if possible. We may, for special purposes, and for a time, debar our thoughts from travelling in this direction ;

but only for a time. The thought will recur. Addison indeed said that we know enough of water when we know how to boil, how to freeze, and how to evaporate it; and Paley endorses the remark with his approval. But neither of them then spoke like a philosopher. For mere material use we do not require much more; but for the higher use of Nature, as a subject of thought, we do require to know more. For we cannot be misled in thinking that we know something of Nature: our minds are in sympathy with it; they have something in common with it; the riddle is partly read, and we are irresistibly compelled to study in hope of reading more. It is therefore from the necessities of the case that some philosophy of these subjects has to be constructed, and Natural Theology is such a philosophy. We all of us, I suppose, think somehow on these matters, and Natural Theology is an attempt to think carefully and systematically about the world on a certain line of thought as to its origin and design; a line that appears to be indicated by reason.

At the present time Natural Theology is somewhat discredited, and for several reasons. First, the sort of progress that science has been lately making is adverse to the popular theological view. Science has been busy tracing causes farther and farther back into vistas which seem interminable: and secondly, theologians have relinquished this field, on which they have suffered some defeats, and have occupied themselves with other studies: and thirdly, the old and standard works on Natural Theology are no longer worthy of the subject. No philosophy of Nature can profess to be complete without dealing with the supremest questions, suggested by Nature as a whole, as to the Author and Object of the world. And yet where do such philosophies exist? My first advice to a student of Natural Theology would be to read no books on the subject. The Franciscan friars, I have been told, were forbidden to read books, and, in consequence, instead of repeating ten-times-told falsehoods in medicine and science, they studied Nature herself at first hand, and laid the foundations of experimental science.

There are times in the history of all sciences when this is the necessary condition of progress, and perhaps Natural Theology is now in this state.

The popular notion of Natural Theology is derived from Paley and the Bridgewater Treatises. Paley's philosophy is briefly as follows. He supposes a man to pick up a watch on a heath: he observes the arrangement and adaptation of its parts to perform certain purposes: and from this he concludes that it had a maker. The watch of course represents some animal structure; the eye, the ear, or the arrangement of muscles; and from the adaptation shown in those structures, design is inferred: and there cannot be a design without a designer.

There are limitations in his view, and defects in his reasoning which I need not criticise, as it is not in consequence of logical defects that his book, brilliant and interesting as it is, is felt to be superseded. The truth is, his flank has been turned. *Adaptation does not always imply design:* and this vitiates his whole argument.

This point is so important that I shall give a few examples.

Consider how perfectly a river bed is adapted to the work it has to do. Placed at the lowest part of the valley, with gentle slope, with depth and width increasing as the river increases, provided with countless small channels that supply it, and regulated by the absorbing power of soil, or by lakes, and suited in size to the rainfall of the district. It would be easy to point out in detail exquisite adaptations. Yet they prove no design. The river bed was not made *for* the water, but *by* the water. No moral cause was at work on it; it was moulded by circumstances.

So again, admitting a certain degree of variability of colour and habits in animals, no conclusion can be drawn from the admirable adaptation of some animals to their environment; the adaptation may not be prior to the circumstances, but the result of the circumstances. The wonderful structure of animals and plants may be to some extent not the result of a moral cause, but the result of circumstances.

It is quite impossible in the present condition of science to draw a line between those structures which we may say, I hope without fear of being misunderstood, are the result of circumstances, and those which are not so produced, but must have had a cause of a different kind. And without attempting to do so, it is plain, which is all I want for my purpose, that the development of Natural History under Darwin and Wallace is thought to have destroyed a considerable part of what used to be thought legitimate materials for Natural Theology, and has cast doubt, for the present, on much of the rest.

This is, I think, the reason why Natural Theology is at present neglected; it is at present uncertain what share of its territory will have to be ceded to its younger sister, Evolution, which is regarded as a rival theory. What the true relation of these two doctrines is would be most interesting to examine, but has no reference to this evening's work. I am certainly not prepared to admit any inconsistency between the doctrine of Evolution and the fundamental truths of Theology. This evening, however, we are discussing the unchangeable properties of water. No one imagines that water is an evolved product, or that it has acquired by any development its present properties. Such as it is, it always was. The inorganic elements of Nature represent to my mind the original foundation, the materials of the stage on which the magnificent drama of Evolution is unfolding itself, and exhibiting in operation the ideas of the Creator. And I cannot help seeing how marvellously these original, unchanged, and unchangeable properties of water contribute to making this earth the suitable place it is for the development of life and of man. The original Oxygen and Hydrogen of our globe, dissociated, it may have been, by intense heat, contained potentially all the properties of which I have spoken : all the world, Life and Mind only excepted, is the result of the properties of a few inorganic elements, and is implicitly contained in them.

Limiting, then, our view to the argument derived from the unchangeable inorganic parts of Nature, of which water is an example, the stages of the argument are briefly as follows. We rise successively, and, I think, inevitably, from the perception of *order* to that of *fitness:* and fitness passes into *adaptation.* From this we infer, in these cases of adaptation of the unchangeable, *intelligence* and *design.* Design implies *Mind* and *Will;* and Mind and Will are nothing but *Personality.*

I need not dwell on the existence of order in the universe. The uniformity of sequence, the majesty of natural laws, impress every mind profoundly. Some are indeed oppressed, and are thrown off their balance, by the pitiless rigour of order in Nature; but none doubt it or ignore it.

But the fact of order is no sufficient account of the origin of order; and we are compelled to see more than order: we see fitness; we see appropriateness of means to ends. It is not by one of our five senses that we perceive this, but by a power of our reason that we cannot do away with or discredit. The eye *is* fitted to see with; the ear to hear with; water *is* fitted to perform the varied functions I have described.

But we cannot stop at fitness. When we perceive a harmony of power and function, a mechanism accomplishing results, we infer that the harmony was not accidental, that the fitness is made; or, in other words, we infer adaptation. If we are wrong in inferring this, our whole intelligence is untrustworthy, and we are the laughing-stock of that Nature of which we are, in a certain sense, a part.

What the adapting forces are is a matter for investigation. In the formation of the curves of a shore-line and the slope of the sand the force is the sea. In the colours of birds it may be natural and sexual selection. It was legitimate for Topsy, in reflecting on her origin, to "spec she growed." But what is the adapting cause in the case of water?

It is contrary to all evidence to imagine an evolution of such properties. We conclude, therefore, that we are here face to face with no secondary cause, but with a primal cause, a cause of a different species, moral not physical.

And in this we cannot but recognise intelligence. Precisely the same faculty we exercise in the appreciation must have been exercised in a vastly higher degree in the operation of that cause to which are due the various properties from the combination of which so much follows. We infer intelligence, resource, foresight, design.

There is, of course, an inherent difficulty in all Teleology to distinguish between purpose and concomitance, between the design and some accident accompanying the execution of the design ; or, as Huxley puts it, to mistake the ticking of the clock for the object of the clock. It will not, indeed, fail to occur to you that if we completely understood the molecular structure of water, we might be able to see that all the properties of it are necessary consequences of some one single property. But the argument does not therefore lose weight, as if there was only one wonder to account for instead of many; there is one wonder which includes many. And it would be vain to say that perhaps after all this single property of molecules, from which all the properties of water are supposed to follow, has some quite different object, as different from the results we see, as time-keeping is from ticking. For, while liable to error in judging of final causes in individual instances, we cannot suppose that we are in error in contemplating all ; and the existence of design and contrivance is obvious in cases in which the final cause is quite beyond our comprehension. No one who looked at Babbage's difference engine would doubt that it had design, even though incapable of understanding the design. Remembering that we, too, are a part of Nature in its wider sense, an intelligent appreciation of contrivance and design shows a sympathy between our minds and the ruling contriving force of the universe. Unless we take refuge in a philosophy which limits our knowledge to our senses, which ignores that most important part of Nature, Life and Mind, which constitute human nature, we cannot stop short of this point; we must accept either *growth* of the properties of water or *design* in them.

There are modern writers who profess to see no design, only sequences, in Nature. The following passages are written by one in whom they would, I think, acknowledge a master:—

"Though the stupidity of men, barbarous and uninstructed, be so great that they may not see a sovereign author in the more obvious works of Nature to which they are so much familiarised; yet it scarce seems possible that any one of good understanding should reject that idea when once it is suggested to him. A purpose, an intention, a design, is visible in everything; and when our comprehension is so far enlarged as to contemplate the first rise of this visible system, we must adopt with the strongest conviction the idea of some intelligent cause or author."

And in another passage the same writer says, "In many views of the universe, and of its parts, particularly the latter, the beauty and fitness of final causes strike us with such irresistible force, that all objections appear (what I believe they are) mere cavils and sophisms: nor can we then imagine how it was ever possible for us to repose any weight on them. The order and arrangement of Nature, the curious adjustment of final causes, the plain use and intention of every part and organ, all these bespeak in the clearest language an intelligent cause or Author. The heavens and the earth join in the same testimony. The whole chorus of Nature raises one hymn to the praises of its Creator. I have found a Deity, and here I stop my inquiry."

These are the words of no less a man than Hume, and are remarkable as showing how a philosopher, regarded generally as the chief of sceptics, yet conceded entirely the irresistible weight of the argument from design. Had he seen the Godlike in Man, as well as in Nature, he might have effected not a breach but a bridge between Science and Faith.

If Hume admits design in this emphatic way, no one

need fear the charge of credulity in following his example.

But *design* is the work of *Mind:* and this brings in a new and wider conception. It is difficult, perhaps impossible, to conceive of Mind as apart from body; but we are none the less driven to conclude that Mind exists or has existed which designed the forces and materials of nature. The inference is the joint result of external nature which shows design, and of human nature which reveals Mind. For how should we suppose that we alone in the universe possess Mind? Our faculties are as surely derivative as our bodies are.

And as we recognise Mind, so also we recognise Will. Here, too, we rise inevitably from non-human nature and from human nature to the same result. We are conscious of only one source of new power in the universe, Will. No argument can deprive us of the conviction that this is a real origin, a true primal cause. And if *we* possess Will, how much more does it reside elsewhere in the universe? Our wills and minds and bodies must be alike derivative, mere morsels representative of the Great Mind and Will that somewhere and somewhen fashioned the materials of the world.

It is true we see now in inorganic nature no proof of Will but of Law: and for this reason. We cannot detect Will except by its being arbitrary, or even capricious: the wiser and nobler the will the less evident is it in its operation. A wilful person is not one of strong and equable, but of fitful and capricious will. Exalt our conception of Will to the uttermost, and caprice and arbitrariness vanish, and we get Uniformity: we get the laws of Nature. It is part of that tendency to a wrong kind of anthropomorphism, wrong because it deifies the lower tendencies of Nature, and not the highest, that makes us look on Uniformity as a mark of the absence of Will. This seems to me to indicate the answer to those ever-recurring doubts that arise from the pitilessness of natural laws.

We do not see caprice: nor do we see the traces of the primal working of the Artificer. What we see is the effect of mind operating in some unknown way *directly* upon matter, and not through mechanism. The *modus operandi* is absolutely unknown, but is neither more nor less inconceivable than the relations of force and matter. It is beyond the evidence of our senses, and something is left to our belief. No evidence from design can *prove* the doctrines of Natural Theology. They can indicate, corroborate, elucidate. And since we must form a theory of the universe, it is at any rate wise and true to form one which from the point of view of Science is not only unassailable, but meets with infinite confirmation; and which brings into harmony the intellectual and spiritual faculties of man with the properties of the external world.

And it is scarcely necessary to remark, but it ought not to be forgotten, that the argument from facts of this kind is in the highest imaginable degree cumulative. What I have been saying is only one brief chapter of a large work; a drop of water is my theme, but the universe is at hand to support the inferences drawn from it. If an argument is bad, multiplication will not improve it; but if an argument from one instance has any weight at all, an argument from ten thousand similar instances has vastly greater weight.

It will now be understood what Natural Theology is, and what relation to the whole is borne by this particular chapter of it. Much of what did form its materials is given up; conclusions once formed in ignorance as to the mutability of organic forms, and opinions thus formed when experience was immature, have grown to be incredible now that they are out of harmony with more exact information. But this can never be the case with inorganic nature. We cannot conceive of a revolution in Science which would overthrow our belief in the permanence of the chemical and physical properties of inorganic elements. And hence the basis of Natural Theology that I am considering this evening is not transient. There *is* a scientific view of the universe, a cosmology, which is identical with a theology: and the development of this cosmology is perhaps especially the work of the coming generations. We have seen growing up the vast Temple of Science, the work of the past and present generation, and men's eyes have been fastened on it as if it were not a part but a rival of the Temple of God. To feel their complete unity is not yet perhaps given to any man, but to work towards the synthesis of science and faith is, in an especial sense, the duty of this generation. It is an unfinished task; and no higher task can be imposed on a generation or a people than to complete it. No nation possesses such qualifications for this task as the English; they combine reverence, subtlety, and knowledge, the characteristics of Israel, Greece, and Germany: and some of our greatest philosophers combine them in a high degree. It is to this illumination, as it has been called, of privileged intellects, which may indeed follow a law, but to us seems fortuitous, that we must look for progress in this synthesis, in the establishment of reasonable beliefs founded on the whole of our knowledge of Nature, human and non-human, and in finding the relation which the laws of Nature bear to the government of the universe.

The rapid and sound progress of Science is a fact of extraordinary importance as affecting philosophy. No words can express the value of the sense of reality, exactness, and truth that Science is conferring on departments of knowledge in which formerly much was conjecture. And when we see these results in their right proportion to other results of human knowledge; when they combine with our instinct for Teleology, distinctively human, and certainly true; and when the spiritual faculties of worship claim supremacy over the whole man, instead of shrinking into an ever-lessening corner, then harmony and happiness will be found in highest measure. It will be possible to many, as it is now to a few, to see God's providence, not in miraculous interposition and contravention of the order of Nature, but in the daily working of that order. We perhaps can only see dimly, but our successors will work themselves into clearer light, and they will look back on this age with the interest that attaches to the history of a generation which devoted itself, perhaps sacrificed itself, to one idea, incapable of seeing its relative value.

In conclusion, to speak for myself—and the expression of individual conviction always carries some weight—I find the riddle of the world best solved by placing behind it the awful Personality of a Creator and God, who is at once the Author of Mind and Life and of all Nature. To ennoble that Conception I know that all the powers I have ought to be devoted. From the noblest examples of human nature, and chiefly from the Highest of all, I infer that He in the highest degree possesses those qualities I most reverence in men ; but to this conception of the Supreme, the study of Science—and it is that only that I am now engaged with—contributes an element which I find of immense value : it contributes the element of boundless admiration for foresight, wisdom, and power ; and the element of awe at a Mind and Will so perfect, so unimaginably beyond our own, that its working is perfect law and order, with absolutely no element of Caprice. I find, moreover, that just in proportion as I allow this conception to be present in my mind and dominate my thoughts, it serves to check the ever-present tendency to an anthropomorphism that lowers the Divine, and that it gives clearness and unity to all my ideas.

For eighteen years I have been studying and teaching Science, and hence the constant co-existence in my thoughts of the methods of Science and the conception of Religion has worked out a harmony between them that at one time did not exist. Perhaps what I have been saying is commonplace, and familiar to other minds. I am glad if it is so. I can only say that with myself it has been the work of years to grasp these truths firmly,—to look at them fearlessly ; and I trust there may be some at any rate to whom what I have said may suggest fertile lines of thought. By adhering to truth, even though it lead us through a wilderness, we are brought at last to a promised land.

It is with the wish to urge that this conception of the position of Science in the realm of human knowledge, as providing the foundation for a reasonable Natural Theology, and as contributing a most valuable element to our Worship, and thereby making it symmetrical, that this conception should be more firmly and universally grasped, that I have ventured to address you this evening.

MORALITY IN PUBLIC SCHOOLS, AND ITS RELATION TO RELIGION [1]

A FRAGMENT

THE subject which I have chosen needs no apology. It concerns every member of our Society, and touches on the principles and practice of the whole profession. I deeply regret that, from want of leisure, as well as from other causes, I am wholly unable to do more than break ground in it.

Public School education is, of course, but one phase of our national education ; but it is so very closely connected, on the one hand, with our whole political, moral, and social condition, and, on the other hand, with all other educational bodies and systems, with Universities, with Private and Preparatory Schools, and even with the education adopted in Girls' Schools, that, in discussing any great question connected with Public Schools, there is no one engaged in education who can say that the subject does not concern him. Further, Public Schools are becoming more and more important as a factor in national higher education. The Great Schools grow larger and larger ; twenty years have seen a considerable increase to their number and magnitude, and they do not seem even yet to have reached their limit. Private Schools are, on the contrary, tending to become preparatory to Public Schools.

[1] Delivered as the Presidential Address to the Education Society, 1st November 1881.

Now, Public School education has become what it is, partly, of course, as a result of the reaction on it of society as a whole. It is an outcome of the national genius and traditions ; its merits and defects are those of the nation, and of the particular time in which we write. This is obvious. But let it also be remembered that schools are not mere passive recipients of external influences ; they are strong enough in themselves, and influential enough by their position, to be themselves a power, a reaction on society. They are in the hands of persons presumably specially intelligent and public-spirited, drawn not from any narrow section of society or clique, clerical or social, but representative as a whole of the widest and most enlightened culture and thought ; and hence they have a real function in the nation, if they can but rightly formulate it. It is in this aspect that we are bound to regard our work, not as a result of society, but as a power to affect it : within no narrower limits lie our work and our responsibility. This responsibility lies chiefly on the Head-masters of the Public Schools *par excellence ;* but, in their degree, on all Head-masters and on all Masters : in a word, on all who take part in education in any form.

The saying of Wilhelm von Humboldt will occur to many of us, that, whatever we wish to see introduced into the life of a nation, must be first introduced into its schools. This is the real text of my discourse.

It is a wide subject. According to this, we must look to schools for a revival of simplicity of life ; for training in truth and moral courage ; for real intellectual training ; for giving men the power of hard thought of seeing things as they are ; and not giving only a superficial culture and a positive distaste for the unsymmetrical facts of life. The schools must educate the young to keen social and political interests ; must bind classes together in an unselfishness that is often wanting in the weary pleasure-seeking classes : in a word, must revive public spirit. The schools must give that self-restraint of the body, that purity of moral tone and conduct, that moral horror of degradation, on which more than anything else the welfare of the nation depends.

And, lastly, the schools must educate, develop, guide, and instruct that spiritual faculty in the child and boy, which, by whatever name we call it, is supreme.

Papers on great subjects like these, the national needs, and the power of schools to do something to supply them, and their lamentable shortcomings in not a few of these respects, may well occupy the attention of your Society. I shall to-day touch on one only, on the question of morality, and its connection with religious teaching, and on the duty and possibilities of schools to affect the morality of the country. What I can say will be, I foresee, a very incomplete fragment.

It must, I believe, be admitted as a fact, that immorality, used in a special sense, which I need not define, has been of late increasing among the upper classes in England, and specially in the great cities. Those who have the best opportunities of knowing, who can from personal knowledge compare the tone of society now with that of twenty, thirty, forty years ago, speak most positively of this deterioration. This is not the place to give details or evidence. There is amply sufficient ground for alarm that the nation may be on the eve of an age of voluptuousness and reckless immorality. Even if the phenomena of so-called philosophy, as well as of practice, which lead many thoughtful people to this conclusion, be otherwise interpreted ; if the increase is not real, but only apparent, and due to the greater publicity of life, it remains none the less true that it is the business of schools to prepare boys to face this evil. When one reflects that the present immorality is due to those who have left school within the last thirty or forty years, it is impossible not to speculate whether something could not have been done during those years to have diminished the existing evil. It is surely the duty of schools *venienti occurrere morbo*. I do not think it can be doubted that the immorality of manhood is often a direct consequence of earlier immorality.

I have said that there are grounds for fearing that immorality is on the increase among the wealthier classes. But it must be carefully noted, as a sign that education is not without a direct influence on conduct in this respect, that at the Universities—I mean at Oxford and Cambridge —this is not the case. There is, I believe, a fair consensus of opinion—I think, an entire consensus of well-qualified opinion—that the Universities are better than they were, and have a standard distinctly higher than that of any similar aggregate of men,—higher, that is, than the standard of the individuals of which it is composed. The traditions and influence of the society act as an appreciable check on its members. Of course, these are most felt in those colleges which are most representative of the University, for it is well known that the difference between one college and another is great in this as in other respects.

Further, it must be noted that the morality of Public School men as a whole is the best. At the Universities a fair comparison can be made between the moral effect of the education of the large Public Schools, and of the private and smaller schools, and the verdict is distinctly in favour of the Great Schools taken as a class. It is of importance to my purpose to insist on this point ; otherwise it might be inferred, from my choice of a subject, that I think the Public Schools are the chief offenders. *I believe that the very opposite is the case ;* that, while what I have to say applies, in very different degrees, to all of them, it applies with still more force to other schools. And I attribute the difference between one class of schools and another, and between the members of the same class (it being remembered that the boys are of the same social rank), chiefly, if not exclusively, to the degree of insight into moral conditions, the sense of responsibility for those conditions, and the spiritual force to control them, which have characterised, in the past and present, the men who, as head and assistant masters, have been in charge of those schools.

Let us now proceed to examine into the causes, so far as they are remediable, for a low standard of school morality, and their remedies, as far as they can be gathered by experience. I cannot pretend to deal with this subject exhaustively. I can only speak of one class of schools. Doubtless the masters of Middle Class schools meet the same problem, and it would be most instructive to us to hear how they face it.

One of the causes of immorality is idleness and luxurious living. This, at any rate, the schools can to some extent deal with. It is necessary, from this point of view alone, that fare should be simple (meat once a day is better than twice), that great temperance in the use of alcoholic liquor, if not indeed total abstinence from it, should be secured; that discipline should be good; industry great; exercise abundant, carried on up to the point of fatigue, two or three times a week; and that time should be fully occupied. Nothing to do is the parent of vice of all sorts. That a boy should be bored at school, from the monotony or the absence of employment, is a blot on the school, because it is a great danger to the boy. It is the business of masters to provide both work and play, and, what is more difficult, a variety of rational and interesting voluntary occupations, which are intermediate between work and play, which occupy time, which fill the thoughts, and break up those deadly blank times in which evil germs breed.[1]

Again, it is necessary that what may be called the mechanical arrangements should be carefully attended to, in respect of dormitories and other places. I shall pass over this very important point without going into detail, though I hold very decided views on the subject; but I think it might be worth the while of the Head-masters' Conference to collect information and opinions on such mechanical arrangements, and on school moral sanitation generally, and digest it into a report for the use of the profession.

Let me, however, say at once that no reliance must be placed on any mere mechanical arrangements. They may form *conditions* unfavourable to some forms of immorality, and we are bound therefore to secure them; but they cannot be regarded as *powers* and influences working for morality. Should any parent, anxious about the choice of

---

[1] I find I have unconsciously almost quoted this sentence from a most valuable article on Rugby, in the *New Quarterly Magazine*, for October 1879, p. 273.

a school, read this address, I would most seriously warn
him not to attach much weight to the apparent excellence
of arrangements.   Some of the very worst schools have
these arrangements in the highest perfection.   They cannot
afford to have them otherwise.   Neat cubicules and spotless
dimity have beguiled an uninterrupted sequence of mammas,
and have kept alive, and even flourishing, schools which are
in a thoroughly bad moral state, and are hopelessly inefficient in every particular.   Of course, many a parent feels
that he ought to judge for himself, and these mechanical
arrangements are too often the only material on which he
can form his judgment.   Let me assure him that they are
entirely untrustworthy.

We must go somewhat deeper.   Some persons advocate
a general teaching of physiology.   They urge that, as
knowledge is sure to come, it is plainly better that it should
come formally, seriously, from accredited teachers, and not
be left to be picked up in a fragmentary way that most
stimulates curiosity from the least desirable companions,
and so be regarded as a guilty knowledge.   They point
out that it is the mystery, the secrecy, that forms one of the
allurements to such knowledge.   They would remove the
mystery.   The knowledge would be accompanied with
proper warnings, and the evil would be checked at its
source.   This is a common view taken by younger men,
and is therefore important.

I cannot, in the least, assent to their view.   In the first
place, I do not think its advocates take into account at how
early an age such teaching would have to begin.   It would
not be at the Public Schools, it would be at the very earliest
preparatory schools.   Perhaps none but Public School
masters and doctors are aware at how early an age such
knowledge is acquired and in some instances bad habits
begin.   To the question which must sometimes be put,
" Where did you learn this ? " the answer invariably is, "At
my first school."   It follows, then, that such teaching, if it
is to anticipate the evil, must be given at an age at which
it would be practically impossible.

It is not, I think, credible that such teaching would do

much to eradicate bad habits already formed. On the contrary, I feel sure it would promote them, partly from curiosity, partly from the consciousness that all the others had their thoughts turned in the same direction. The freedom of conversation that would follow would be an incalculable evil.

In the next place, whether the facts above stated be admitted or denied, there is the fatal objection to the proposal, that it is so utterly repulsive to our nature to give this teaching that men and women of high character and refinement could not and would not do it. What sort of man would he be who would face a class on such a subject? A certain doctor pressed this method very strongly on the late head-master of one of our great schools, and he was met by the objection I am now urging. The doctor made light of it, saying he should at any rate teach his own son, then a fine open-faced youngster, before he went to school. Years after, they met again, and returned to the subject. " Did you teach your son as you intended?" was the question. "No," the answer was, "I found myself absolutely unable to begin." This is, I believe, a typical instance. I think the doctor was wrong. But if he could not teach his own son, how could he have taught a class?

Further, we have no reason for thinking that knowledge would produce purity. There is, in fact, a good deal of experience, open to any one, that would lead one to the opposite conclusion. A very large proportion of boys grow up in entire ignorance of certain forms of immorality. To mention these in the presence of such boys would be a great crime and cruelty. Whatever may be the right solution of the question, it is not in this quarter that we must look for it. There is, perhaps, an age at which some information may well be given, but it is not at this early age.

Another and very different solution is, for a master, or person *in loco magistri*, to have frequent private conversations with each boy, studying his individual temperament, ascertaining his special difficulties and faults, and giving him the necessary instruction and warning. This is not open to the same fatal objection of publicity as the former method; but it has peculiar and great dangers of its own. It is, in fact—I do not use the terms in any invidious sense —the system of confession and direction. Now, if this method were not earnestly advocated and actually employed in certain schools, not necessarily under these names, it would not be worth while to discuss it. As facts are, however, it may be worth while to point out some of the objections to it.

To obtain a confession from a boy is an easy feat; but it is to tyrannise over the weak in his hour of weakness. A time will surely come when the boy will repent having given his confidence. It will have weakened him; for which of us will not admit, in his own case, that he derives strength for action, for self-recovery, for self-respect, from the fact of his sins being known to God only?

Again, it compels the boy's mind to recur to the subject; it keeps the fault in view; it is keeping him in a tainted atmosphere. The boy ought not to be compelled to revert to it. It ignores the one great truth on the whole subject, that the real safety from such sins is always to be found in flight. Temptations of the devil we can fight; temptations of the world we can control: but temptations of the flesh we must flee from; and there is no other way of dealing with them. A struggling penitent, who is just safe by keeping the whole subject out of his thoughts, is perforce by such confession reminded of past sensual pleasure, and is weakened sometimes more by the memory than he is strengthened by the words of warning. One who is not penitent, and not struggling, of course gets harm unmixed with good.

Further, it is inevitable that such matters would come to be spoken of with a certain degree of conventionality, and this would be—indeed, I may truly say, is—most fatal. The tone of its being a matter of course is most deadly. The loss of respect for the master is certain. I attribute much of the evil at certain schools to this cause.

These objections would hold, even if the director were exceptionally gifted with sympathy and insight and purity. But what would be the case with the ordinary run of schoolmasters ? Even if one could answer or counter-balance these objections, how many men are there whom one could trust on such delicate matters,—trust neither to suggest, nor exaggerate, nor terrify, nor misuse their power, who would cheer and strengthen, and not confuse and paralyse and distress ?

Nor, I may add, do we seem to have the slightest ground of experience in trusting to this method, here, or in other countries. Indeed, the verdict of experience in English schools would be found most unfavourable, as has been reluctantly admitted to me, more than once, by men who know what that experience is.

There may be, and are, cases, usually at a much later age, in which there is unsolicited request for advice. And advice so given may change the current of a life. But, as a general method, it is not less wrong and impracticable than the proposal to give general physiological instruction.

Between these two extremes lies the method which is generally adopted at the Great Schools with more or less of care and completeness, varying from a *laissez-faire*, which is obtuse and loveless, even where it is not indifferent and coarse, to the most strenuous and effective, though unseen and almost unrecognised, influence. It consists in saying a few private words to boys when they first enter a school, and on other special occasions ; in keeping a close look-out on anything that looks wrong; in associating the elder boys with the master in stopping anything that is low ; and in doing all that may be done to keep up a healthy tone. A very general and vague description of a method, perhaps, scarcely up to the requirements of a scientific society ; depending entirely on the persons who apply the method, and on the spirit in which they apply it.

Now, I think that, with one proviso, of which more will be said presently, this is the right method ; and that the general high character of Public Schools, at the Universities and elsewhere, is due to it ; and further, that the schools which fail to deserve this high character fail because they neglect it in some important particular.

Let me go through it with rather more of detail. It is

very desirable that before a boy leaves home he should be warned that he will meet with boys who have dirty and nasty ways. He must be taught to regard all dirty talk as being low and ungentlemanly, and only fit for cads. He must be told that any offence will be followed by a whipping. It is premature to make a sin of it. So few parents will do this, that it is needful for the schoolmaster to see that it is not wholly omitted. And it must be remembered that it is at the schools for the youngest boys that this is most necessary. It is among young boys,—boys under fourteen, even under eleven,—that evil chiefly breeds. Over and over again, boys coming from middle class and preparatory schools will speak of the astonishing relative purity of the best Public Schools. Incredible as it may seem to those who do not know the best Public Schools, the fact is unquestionably so. The pure-minded boy is exposed to far less annoyance at a good Public School. The coarse is suppressed, intimidated, and sometimes cured. The large class of waverers who have previously joined more or less, not without qualms of conscience and some degree of disgust, in what seemed the fashion, are able to give it up.

The attitude of incessant watchfulness is difficult, because it must not be an attitude of incessant suspicion. The thought ought not to be in our minds. But we ought to watch for the slightest indications of a boy going wrong, —a look, a smile, a gesture,—and help him at the right moment. Many masters would confidently and almost indignantly assert that nothing is wrong in their schools. It is not to such that I should look for a really high standard.

The skill and judgment of a master is perhaps more shown in his power of selecting the right boys to co-operate with them, and in influencing them to do so in the right way, than in anything else. Certainly, without such co-operation, all else is vain. The tone of the school, though it may be suggested and inspired by the masters, must be independent, and dead against the faults we are discussing. It is made so, not simply by arming the older boys with

authority, though this is much ; it is by giving all the older
and leading boys, without saying much to them, the feeling
that they are working with the masters, and for the school,
on the most important of all points ; it is by trusting the
boys, and educating them to be trustworthy.

I need scarcely say that stern treatment of public
offences is essential.   In no other way can the right public
tone be maintained.

Δεῖ γαρ ἀπειθοῦσι καὶ ἀφυεστέροις οὖσι κολάσεις τε καὶ τιμωρίας ἐπι-
τιθέναι, τοὺς δ' ἀνιάτους ὅλως ἐξορίζειν.   (Arist. *Eth. Nic.* x. 9.)

(The whole chapter is well worth studying on this
question.) They must be got rid of, and got rid of in
silence.

The healthier and manlier the general tone of the school,
the less power these temptations will exercise.   They are
bred by indolence, by luxury, by lounging, by swagger, by
indifference to games and school interests, by loose literature, by want of discipline, by being bored.   I do not
mean that either the hard-working boy, or the athlete, or
one who is both, is necessarily free from these temptations,
and even these faults, but that he has some of the best
safeguards and antidotes against them.   His mind is occupied ; he is in health ; he has some self-respect.   I would
say to all parents of day boys as well as boarders, co-operate
heartily with the schoolmaster in enforcing school games ;
they are essential to health, to the *esprit de corps*, and to
the employment of time.   If you keep your little boys away
from games on all sorts of frivolous excuses, as they grow
up they will not care for games, they will not be induced
to join in them, and you will regret and wonder why it
should be so, why they have turned out the poor mannish
strutting creatures they are.   You are exposing them to
risks a thousand times worse than taking colds, or getting
their shins kicked.   Did you ever think what a priceless
boon is the innocence of school games as a subject of conversation ?   You are perhaps bored by the incessant talk
about matches and runs, and place-kicks, and scrimmages ;
you think games occupy a disproportionate share of the

boy's mind. You may be thankful it is so. What do French boys talk about? Talk is one of the chief uses of games. The talk about them is more than innocent,—it is a training in politics, loyalty, patriotism, hero-worship, justice. I wish girls could have a little more of such talk. Lawn tennis is doing something for them perhaps.

The free intercourse of masters with their boys,[1] the genuine and unaffected interest they take in their games and occupations, and the general healthy tone of the masters' society, are of the highest importance. If a master is fast and coarse-minded, or even indifferent on these points, he has mistaken his profession, and the sooner he is got rid of the better.

It will be noticed that I have said little of direct religious motive : that I have laid more stress on the tone of manliness than on that of godliness. And this represents my conviction, after some experience. I have not found, nor have others told me that they have found, that direct religious teaching exercises much permanent influence on young boys in protecting and rescuing them from these faults. There are some who will hear this with surprise, and a sense of despair; others may listen with something of a sneer. To the first I would say, that each age has to be educated by suitable methods,—that teaching may be good but untimely. It does seem to be indicated by experience that it is better, with young boys, to treat these faults as disgusting than as sinful ; to cure them with " kicks and contempt rather than by prayers and lectures " ; to consider them as unmanly and ungentlemanly rather than as unchristian ; as a disgrace to a school and to self-respect rather than as a defilement of the temple of the Holy Spirit ; and even where boys grow older and begin to know what impurity really means, it is moral repulsion, not religious enthusiasm nor religious terror, that aids them most in resisting temptation. And though it is essential

---

[1] A friend writes to me, "When I first took my house, the worst offender I ever knew said to me of another boy, whom I held up to him as healthy-minded, 'I should have been all right if I had known the masters as he does.'"

that the atmosphere of the school should be religious, in order that any mode of dealing with the evil should be effective, it is not on the religious side that the evil is best attacked. Further, I would add, that while the number of masters and elder boys who could treat them in the former way is very large, the number who could treat them in the latter way, without some considerable degree of unreality, is extremely small. And if any one doubts still, whether the highest motives would not be the most powerful if they were rightly and strongly brought before the boy at the right time and by the right person, I would ask him to weigh well the additional facts,—that the boys whose temperament specially exposes them to these faults, are usually far from destitute of religious feelings; that there is and always has been an undoubted coexistence of religiosity and animalism; that emotional appeals and revivals are very far from rooting out carnal sin; and that in some places, as is well known, they seem actually to stimulate, even in the present day, to increased licentiousness; that, along with an increased immorality in society, has arisen an increased demand for stronger religious excitement; and that somehow, in our complicated nature, room is found for both; strange to say, they coexist in the same society, and even in the same individuals.

But to those who would treat this admission with a sneer, and infer that religious motives are powerless and unsuitable in education, if not absolutely prejudicial, I must reply at somewhat greater length.

I once asked the head-master of a school, in which there is no religious teaching, his opinion as to the effects of the absence of this element from the school. He had previously been an assistant master at a Public School. He replied that he did not miss the chapel or the religious teaching for the boys at all, or very slightly. He missed the Latin Verses very much more.

This was of course an epigram, and must not be taken as expressing my friend's deliberate judgment; but it is, I think, sufficiently representative to be regarded as a pointed statement of an opinion which, if not widely spread, has a

good many tacit and some open-mouthed supporters ; it is
the opinion which prevails in our colonies ; and I think it
is worth while to direct the attention of this Society to the
most important of all things connected with the practice of
Education, viz. the position that should be occupied in it
by religious instruction and influence, giving these terms
the most liberal interpretation, and its connection with
school morality.

I said above that, *with one proviso*, the method of dealing
with immorality at our Public Schools is the best.   This
one proviso is, that the whole atmosphere and tone of the
school, and recognisable influence of the masters, is religious.   And thus I pass to the second part of my paper.
The method is not distinctively religious ; but, to be suc-
cessful, it presupposes, both in the man and in the boy,
that fear of God and that conscious service of a Master
which is implied in any high sense of duty, and which
constitutes the essence of religion ; and it presupposes,
further, a mutual understanding between master and boy,
that they have this common ground, even where it is not
directly appealed to.   Such, at least, is my deepest conviction.   I should not have much cared to address your
Society on any other topic, for at the present time this
surpasses all others in importance.   For we schoolmasters
are brought face to face with religious problems in a way
that perhaps no one else is brought, unless we simply
shirk them.   A schoolmaster who really sympathises, feels
with his boys, whatever his past mental history may have
been, is compelled to think of their religious education.
Many a father has been similarly compelled, unless he has
been too busy to think about such things.   He may have
persuaded himself that he can let his own problems alone,
and that he gained nothing by his own early religious
teaching, fastening in memory on its transient errors rather
than on its permanent effect; but put a sympathetic fatherly
nature face to face with the young, and these theories vanish
like a fog,—we discover that our children or our pupils
have inherited our own early religious instincts and feelings
of need, and not our later uncertainties and compromises.

There are, of course, men who are, so to speak, blind on this side. I have known men quite out of sympathy with the religious feelings of boys, and as a consequence, with all their great ability, curiously, and otherwise inexplicably, destitute of influence. There are many, doubtless, who regard such feelings and aspirations in the boy as negligible idiosyncrasies, transient feeblenesses. But such men can only fulfil part of their functions as educators, and not the whole. An entire region, in which their influence ought to be felt, is unknown to them. Round them, among their pupils, are being worked out countless spiritual problems of which they are as unconscious as an ox. It will not, therefore, surprise me if some teachers dissent from these views. But nothing can be gained by argument with them. Ultimately, as in all educational matters, the value of religious education is to be determined by observation and experiment, and it is to this I appeal.

There is no other restraining power. Sympathy, the innate horror of doing wrong to a fellow-creature; self-respect, the innate horror of wronging ourselves, are real powers with all finer natures, but are meaningless τῷ κατὰ πάθος ζῶντι. It is vain—it may easily be proved—to rely on any convention of society, on good taste, on prudence, on laws, on rival and overmastering passions. The tendency to immorality cannot be treated in an individual instance as a question of Ethics on any basis, utilitarian or hedonistic. We cannot help another by pointing out the public condemnation of such vices, as inducing distrust in society; or the probable evil effects on the individual. These are after-thoughts that justify on philosophical grounds an already existing morality, but do not originate it. Legislators can appeal to these principles; but no individual finds his instincts raised, his love of purity quickened, his strength increased, by an appeal to such principles.

Again, a restraining power is needed. For the gratification of passion is an intense reality, and can only be held in check by a still more intense reality. This must be physical or spiritual. It must come from the legislator, the doctor, or the teacher. The legislator can only help to diminish crime, and does not really touch the case. The motive must come from science or religion. But science gives a feeble sound. Science admits that immorality is damaging to the body,—but talks of recuperative powers, advises moderation. Science, as yet, does not speak of its effects on character. It is not in science that we are to look for a restraining power.

Again, let us observe that, as a matter of fact, the public opinion already existing in the best schools has been almost created, certainly profoundly affected, by religious influences. They make the only standard to which we can now appeal. This is undeniable. It is needless to dwell here on the effect of Arnold's teaching, or the aims of his spiritual successors. He added a new hemisphere to their work. He taught them to educate school morality through school religion. Some of them have done so. His aim and theirs ought to be the aim of the profession collectively, if experience is to be our guide. I do not see how the abandonment of his aim can lead at last to anything but pre-Arnoldite school morality.

If any one will fairly face this problem in thought, he will be driven to the conclusion that it will be solved by the religious motive or by none. In so far as sin is the product of circumstances, we must strike at the circumstances, and every schoolmaster ought to have his wits about him, and scrutinise circumstances, as if everything depended on them : but if sin, and in so far as sin, is in human nature, it is necessary to give boys some fresh power to cope with it. If this is attainable in any degree anywhere, it is attainable in schools such as ours. Young, educated, docile, refined, public-spirited, loyal, how incomparably better is our material than that which one meets anywhere else. To give this fresh power, the power of conquering the selfishness and passions of our lower nature, is surely the aim and end of all education.

Yes ; but how is it to be done ? How is it even to be attempted ?

We schoolmasters—who as a class are highly strung,

and feel with peculiar intenseness the forces of the time—
are in more danger than any other class of pressing into
extremes one or other of the two axioms of education :
religion cannot be taught ; religion must be taught. We
must keep both constantly in view. Religion cannot be
taught. Each human soul finds it for itself. All alone,
each soul weaves out its own web of truth, grows by its
own inner vitality, and shares its inner life with no one.
The thought should fill us with respect for each young soul
around us, fill us with a divine awe of the inaccessible
depths that seem so close to us and are yet so far. But
that other truth must be equally in our minds, and needs
the more insisting on. As the young soul grows by its own
inner vitality, so it needs its natural food, its mother's milk.
The teacher can in part supply this, if he has it,—the sympathy of a living soul, the truth on which he lives. That
this food is necessary and longed for,—that, when it is
wanting, the education is partial and poor,—witness the
great teachers of all ages. Consider one point only. Consider who those teachers are who have won the *affection* of
their pupils. There is nothing else that boys love. The
instinct of the young soul is true. Look at the love
cherished for Arnold, for Pears, for Temple, for Moberly,
for Percival, and many another,—nay, for all such men in
all ages from Socrates of Athens to James A. Garfield of
Hiram's College, U.S. Let any one who knows a great
school reflect which among the masters has the enduring
affection of his boys,—not the popularity that comes of
agreeable manners, or hospitality, or intellectual brilliancy,
but the deeper and rarer respect and affection,—and he
will find it is the man of true unassuming religious character. Of all the intellectual and moral elements which
go to make a master,—the originality that does not despise
method ; the flexibility of mind and sternness of character ;
the sympathy with learners, and attitude of ever learning ;
the instinctive appreciation of small traits of character ; the
love of human souls that will count no pains too great to
save a boy, that " never despairs of a lad " ; the sense of
duty that sustains in wearisome routine ; the deep under-

current of character that makes the whole life a conscious, though often very secret, service of God,—the last is, as any wide experience will show, the most precious of all. Many a master, as he looks back and reviews the experience of his life, will find that this is the key to the position held by some of his colleagues,—a position inaccessible to him, however superior he may have justly felt himself to be to them intellectually. The experience of schoolmistresses will confirm this. The really loved mistress,—she who has influenced the whole life, whose approval is valued, whose words and memory are cherished,—she, in a word, who educates the girl,—is the one who, to sufficient intellectual power to command respect, added a natural and transparent simplicity and truthfulness in dealing with questions of duty and of all things spiritual; who brought her heart to touch the hearts of her girls, as well as her mind to touch their minds.

Now I regard this fact as a strong scientific testimony to what I am asserting. It is a part, a very small part, of the testimony of experience to what some one may call the usefulness of religion in education, but what I should prefer to call its proved supremacy.

The hope of education in England lies in the increasing recognition of this usefulness or supremacy; and, along with it, in a juster idea of what religion is, and what influences ought to be brought to bear on the young. It is not to be despaired of that we schoolmasters—brought as we are face to face with facts, made more tolerant, let us hope, than some others by our associations and experience —may help to work out a solution of the religious problem of the day: that it may be from the schools that the new Reformation may spring.

We may be certain that religion is very simple. There is endless discussion about it; there are books, societies, meetings, congresses, sermons, newspapers, without end. It is in everybody's mouth. Yet there is real danger lest we, like so many others, should never know what religion is,—lest we should never see the wood for the trees. Can we, a scientific society, close our doors for a moment against the buzz outside? Can we still the heart that already begins to beat as if drums were sounding, at the prospect of a few words on such angrily debated ground, and approach this subject as educators of the next generation of men and women that shall live in our land, with the humble desire to speak and to tolerate the simple truth?

I have already detained you long, but what I have said would be obscure, and almost valueless, unless I go on to explain what I mean by religious influence.

Religion is not the holding of certain opinions. It does not consist in certain views of difficult questions. We all agree that the kingdom of God, however we choose to express the idea, must be entered by us as little children; and little children know nothing of views or opinions. Views and opinions and creeds are not of the essence of religion; they are its superstructure. They belong to its intellectual and speculative side,—profoundly interesting to some minds, sometimes highly important, but not religion,— only accessory to religion.

Religion is not identical with religious services, any more than it is with religious views. They are at once a natural, and almost inevitable, sequel and manifestation of religion, and a stimulus to it; but they are not religion. The performance of acts of worship is only accessory to religion.

Picture, I pray you, the mind of an average schoolboy of thirteen to sixteen. What is his religion? has he none? He is, doubtless, if he is thoughtful, sore bewildered by the aspect of the world. He cannot see the wood for the trees. Who can analyse his thoughts? Not one of us. But cannot we educators, as we call ourselves, with all our experience and united wisdoms, help such a boy? Have the past ages absolutely no resultant experience in which all can agree? Must we tell him that we too, or perhaps that every one else except our own particular selves, are as much in the dark as he; that we are not quite sure whether there is any religion; and that, as the *Daily News* said the other day, in speaking about schools in Wales, "It is far better to leave religion to be taught by parents and clergymen." It is *our* fault that the *Daily News* should have to say this, that religion should have come to mean what the *Daily News* means by the word.

The religion of a boy means learning what duty is, and caring much and always for it. All else is accessory, this alone is of the essence. This is also the religion of a man. Shall we leave this to parents and clergymen? Can we do nothing to help our boys, who are with us during so many of those years in which they imbibe most of the principles of life, to learn from all noble examples and lofty words what duty is, and to care much and always for doing their duty?

We possess the ear and attention of a boy during all those years when his aspirations rise highest, when the power of conscience is strongest, and that of passion weakest, when reverence is most natural, when goodness and greatness are most inspiring, when the range of future duties and possibilities is most unlimited, when high public spirit finds its most appropriate sphere, before the pressure of care can have driven out all thoughts that kindle, and habitual hardening sins can have dulled all spiritual life. We have the opportunities of teaching boys their duties in their widest sense. What is our education worth, if we leave all this side of it neglected? Who can deny that we ought to educate our boys in self-respect and thoroughness and modesty and purity and singleness of mind as positive duties? or in self-culture and diligence? or in public spirit and helpfulness and love? or in reverence and unworldliness? It is at the age at which boys are with us that these ideas are most easily assimilated, at which boys delight to hear of them; for boys prefer nobleness and goodness to everything else. This, too, is the time for warning them against the faults of vanity and cowardice and aimlessness, against littleness of mind and coarseness; and that by such analysis and sympathy as come home to them and help them. If this is religion, if the master can really help his boys to this, shall we put it rather below Latin Verses as an element in education? Or shall we say that these things are best not spoken of: let the boys copy them, if they can see them, in silence; let the only voices they hear be such as are wafted to them by chance, or sought by their own unguided will?

I say, then, that a school is only performing half its duties if it does not so educate its boys; if it does not enable and induce its masters, not clergy only, but lay also, to bring their very best and loftiest influence to bear on the school; if it does not thoroughly bring out the best side of the best members of the staff. These great moral or religious ideas, and such as these, must come within the sphere of ordinary school education. They can do this without being entered on the time-table. It should be our aim to transmit to the young the best thoughts and aspirations of the best of the generation above them, and so aid in the progressive development of the nation in all that is good. We must not rule all this department as outside our sphere. We must claim it as within the province of every school, from the Board School upwards; and if we can claim it temperately, and use our opportunities wisely, no one will deny the value of the teaching.

It is astonishing how much of life is left outside the sphere of education. Our teaching stops short at almost all points of the needs of real life. It would be easy to dilate on this. The education of the Greeks and Romans aimed, at any rate, at the requirements of actual life. Ours is more than ever antiquarian and elementary. Except incidentally, we teach no political philosophy, no physiological philosophy, no ethical philosophy; in a word, no science of individual or social life. Each generation faces its problems afresh: the young mind is not brought into contact with the thought of the generation above, except by books which lie quite outside the lines of education, and on which we give no guidance. In old times, the education of a youth was to put him with a tutor, a sage if possible, one impregnated with learning and thought, and so by the intellectual and moral contagion to develop the youth's latent power. Of that there is little now. What I plead is, that religious instruction in schools is almost the only remnant left of this education of the inner man, that brings the very soul of the pupil and the sage—if he exists—into contact. To hold this cheap, to put it a little below Latin Verses, is a proof of a most inadequate notion of what the actual capacities and effects of religious teaching are, of its width and depth even now, and still more what it may be in future; or a deadness and blindness to one whole region of the human soul, a limited conception of it as an examinable and more or less intelligent entity.

"But is this teaching to be merely hortatory or theological?" I hear asked; for this makes all the difference.

Well, I reply, religion is the caring for duty in all its varied aspects of self-culture, duties to others, duties to God; and it is a subordinate, though very important question, what helps we shall use in bringing this religion home to boys. We must use those helps we truly find most effective ourselves, being perpetually on our watch against unreality and self-deception. The natural consequences of sin impress one man; the elevating charms of greatness and goodness move another; the inspiration of public spirit is a power with a third; another finds his inspiration in the life and example of Jesus Christ. To one the inner voice of conscience; to another the voice of the Bible; to another the teaching of Nature: each finds a revelation somewhere. All will teach one religion,—the religion of caring for duty,— though they may differ in the motive they apply. One whose whole nature is sceptical to his heart's core, sceptical on the use of all these helps equally, may yet be thoroughly religious; and he may do good service if he will enlist himself on this side, and not permit himself to be driven into opposition. One who doubts, and on speculative grounds would deny, all that most men who are called religious hold as truths, may feel keenly the duties of life, may care much and care always for them, and be a hearty ally in all true and noble education, if he will loyally help in this its highest aim. But this implies that he will extend to others the toleration that is extended to him. He must not condemn as useless and false what others find useful and true helps. In a word, he, and all of us, must care supremely for the end, and be modest in judgment about the means.

One will speak in one tone and another in another; but what I want to insist on is, that the ethical side of all our education is in danger of being crushed out by conventional reticence and tacit abandonment; and that this is a mistake of the highest order. We have lost sight of the true perspective. The old division of Educational Subjects, adopted in the schools of the Stoics, was Physics, Logic, Ethics. And it stands as sound as ever. Still men have to learn the basis of facts, physical, social, political, on which life is based; still men need the training in logic and language which shall enable them to grapple with facts and construct sound theories; and still they need the application of theories to the concrete facts of their own life. Life is not long enough to deal with the vast array of sciences that now come under these three heads; the first alone bewilders our generation: but I plead that the third, in its modern form, which is practical, sensible, religious teaching, shall not be ignored and quietly turned out by our modern theorists and practitioners in education. It is not to be placed below Latin Verses.

I have said that the modern form of Ethics is practical religious teaching. It is true that the lines of ethical and religious thought have different origins; but they converged once under the mighty influence of early Christian philosophy, and, if now once more separated, that separation is not necessary, and signs of convergence are not wanting. But this is a subject for an essay in itself, and I will not enter on it.

Few, I imagine, whatever their speculative conclusions may be, do not feel the attractive power of that grand ideal life which they may think existed only in the imagination of the writers of the Gospels, but which others believe to have been truly divine. Those who do so believe it, find in the service of that Master the greatest help to religion. *Help*, I say, to religion, because it helps them to see their duties, to care for them, and to do them. Let no one say this who does not, from his soul, believe it; but let no one deny the existence of a help which he cannot himself use. Let us schoolmasters, at any rate, with our high calling ever in view, work together in any way we can to implant great aims, powerful motives, purity of life, in our boys; and let us, supremely caring for our great aim, never try and discredit the means our brothers use. Rather let us be honourable rivals in our work, and be ready, on all sides, to admit that where the fruit is good there the tree is good. He that is not against us is for us.

And let all whom it concerns know that in school is a field for noble work, and for the expression of their best selves. School work may be elevated far above the region of gerund-grinding and drudgery to one who, in his gerund-grinding and drudgery—which are very real and necessary —sees the opportunity for that intellectual contact from which permanent religious influence springs. A schoolmaster need not be a brilliant speaker, for his power rests on what is deeper than eloquence,—the transparent principles of a life lived in the sight of his hearers.

We are to leave religion, says the *Daily News*, to parents and to clergymen,—and thus deliberately cut it off from the reality it gets from its association with other teaching; sacrifice that inspiration to goodness and duty, which comes only in early years, and comes most effectually from a voice which also kindles by its intellectual fire.

Let the very opposite be the view of all who take a wide and thoughtful view of education as the work of implanting in schools what we wish to see reproduced in the life of the nation. Let our highest aim be to put before our boys the life of duty, in all its width and depth, and inspire them, if it may be, with the love of it; and let our most earnest thoughts be devoted to finding the most effectual helps, whether in regulations and discipline, or in admonition and literature, for accomplishing this aim. And let it be part of the work of our Society, which claims so lofty a name as the Education Society, to observe faithfully and record truly what methods and helps are best.

To this end I have contributed this paper, of whose lamentable shortcomings no one is so conscious as myself. I have, however, attempted to describe what methods I have observed to be most effectual in promoting a healthy tone of morality in a school, viz. in brief, great care in arrangements, the hearty co-operation of elder boys, sternness in dealing with the fault, full occupation of time and thoughts with many interests, and a general treatment of the subject most earnest indeed, but which would commonly and rightly be called non-religious, based however on a strong undemonstrative religious tone pervading the whole life of the school. I need not, before such an audience, emphasise my conviction that it should be a life of action, not of talk and ceremonial; in other words, that it should be a life which aims at the result, and shows the result, and is not so incessantly occupied with one particular set of means that the end is lost sight of. In this you will agree with me.

But it is, perhaps, more necessary to emphasise here, that for my part I see no argument from experience—to which we all appeal—in favour of secularism, though secularism may be, I admit, a religion, as Stoicism was. My own personal conviction, based, as I believe, on facts alone, is that morality cannot become religious, that is, be penetrated with the love of duty, and so secured, without the sense of service of a Divine Master. This is a subject which I feel it would be inappropriate to handle here.

Finally, let me sum up very briefly. Don't bring religion into this cloacinal region of morals prematurely. Treat the fault with moral horror, silence, and great sternness; and get your boys to work with you. Look after the conditions, physical and social, that all may be healthy. But let religion, a stern and eager love of duty, be the tone of the school, or all else fails; and the best help to religion, I believe the only help, is what I have just briefly indicated.

And now, with two more remarks, I will at last conclude. First, let me say that the distinctive doctrines of the Church and many of the Sects are utterly unimportant at schools and everywhere. No genuine schoolmaster in any rank can for an instant digress from his religious teaching into such debatable ground; it is one of the stupendous and far-reaching blunders that the world outside our profession make, when they say that masters cannot be trusted to speak on religion, because they would *proselytise*. We have no time to proselytise, even if we had the wish. It is to misconceive the nature of the only possible religious teaching at school.

And lastly this. The great change in education going on before the eyes of this generation is the gradual passing away of education out of the hands of the clergy into the hands of the laity. What I would say, then, to laity and clergy alike is, See that the element of religion is not thereby eliminated. Religion is not the peculiar province of the clergy. I do not see that clerical masters are more religious than lay. If I were to name the twelve best living schoolmasters that I know, merit being estimated in the way that you now know I should estimate them, two only are in orders. The speaker is neither of those. And this leads me to deprecate one criticism, and one only, on this paper,—that it should be said that I have been describing my own estimate of my own attempts. Say, rather, a vision sometimes seen, oftener forgotten, suggested by the work of others: a vision which may be useful to some of you. But, to resume. If education has passed, or is passing, out of the hands of the clergy, if you rejoice in what you may call its emancipation, and I see no reason for necessarily re-gretting it,—then see that you do not repudiate the respon-sibility you inherit, nor leave untrained those faculties which you deemed mistrained before. Let it be our business as schoolmasters to make our schools, in a higher sense than ever before, places of true religious education.

With this thought in our minds, let us go back to the great saying of Von Humboldt, " Whatever we wish to see introduced into the life of a nation must be first introduced into its schools."

III

THE NEED OF GIVING HIGHER BIBLICAL TEACH-ING AND INSTRUCITON ON THE FUNDA-MENTAL QUESTIONS OF RELIGION AND CHRISTIANITY[1]

THE Rural Dean has done me the honour to invite me to read a paper on this subject, which I understand to be the need of Higher Teaching and Instruction, other than what is given by Sermons, to meet the wants of our fellow-citizens.

I do not propose to read more than a very slight paper, not ten minutes in length, with the aim of starting a discussion, and if possible, after obtaining the advice and co-operation of those who are present, of setting on foot a definite plan of work in the form of classes and lectures.

I think it must be obvious, if we reflect, that we clergy do not do the whole of our duty to the most intelligent portion of the city. I fear they "take hurt and hindrance by our negligence." Laymen have frequently spoken to me on this subject. I may mention that the Mayor[2] spoke recently to me on the need of some such lectures as I propose. "Parochial Sermons," he said, in a conversation that I do not profess to report verbatim, "do not meet our intellectual needs. They seem to be intended for the young or for the uninstructed. They rarely touch the

---

[1] A paper read before the Ruridecanal Conference of Bristol, on November 8, 1882, printed at the request of the Lord Bishop of the diocese.   [2] Sir Joseph Weston.

points on which men want guidance as to principles, or information as to facts. We do not know what you clergy really think on some of the most important and fundamental questions of religion, questions which underlie what are commonly called doctrines. The cause of religion among the laity suffers more than you can easily imagine from a general and vague mistrust that Christian advocates are wanting in candour, and have a logic as well as a dialect of their own. The avoidance of important questions may possibly be wise in a mixed congregation of women and children, and it is certainly wise on the part of those who are unable to handle them; but that they should be avoided universally by the clergy produces the impression that you shirk awkward facts and awkward questions, and that at bottom you are as sceptical as we are. You underrate the intelligence of the laity and their interest in religious questions. We in our turn perhaps underrate your intelligence and comprehension of questions which occupy our minds, which seem to be not identical with those which occupy yours. We read the reviews which are full of apparently well-reasoned papers, which seem incompatible, or at least incommensurable, with much that we hear in church; and we cannot tell what you, our professional advisers, think on these questions. They are rarely touched on at Diocesan or Church Congresses. We hear of protestations enough from intolerant and half-educated clergy against facts of science which are not shaken by their protestations; but these do not help us. Pardon me if I speak too plainly," he said, with his usual perfect courtesy, "but you clergy hardly seem to know what we laymen want, or you are unable or afraid to give it to us. Either alternative suggests uncomfortable feelings of distrust and doubt."

Intelligent men of the middle classes and artisans say the same thing. They want first principles, in religion as in other things; they want plain speaking; they want facts; and they want answers to questions. "What is knowledge worth," they say, "if it cannot stand the test of questions?" And in the ordinary sermon they get no first principles; they get conventional language—really an unknown tongue—which they very imperfectly understand; reasoning based on assumptions which are not stated; they don't get facts; and they can't ask questions. Exhortation and advice are very well, but men want reasoning also; and not sham reasoning. They want above all things to be convinced that we are candid and fair, and that we can see both sides of a question.

Another class which we ought to consider is the young women of education and intelligence in our society. What instruction is given to them? Higher education in other subjects has made them somewhat more exacting as to the quality of what is laid before them, and much more desirous of real information and guidance. What do we do for them? Some instruction is given to those who teach in Sunday Schools; but this is given for immediate reproduction for the use of inferior minds, and is a totally different thing from what I have in view. There is sound teaching at our High School, and girls who have left avail themselves of the privilege of going back to attend the classes. There are books. But the best books are almost inaccessible to them, or are disfigured (for their purposes) with Greek words. And no books take the place of the living voice, especially the living voice of men whose lives and works, whose faces and tones, are known among us. There are young women, destined to be the teachers and mothers of the next generation, whom we ought to interest in religious questions. The cleverest of them put these questions aside now with some contempt because they are so badly handled, and because they are unable to get any better teaching. I may mention that at Newnham College a class for Biblical instruction is formed; and at King's College, London; and I hear of similar movements elsewhere; but there is nothing in Bristol.

Such then are the classes to be considered, and to them may be added the small but important class of lay helpers, readers, workers, of Church and other denominations, for whom some definite, stimulative, expansive teaching, some contact with deeper thought and greater learning, is wanted beyond that which the arrangements of the Church at present offer to them.

In fact I am advocating a mission : not a mission to the ignorant, but a mission to the educated. Our Prayer Book and our services contemplate Churchmen ; they are intended, not, as the Mayor assumes, for the young and the uninstructed, but for convinced and converted worshippers. Outside these are the masses of our city who need a mission of one sort ; and the educated, but alienated or indifferent, who need a mission of another sort. They must be approached in a very different way. There are people who with familiarity with the externals and words of religion combine more or less complete and explicit disbelief of the very elements of it, as it is ordinarily presented ; and complete uncertainty as to the relation of religion to the other spheres of human thought.

The next point to be considered is the subjects of the lectures. I have spoken of Higher Biblical Teaching ; I should include under this head such questions as these. Lectures and essays on—

> *Inspiration.* What we really nowadays mean by it. What will stand investigation ?
>
> *The Authority* of the Bible is a closely connected subject.
>
> *The Canon of the O. T.* and the degree of importance of questions relating to it. How far they affect the nature of Revelation.
>
> *Special Studies* on various books, such as the Pentateuch, the Psalter, Job, some prophets, some epistles ; or on special portions of books.

There would be some special advantages gained by adopting the books selected by Cambridge for the Higher Local Examination. It is probably not known to all present that Cambridge examines men and women over seventeen in religious knowledge all over the country. Bristol is one of the centres of examination. The subjects for this year, for example, are—The Captivity and the Return; the Psalms, Book III.; St. John, the Galatians, Ephesians, and St. James; Butler's *Analogy*, Part II.; Hooker, Book I.; *Horæ Paulinæ*, 1-5. Now from our places of higher education like University College this teaching is excluded: and so it results that a young man or woman in Bristol is offered help in every other subject but these. Why so? Are these subjects so very easy? so very unimportant? Is there no one that professes knowledge on these subjects? No one whose business it is? What if it should be ours?

Among questions that may be called fundamental questions of religion and Christianity I might name the following, merely as specimens, to make my meaning distinct, not of course with any thought that all these subjects should be at once handled :—

Relation of Christianity to the other great Religions.
The Limits of Science and Religion, and their Borderland.
Miracles : what we really maintain about them.
Relation of Socialism to Christianity.
Evidence for the Resurrection of Christ.
What is meant by External and Internal Evidences for Christianity.
The Common Ground between Christianity and Agnosticism.
The Theory of Prayer.
The Authority and Value of Creeds.
The Authority of the Church in matters of Faith.
How far Morality is dependent on Religion.
Relation of Religion to Political Economy.
Effect of the Theory of Evolution on Natural Theology and the Doctrine of Final Causes.
The Meaning at the present time of the Imitation of Christ.

It is good for us even to hear such a list read, and to reflect how exceedingly difficult we should find it to lecture a highly intelligent and interested audience on any one of these subjects. And yet—how shall we excuse ourselves?

May I venture to say that these and such as these are the questions which our clergy and devout laity ought to meet to discuss. I confess I listen with some degree of impatience to the discussions on minor points at our very pleasant Greek Testament Class. And if we did so meet, and gravely, and humbly, and courteously tried to ascertain the truth on these matters, we should perhaps not so much shudder at the thought of addressing others on them.

But whoever takes them, it is obvious that they will tax him to the utmost. They must not be sermons, padded with homiletic instructions; not written in that "peculiar combination of Elizabethan English and Hebrew poetry which is considered to imply reverential treatment"; not goody little books, intended for children and the unintelligent, or to win a reputation for undoubted orthodoxy and soundness: but essays, hard-headed, stimulative of thought, candid, solid, worth a sceptic's coming to hear. They must, above all, be modest, not over dogmatic; constructive, restful: not timid, apologetic, wavering; and they must face fundamental questions.

If such essays cannot be written by clergy holding the doctrines of the Church of England; if our Bishops enjoin silence on these subjects; if they have none on whom they can rely for a right use of our Christian birthright of παρρησία, none except those οἷς δεῖ ἐπιστομίζειν, what are we to conclude either as to the clergy or the doctrines?

I believe the essays can be written if the men can be found to write or speak them. And so we pass to the next questions—Who will deliver them, and who will arrange the courses?

I should propose to limit the lecturers to the clergy of the city and neighbourhood in general, giving power, however, to a certain committee to invite others occasionally, whether clergy from a distance or others. I should eschew the apologist; the professional lecturer on

Christian evidences: I should plough with our own oxen, or even with our own asses. These lectures would be more valued if they were delivered by men whom everybody knows. Why should Bristol look outside itself?

The lectures on portions of the Bible might be left entirely in the hands of men selected for the purpose. But the lectures on the *subjects* named, or subjects like them, need greater care and some supervision. What this should be is a matter that will need our consideration.

As regards details, I would suggest that the lectures be at regular intervals, and advertised beforehand, with some brief analysis of contents ; that discussion be allowed after the lecture, or after some of the lectures ; that they be free ; and that if no diocesan fund can be used to pay for the necessary expenses, a statement be issued periodically of the expenses, and subscriptions solicited. Of course in this case there must be guarantors.

It might be well to use the fact that the Mayor has authorised me to present his request to the Ruridecanal Conference to establish such a series of Bible Classes and Lectures.

Perhaps a few words may be added as to the nature and tone of these lectures and essays.

It is not at all necessary or desirable that these lectures should be made vehicles for party war cries, or for what is commonly called edification. They are intended primarily for them that are without, at any rate in all but name. All these subjects must be treated in a deep religious spirit, but we must get far below party watchwords, and even the recognised religious phraseology. Men will not believe that the most important truths can only be expressed in a single dialect. I am sure it is possible to have this deep religious spirit without being what is derogatively styled latitudinarian ; and to make these lectures truly Christian and Catholic, and tolerant and modest ; tolerant because they are deep ; tolerant because conscious of the conditioned character of all our knowledge. The teaching ought not to be identical, though it must not be contradictory, to that which we give in the pulpit.

Real unity is what we long for. It is to be found by digging down to first principles. It is not in these that men differ. It is confusion, not lucidity, that causes misunderstanding. In a Christian country like this, depend upon it, men are *naturaliter Christiani:* it is bred in their bone and blood; and, unless I am mistaken, men are wearying of negation, hungering for faith, but unable to accept truths in quite the old forms.

It is not possible to effect the purpose of these lectures by our sermons; and it would be wrong to attempt it. Our sermons ought to add to the effect of our services, and be directed primarily to warm and foster the spiritual life, to touch the heart, and direct the conduct; and can only rarely touch on questions of philosophy and reasoning.

Some one will naturally say, It is our business to preach Jesus Christ and Him crucified, and to know nothing else among our people, and so be like St. Paul among the Corinthians. I don't feel sure that this is quite applicable. I think of the caution of St. Augustine, " Let not the artless, simple brother think himself a holy man because he knows nothing." I think that St. Paul knew a great deal besides what we, perhaps, mean by " Jesus Christ and Him crucified." I think that when he speaks of " power and a sound mind," he means strong convincing reasoning based on knowledge. There is no necessary connection between orthodoxy and ignorance of science, or between scepticism and logic, though I believe if hearts could speak there are some of us that have a dire fear that it really is so.

But I have run to greater length than I intended, and will conclude with a very real apology for the inadequate way in which I have been able to bring before you a subject which seems to me one of very high importance. I await with deep interest and anxiety your opinions on the advisability of establishing such a course of classes and lectures; opinions that will doubtless be delivered with a deep sense of the gravity of the subject, and which will deal, not with minor details which may well be left to a committee to consider, but with the broad principles, the needs, and the way of meeting them that I have attempted, however imperfectly, to describe.

Resolution passed :—" That a Committee be appointed to consider the whole question, and to take what action may seem desirable."

In the years 1883, '84, '85, and '86, lectures were given by clergy and Nonconformist Ministers of Bristol on all the subjects set in the Cambridge Higher Local Examination. The Council of University College, Bristol, granted the use of its lecture-room for this purpose.

THE THEORY OF INSPIRATION ; OR, WHY MEN DO NOT BELIEVE THE BIBLE

PREFACE

THE two lectures that follow were delivered in the Temperance Hall, Bristol, on Jan. 31 and Feb. 14, 1883, to audiences chiefly consisting of artisans. The Bishop of the Diocese was in the chair at the first lecture, and the Chairman of the Trades Council at the second. They were delivered at the request of a Committee of the Ruridecanal Conference of Bristol.[1]

The selection of the subject was not my own, and I am very conscious how incomplete my treatment of it has been. It has been impossible in the space of these lectures to enter upon the application of the principles they contain. The application to history, interpretation, and doctrine offer indeed a wide and most interesting field. But it is of importance to note that this field is unquestionably open to Christians in general, and to members of the Church of England in particular. The principles of the Church of England are happily wider on this question than is usually avowed. And it is only by such principles and such applications that Christianity can reinforce itself by the revelations that God is making to the world in the wider and more philosophical study of antiquity, of textual and Biblical criticism, of comparative religion, and of the various branches of science. No view of divine inspiration of the Bible can be correct which precludes men from fully availing themselves of other revelations of truth. The popular opinion which prevails at present on inspiration does so preclude men : orthodoxy, whether witnessed by Councils and Creeds, or by the profounder study of the Bible, does not.

I briefly repeat my conviction that it is the misrepresentations of the essential nature of Christianity which seriously diminish its influence, and especially among the thoughtful, and that it is the duty of the authorised teachers to remove, and not humour, those misrepresentations : and I will quote, by permission, a passage from a letter I received from Archbishop Benson, to whom I had sent the first lecture.

---

[1] See p. 59.

It is dated Feb. 11. His weighty words need no commendation from me to the hearts and minds of all thoughtful Christians and thoughtful Secularists into whose hands these lectures may fall :—

"I need not shrink from saying that I have often gone over the pages of some anti-Christian journal with care, and failed utterly to find one of the assailed beliefs really understood. There was not what I (or any Christian I know) believed, but what some (probably honest) persons imagine we believe.

"You show from authorities how different is the Church-thought on inspiration from the straw-figure set up by objectors as if it were Church-doctrine, and so easily destroyed.

"All scientific ideas are difficult to grasp, whilst it is easy enough to take in some rough caricature of them. But I am mistaken in the intelligence and love of truth in the class now affected by misapprehensions, if they do not press on to gain, as other scientific knowledge advances, some true and scientific knowledge of what the teaching and basis of Christianity really are.

"I cannot of course pledge myself to every or any particular expressions or arguments which another may use ; but I know you are to be thanked, first for pointing out that there are such scientific ideas, as opposed to popular illusions about Christianity, and again for showing that what the Church holds about inspiration is something very different from the idea of it which objectors put out."

J. M. WILSON.

Clifton College,
    June 1883.

These lectures are published by the Christian Evidence Committee of the Society for Promoting Christian Knowledge, and are republished here with the kind consent of that Committee.

I

It has been thought better that these Lectures should be continued by one who is a resident among you,[1] and accessible to further inquiries ; by a clergyman, and by one who is already more or less known to many of you. We feel that this is our work, not a stranger's. And, on these grounds, I have been asked by some of you, and by the Committee, to give this Lecture. It is a duty quite un-

---

[1] One Lecture, on the Witness of the Bible to its own Inspiration, had been given by a very able lay friend from a distance, at the request of the Committee of the Ruridecanal Conference of Bristol.

sought by me. I am no debater; I have never spoken on this subject before. I have had but very scant time for preparing the address in the midst of much pressure of other work. My one qualification is an intense and burning desire to help my fellow-men who are inquiring into religious truth; to remove the painful barriers that seem to separate men equally honest and truth-seeking; to show what seem to me the truths I have slowly and painfully acquired.

The difficulty of the address lies in the fact that it will be listened to by very different classes of persons, who are, perhaps, very little acquainted with each other's way of thinking; by clergymen, to whom what I shall say will be familiar in their reading, though necessarily rare in their own addresses; by believers, who are, nevertheless, harassed by doubts which they do not know how to look into, and by objections which they constantly hear and see urged, and which they are unable to meet; by professed Secularists and disbelievers, such as spoke in this room a fortnight ago, who seem, nevertheless, to misapprehend the essence of Christianity, and to be fighting with an idol which they mistake for Christianity; and by believers, it may be, who have been troubled with no doubts, and to whom objections and difficulties are all alike new. These last will perhaps be pained for the moment at Lectures like these. I can only assure them that these difficulties, unfamiliar to them, are familiar enough to others; and that it seems, after anxious thought, a plain duty to attempt to discuss and reply to them in public. I have no fear of real unsettlement or permanent distress where there is earnest desire for truth. Many, moreover, would say that they have no doubts, yet have had misgivings, and have suppressed them from the thought that such misgivings were wrong. They feel neither the power nor the inclination to face these misgivings. The object of this course of Lectures is to reassure: to tell you that those who have leisure, and power, and inclination to investigate misgivings on these points are, nevertheless, strong in faith.

I am, however, chiefly addressing Secularists: and I wish to make it plain in what spirit I address you. I am not going to preach you a sermon; I am going to speak with the same freedom and unconventionality that I would use on my own hearthrug, as a man to brother men. I desire to remove some misunderstandings between Christians and Secularists; to mitigate strife; to separate essentials from matters of opinion. We shall understand one another better. If you love truth first, you are no foes of Christians. The Word of God, the Spirit of truth, is in the heart—dormant it may be—of every lover of truth. Christ lay asleep in the boat that was tossed on the waves of the Galilean sea: and so He sleeps in the heart of many a man who is agitated by doubt. But Christ may awake and still the storm.

My last prefatory remark is this—that for what I say I alone am responsible: at the same time, I am giving you nothing that is in any degree peculiar or original. The only originality is in offering it to an audience of artisans. And in this I trust I am not mistaken. You will perhaps find these Lectures difficult; but that arises from the nature of the subject: if any one thinks it obscure, I would remind him that all things cannot be expressed with the same clearness that some things can; and ask him—as Bishop Butler asks his readers—to reflect whether he could have expressed the same things, and not other things, with greater lucidity.

The Lecture is on the Difficulties of Belief in the Bible —"Why men do not believe." I shall try to give an abstract of these difficulties as far as I am acquainted with them: not stating them of course at full length; not urging them in such detail, and with the enforcement with which some of you might perhaps wish them to be urged; for this is plainly unnecessary and foreign to the purpose of these Lectures. But I will state them as fairly as I can, gathering them from ancient and modern sources. Some of them you will recognise as having been urged in this room a fortnight ago. I will then give at some length a reply to one group of these difficulties which I find sufficient to my own mind. Another group of difficulties I will reserve to a subsequent Lecture.

The first group of difficulties consists of those which may be called intellectual difficulties of the Bible. Among these is the improbability of facts related—the accounts of the Creation, the Fall, the Flood, the appearance of God to Abraham. You wish to know in what sense you are required to read these narratives. There is further the miraculous character of certain recorded events which you find difficult to accept. You ask, "Does the belief in inspiration require us to believe these records in the plain sense of the words?" Lastly, there are variations in the texts and in the versions, which the Revised Version has brought into public notice, and inconsistencies of narratives, discrepancies, or seeming discrepancies, in dates, numbers, and minor events. These and the general tenor of the historical narratives give the impression that the writers were dependent on ordinary sources for their information—on their memory, on tradition, on ancient documents, on information received from others. You ask, "Does the belief in inspiration compel me, in the face of cumulative evidence, to deny that any such inconsistency exists?" This is the first group of what I have called intellectual difficulties.

The second group consists of moral difficulties, which are, I know, deeply felt by some of you. I shall not forget the earnestness with which some of these were urged by one of you a fortnight ago. These I shall state and deal with in my next Lecture.

The third group contains what may be called philosophical difficulties—the difficulties we find in conceiving a future existence, in realising any divine influence on the world; the arguments of materialism and of certain facts of science on the one hand, and of idealism or certain aspects of reason on the other. With these you are probably less familiar. I mention them because I wish to leave none out, though they are in fact not difficulties connected with the Bible, but are in part involved in all philosophy of consciousness.

The fourth class of difficulties arises not so much from the Bible as from the popular religion and opinion of the present day, which indeed appeals to the Bible as its authority for all it says, but not unfrequently strains, distorts, exaggerates the passages which support a particular view, and ignores or explains away passages which should modify that view. Such are certain views as to the judgment of the heathen, as to the state of the wicked after death, certain ways of expressing the doctrine of the Atonement, certain views as to the infallibility of the Bible. On all these points there are held by some Christians strong views, which are not held by other Christians, and must be regarded as matters of opinion, and not as of the essence of Christianity. These are difficulties in the minds of many. To judge these rightly requires large historical knowledge; and it is not surprising if confusions often arise between what is divine and what is human, between the foundation and the superstructure. And these confusions are increased by the unfortunate tendency of human nature to be positive in its assertions in proportion to its ignorance. Fools rush in where angels fear to tread. I wish that all of us, including myself, may ever remember the words in which Cromwell addressed an assembly of Scotch divines: "I entreat you, my brethren, I entreat you by the mercies of God, to remember that it is possible that sometimes you may be mistaken."

These are not in truth difficulties primarily of the Bible; they are difficulties superadded to those of the Bible; superadded by human ignorance, prejudice, infirmity, passion. Alas that it should be so!

The last group that I shall formulate is that to which some speakers among you alluded a fortnight ago—the abuses of Christianity in practice. There are in all our memories the scandals of monasticism, the horrors of the Inquisition, the crimes of Alva, the fires of Smithfield, the profligacy of some professing Christians, the divisions and hostility between opposing parties and churches. There is, further, an alleged tacit alliance between the Church and the upper classes, and an alleged want of sympathy

F

with the aspirations of other classes and with the upward progress of man.

You do not perhaps see as plainly as we do that these are abuses of Christianity, and contradict its spirit, and are not a part of Christianity. But you have a right to ask, If Christianity comes from God, how can Christians have done such deeds? If it was by misunderstanding Christ's teaching, you ask, Did not Christ foresee all this, and could He not have prevented it by plainer teaching?

I have now concluded this summary of difficulties. I do not profess that it is exhaustive in detail; but I claim that it is representative and fair, so far as the book itself is concerned. I am not now concerned with the difficulties that arise from the head and the heart of the man himself. The difficulties will scarcely be really new to any one present. Some of us are familiar with them from the study of history and literature; others have met with them in the current Secularist periodicals of the day; and others, from their own thoughts and from conversation with others, have become acquainted with all, or nearly all, that I have said. These are the ghosts that haunt and terrify believers, that drive some men into timidity and silence, and others into infidelity and blasphemy. Let us drag these ghosts out to the light of day and look at them. Surely it is felt by all of us to be time for Christians to give a reason for the faith that is in them, and to give it, if necessary, on the platform or in the streets. If these were uncommon objections, dug out of obscure books and blasphemous periodicals, it might be urged that it would be unwise to speak of them, to give them a wider circulation. But I believe it is impossible, or nearly so, to circulate them more widely: they are felt as misgivings, if not as formulated doubts, more or less, by every man of every class.

Now the latter (the fourth and fifth) groups of these difficulties arise from human imperfection and sin. It would be bad logic to say that Christianity is false because some Christians have been wicked; as it would be bad logic to say that trades unionism is a crime because some trades unionists have been cruel or unfair. You must judge a system by its tendencies, its best fruits, its capacities. These difficulties arise from its abuses, and abuses seem inevitable while human nature is what it is. Moreover, they have no immediate connection with the theory of inspiration of the Bible, and I need not further allude to them.

There is the very important group of moral difficulties. They arise partly from the common mistake of contrasting what you would expect with what is actually the fact; the slow emergence of man from barbarism and savagery, with the sudden and complete illumination of man, which you may have imagined as the only work worthy of God, the only way in which He could work; and partly also from misunderstanding the dramatic character of some of the Old Testament narratives, and from an erroneous view of the nature of inspiration. With these difficulties I propose to deal in the next Lecture.

Finally, there is the group of difficulties I classed as intellectual, which are the consequences of a particular theory as to the necessity of a literal interpretation and the verbal accuracy of the Bible: difficulties which disappear before a higher, a more spiritual, more scriptural, less mechanical theory of inspiration. It is to this group of difficulties that I must of necessity be confined for the remainder of this Lecture.

Many people imagine, though they scarcely know how or why, that a particular view of inspiration is inseparably bound up with Christianity itself. The very high value, the absolutely inestimable value, which we believers set upon the Bible, as our guide to heaven and comfort on earth, to some extent dazzles us when we try to reflect on the nature of the Bible: and we are apt to attribute to it qualities which are claimed for it neither by the book itself, nor by the formal declarations of the Christian Churches, nor by their most representative teachers. What I shall say will surprise some of you, both Christians and Secularists, often as it has been said before; but it is an undeniable fact that no creed or formulary of any Church has ever asserted that the Bible is to be literally and prosaically interpreted, or that its accuracy and historical correctness are supernaturally guaranteed. It is not in any decree of Rome, nor in any creed or article of our Church, nor in any pledge exacted from laymen at baptism or from clergy on taking orders. The Church has never laid down any theory of inspiration.

You will ask with surprise, How then has this belief that inspiration means infallibility become so common? Is it not commonly thought that a belief in the inspiration of the Bible makes all criticism of its contents impossible, inasmuch as we can only criticise what is human?

I can only reply by going into the history of the theory of inspiration.

The books of the Old Testament had been treasured by the Jews through the captivity, through the terrible persecutions of Antiochus Epiphanes, and were at once the history, the law, the prayer-book, the hymn-book, and the centre and subject of the literature of the Jews. They copied and recopied and valued and counted every letter. It was the text-book of the past, the present, and the future; it was the treasure and pride of the learned classes. But they were slaves of the letter. Christ came and taught them to look at its spirit. He taught them that the law was but a stage in their education, that it was time to advance. He corrects and supersedes its teaching. He shows that it was in its nature temporary. He treated it with boundless reverence and love, but with absolute freedom. He asserted, in modern phrase, the continuity of spiritual progress, just as the prophets had done: and, further, He promised that divine guidance would be given to continue that progress in the future. It is plain that any teaching of verbal inspiration or infallibility of the Old Testament is not traceable to the teaching of Christ.

On the death of Jesus Christ His followers went into all the world proclaiming Him. They preached His life, His sayings, His wonderful works, His cross, His resurrection: they preached forgiveness of sins, and the new revelation of God as a loving Father. And the world opened wide its heart to these men. They brought to the

world fresh aims and hope and life.   None were excluded
from this influence: Syrian slaves and Greek philosophers,
Pharisees and Egyptians, Roman centurions and outcast
women, all believed on Him.   The world awoke to an
inheritance of joy.   All this is indisputable.

But what did they preach?   Not the Bible.   They did
not proclaim "Believe in the story of the Creation and
the Flood, or you shall perish."   They preached "Believe
on the Lord Jesus Christ and you shall be saved."   They
preached the joy and hopes, the brotherhood and renova-
tion of humanity: I may almost say they preached the
rights of man as well as the revelation of God.   There is
no theory yet of the nature of the inspiration of the Old
Testament.   The fact of an inspiration is assumed, but
there is no theory as to its nature.

The generation began to pass away, the work of spread-
ing the Gospel was vast, the harvest was plenteous; but
the labourers who had seen Christ were but few, and so
the Gospels were written.   They are memoirs of Christ:
they contain the substance of the early preaching of the
Apostles.   They are not a treatise on evidences.   They
make no special claim to supernatural guidance, though it
is plain that they felt the guidance and inspiration of a
Power higher than their own.   St. Luke simply says that
as many others have written accounts of Christ's life, he
has taken great pains to investigate the whole narrative
and arrange it in order.   St. John says that he was an
eye-witness, and assures his readers that he spoke the
truth; he knoweth that he saith true.

Then letters of the Apostles are circulated and
treasured, and other books are written, and the Canon
or list of books of the New Testament is being slowly
formed; but for a long time there was no hard and fast
line between the books admitted into the Canon, and
other venerable writings which were read in some of the
churches for edification.   Christianity had conquered the
Roman empire, and became the established religion, before
the Church had formally adopted a complete Canon of
Scripture.   Still there is no thought of a divinely guaranteed

accuracy. The human element was frankly admitted side by side with the divine, and no attempt was made to separate the two, or to formulate a theory of inspiration.

Meantime came the age of persecutions. The marvellous personal influence of Christ and His Apostles was gone; believers had nothing but the books, and the loving interpretation of the books by the teachers, and the organisation and Sacraments of the Church. Against the books the persecution was soon specially aimed. And therefore they loved them the more, and would lay down their lives for them. Fidelity to them was the fidelity of a soldier to his standard. A Bishop was charged with having once surrendered a copy of the Bible : he was branded as a traitor, and ordination conferred by him was deemed invalid. The books became identified with Christianity through the persecutions.

Still no theory was formulated. The great fathers, Origen, Chrysostom, Jerome, dwelt at times on the human element of the Bible, and though they gave no theory, they held generally that inspiration was continuous, and that the inspiration of all Christians was the same in kind, though far less in degree, as that of the sacred writers.

But time will not permit me to go on through the history of biblical interpretation in the Middle Ages : to show how there grew up on the one hand, side by side with the Bible, a mysticism which gave great prominence to the communion of the spirit with God, the inspiration of the individual; and on the other, a Church tradition which has culminated in the dogma of the infallibility of the Pope. Between the two the Bible was almost eclipsed.

Then came at last the glorious and ever-memorable Reformation, when the abuses and superstition and slavery of the human intellect had become intolerable : the Bible was unearthed, and became the proclamation of national and individual liberty. The keynote of our Reformed Church is in our Sixth Article: " Holy Scripture containeth all things necessary to salvation, so that whatsoever is not read therein, nor may be proved thereby, is not to be required of any man that it should be believed as an article of faith."

Still there is no *theory* of inspiration. Among the un-educated it is not unlikely that some mechanical theory of infallibility was assumed, though unformulated; but the value attached to the Bible was that it liberated men, not that it bound them. The power it exercised was the consequence, not the cause, of its study. And among the Reformers, while they held the Bible to be divinely inspired, yet its human element was fully recognised: all that they con-tended for was that nothing else was necessary. In that free air, in that truth-loving spirit of the Reformation, we still live.

And now begins a more generally diffused and popular study of the Bible, and with that study begin theories of the nature of inspiration. "Men began to attribute to the Bible the same mechanical infallibility which the Romanists had claimed for the Church. The Calvinists maintained the direct and supernatural action of a guiding power on the very words of the inspired writer without any regard to his personal or national position. Every part of Scripture was held to be not only pregnant with instruc-tion, but with instruction of the same kind and in the same sense." [1] Men like broad, simple, unqualified state-ments which save the trouble of thought. Such a state-ment was the Calvinistic theory of inspiration, that it was an external influence on man which gave a divine guarantee against all error; that from Genesis to Revela-tion not only is the Bible the Word of God, but the words of God; and it is this theory which lands men in endless contradictions. Such is the historic origin of this theory—fifteen centuries after the books were written. But is the theory true? Listen to what is said of it: "The purely organic (that is mechanical) theory of inspiration rests on no Scriptural authority, and, if we except a few ambiguous metaphors, is supported by no historical testimony. It is at variance with the whole form and fashion of the Bible, and it is destructive of all that is holiest in man and highest in religion."

These are the words of one writer. Now I will read

[1] Westcott, *Introduction to the Study of the Gospels*, p. 5.

you the words of another: "It will not do to say that it
is not verbally inspired. If the words are not inspired,
what is?"

Now who are these writers? Who is this Secularist
who thus denies the verbal inspiration of the Bible? He
is the greatest living authority on the history of the Bible,
the Professor of Divinity at Cambridge, Canon Westcott,[1]
whose text-books are used by all candidates for the ministry
in our Church, and are almost universally studied by
Nonconformists; one, I need hardly say, who holds the
Inspiration of Scripture not less tenaciously than I do.
And who is this theologian, this champion of the faith,
who so stoutly asserts verbal inspiration as the theory held
by Christians? He is the well-known Secularist writer of
America, whose works are diligently circulated among some
of you, Colonel Robert Ingersoll.[2] But I ask what right
has he to put into the mouths of Christians a definition of
inspiration which is so utterly unsubstantiated by Scripture, and by historical testimony, repudiated by the
greatest living theologians, and by the vast majority,
if not the whole, of the educated Christian ministers in
the world?

I do not charge him with dishonesty; I see no trace of
dishonesty in his book. I see ignorance of historical facts,
and an insensibility to the spiritual side of human nature.
But is it not deplorable that such a writer should dress up
a caricature of Christianity in his ignorance, and hold it
up to ridicule in his presumption?

I am stating the doctrine of the Church of England,
and I have given some few authorities, for to give many
would be endless. But I will give one more.

I will quote from the Bishop of Winchester, a living
bishop, to whose moderation and judgment and learning
all defer. He says: "It is a secondary consideration, and
a question on which we may safely agree to differ, whether
every book of the Old Testament was written so completely
under the dictation of God's Holy Spirit that every word,

---

[1] Westcott, *Introduction to the Study of the Gospels*, p. 6.
[2] *The Christian Religion*, p. 41.

not only doctrinal but also historical and scientific, must be infallibly correct and true." "These are all questions on which persons believing in the Gospel may differ." [1]

The importance of clearing up this point is immense. If Christianity and the literal accuracy of the Bible stood and fell together, as Renan in his autobiography professes to have fancied they did, myriads of Christians would be compelled to be Secularists. If they do not stand and fall together, scores of Secularists are Secularists by mistake. It is on this erroneous assumption that they argue, and argue very cleverly. On their own data they are unanswerable, but their data are mistaken.

Do you ask me, Can I then become a Christian without having first believed in the divinely guaranteed accuracy of the Bible?

A thousand times I answer Yes. But the Bishop of Winchester shall again answer for me. "All the history," he says, "and even all the great doctrines, might be capable of proof and so deserving of credence, though we were obliged to adopt almost the lowest of the modern theories of inspiration." [2] He might go further still, and elsewhere he does go further. The truth is that the belief in inspiration is not the portal by which you enter the temple: it is the atmosphere you breathe when you have entered. You may become a Christian, most men do become Christians, from finding in the life and sayings and death of Jesus Christ something that touches them, something that finds them, something that is a revelation of divine love to the human heart. Men find that there is something in them dear and precious to God. And then love springs up in them, and a new life begins. They look out on the world with larger and more loving eyes. They see God in their brethren, God in nature, and God in their Bibles. In their Bibles they read of the Christ whom they love. Those pages are filled with power that moves the soul; never man spake as this man, never book spake as this book. And this, and this only, is the theory of inspiration that Christians must needs possess.

[1] *Aids to Faith.*   [2] *Ibid.*

It is primarily an internal question among believers, not an external question with the world. It has little or no relation to the convictions which make and keep a man a Christian. It is not a question which I or any one would care to talk about to one who is not already drawn to Christ. It is premature to talk with others of the exact limits of inspiration. Let them first read the Gospels, read them as they would read any other book, with any theory of inspiration or with none, with the one aim of learning the truth about Jesus Christ, of finding in the book what is pure and noble and elevating; let them first learn to admire, to love, to copy, to serve Jesus Christ; and I care not what theory they may form of inspiration; they will have got the thing, and then they will not be over-anxious to define it.

Definition is not essential to belief. I believe in God, but I cannot define Him; I believe in matter, but I cannot define it; I believe in my own personality, in space, in time, but I cannot define them. He who believes in a Divine Being, of whose will the world of nature and man is the expression, believes, for he cannot but believe, in the action of that Divine Being through the mind of man. Inspiration is not a definable quality of a book, to be canvassed and weighed and measured by intellectual processes: it is as imponderable as heat. It is felt by the spirit, not demonstrated to the understanding. To prove the inspiration of the Bible is as impossible as to listen to the colours of a rainbow. It is to apply the wrong sense. But even before inspiration is felt by the spirit, it may be seen not to be inconsistent with the understanding.

This Lecture was on the question, Why men do not believe the Bible? I have now in part answered the question. There are men, probably there are men in this room, who do not believe it, because they think that believing the Bible means their interpreting tradition, poetry, rhetoric, and metaphor, as if it were scientific statement; interpreting the dramatic phrases, dialogue, and dress of Oriental narratives and poems of long-past ages as if they were nineteenth-century prose; in a word, they do not

believe the Bible because they misunderstand it, and misunderstand the spirit in which they should read it. Apply
what I said to the difficulties that I classed as the intellectual group. They all vanish into thin air. Certain
statements seem to be inconsistent—with what? with a
theory which was rightly described by Westcott as "at
variance with the whole form and fashion of the Bible,
destructive of all that is holiest in man and highest in
religion." The difficulties are not. We have conjured
them up like ghosts in the dark, and now they vanish like
ghosts in the daylight.

To speak without metaphor, you need not open your
Bibles, you need not begin to study the question of Christianity, with the thought (I have seen the assertion made),
Before I can become a Christian, I must believe that
Balaam's ass spoke, that an axe-head floated on water, and
that all the animals of the whole world went by pairs or
sevens into an ark. You may open your Bibles with any
preconceptions about those and similar narratives that you
please. That is what I mean by saying that inspiration is
not an *external* question : the belief in it is not a condition
of approaching the subject. But you may not, on the
other hand, open the Bible with the preconception that it
is an imposture and a lie. Read your New Testament
candidly, with a prayer for enlightenment, and it will be
strange if you do not rise from it with the thought, This
is noble, this is true, this is none other than the voice of
God. You will then know what inspiration is : you will
know that opinions as to the historical accuracy of these
narratives have no vital connection with the theory of
inspiration. But you will find, as all students find, that
the more closely you study the Bible, the more reason
there is to trust its general accuracy and its faithfulness to
truth.

But do not misunderstand what I have said. We are
not discussing whether miracles are credible, but whether
our belief in them depends on our holding a particular
theory of inspiration, and on our holding it as a condition
of approaching the Bible at all. The subject of miracles

is too large to touch on here. But I will say, first, that the evidence for them is wholly independent of any theory of inspiration; secondly, that it follows that all miracles do not stand or fall together; thirdly, that the evidence for what is commonly called the miraculous element in Christianity appears to my own mind convincing.

But this is parenthetical, to remove possible erroneous inferences from what has just been said: it is, strictly speaking, foreign to the subject, as I have shown, and questions relating to it would scarcely be considered relevant.

O my friends, who are at present Secularists, believe me that you may be nearer us than you think, as we are nearer you than you thought. You may yet find in Christ a Teacher and Master whom you will love and reverence: you may find in the Bible a continuous record of the striving of man after higher things, and of God's continued revelation of Himself as man was able to bear it. You may find, above all, that the deepest and sincerest Christianity is compatible with a clear and powerful intellect, and with the deepest and sincerest love of truth. Human misunderstandings, human misrepresentations, human prejudices—for we all have prejudices—may have hitherto obscured some truths from your eyes. Possibly my words may help you to rend away the veil and see the truth with clearer vision.

And you, my friends, no less dear as fellow-men, and dearer as fellow-Christians, be not afraid of the truths I tell you. In this, as in all else, the truth and the truth alone shall make you free; free from the haunting terror of secret disbelief. Doubt comes in at the window when inquiry is denied at the door. You may learn to value your Bible more and not less, with a more vivid and sustaining intelligence. And you may learn to see that in criticism and science and secularism there is a spirit not wholly evil. They are serving in God's hands to purify Christianity from its errors and accretions, and it shall come out as gold refined in the fire. In their blindness and ignorance (and who but we are to blame for their blindness and ignorance?—God forgive us)—in their blindness and ignorance, and sometimes in their rage and profanity, they strike at things sacred, and insult the name which we most reverence: but it is literally true that "they know not what they do." We are partly to blame, we and our fathers. Let us try to make Christianity once more shine out as it shone in the days of Christ, as good news, and glad tidings of God, as the source of faith and assurance and hope and salvation, as the charter of freedom and progress and the upward march of man, and not fetter and encumber it with human additions of which our Master and His disciples never heard. Let us "stand fast in the liberty wherewith Christ has made us free."

II

I CANNOT begin this second Lecture better than by quoting a few warm and kindly words addressed to you from a letter I have received from our Bishop, who was in the chair at the last Lecture. "Tell them, please," he says, "that their real earnestness made a great impression on me, and that I am as convinced as I am of my own existence, that such men will never seek without at last finding." This is the spirit in which I wish to enter on the gravest possible subject that a man can engage to speak on to others—The Moral Difficulties of the Bible. Do not think that I, or any of those who are co-operating with me, approach men staggered by doubt on these points in any spirit of moral or intellectual Pharisaism, in any spirit which tacitly says, "Stand aside, I am wiser and holier than thou." Our feeling is, I suppose, this: We see men, once children of simple faith, very much distressed by hideous conflict of thought, by wild rebellion against what they hear. I can no more see this without the desire to relieve such pain, than I could pass by bodily needs. Indeed this is acuter pain than wounds or hunger. And I am certain it can be relieved. I have learnt to see that this Bible, this Word of God, as I hold it emphatically to be, is a word to all men. I see that it had in it a message and suitable teaching for such diverse races as the Jews of old, and later on, after Christ came, for Greek and Roman, and for our great sturdy Anglo-Saxon race too. So universal was its power in the past, that I cannot but be convinced that it has a message for us all in the present, if we can but read it right: a message for scholar and simple, for sceptic and child, for him who proves all things, and for him who accepts, doubting nothing. I start with the conviction that if it is God's Word in any sense, it is meant for us all. We shall never understand it right if we attempt to narrow its scope. There is something there for all. It is just as mistaken and wrong in a critical Secularist to ridicule the simple faith of a Christian man less critical than himself, as it is mistaken and wrong in a Christian to say to the Secularist, You shall find in the Bible exactly what I find, or I shall treat you as an outcast. Contempt is always wrong. It is as wrong to count a man a fool for believing as for unbelieving; to have the Sadducaic pride of scepticism as the Pharisaic pride of religion.

I wish to add one further preliminary remark, as it is the justification of these Lectures. Scepticism was once confined to the comparatively learned: now it has passed into a less instructed class. Cheap periodicals, and an endless flow of Secularist leaflets, are familiarising the artisan class with the moral difficulties of the Bible in a very crude shape. Scientific difficulties also a few years ago were discussed only by the learned. Now any man in a workshop can get up and show how little Moses knew compared to Darwin and Lyell. But meantime the learned, and the real kings of modern thought, have moved forward a stage; they are engaged with fresh problems, as little known to you as those I have just been speaking of were known to your grandfathers. They are engaged, not in pointing out moral difficulties, but in removing them; not in dividing religion and science, but in showing that they are and must be inseparable allies. They are thinking

modestly, quietly, diffidently. Great men and wise men
have learnt how to suspend their judgment. It is not the
wise who are always "cocksure" of everything. And
further, it has not been in vain that the vast researches of
the last half-century, biblical, ethnological, scientific, psycho-
logical, have been made. They have put the Bible and
religion on a fresh and firmer footing. Now you don't
know this, and can't know it. I read your Secularist
journals, and I see that for the most part they are slaying
the slain, or at least the dying, on the old fields of battle ;
while the true life and spirit of Christianity and of the
Bible is soaring above them. I am sanguine enough to
think it is not impossible to open to you this higher region ;
and that by so doing most of the moral difficulties of the
Old Testament will disappear. Not of course that I am
shallow enough to fancy that all philosophical and religious
problems can be solved by man. *That* they will never
be on any basis. The finite will never comprehend the
infinite. But I am sure that a very large part of the difficulties which gather round the Bible, among those who
think and have some knowledge, is removable by clearer
thinking and more knowledge.

Once more let me repeat that I claim no originality or
liberality in what I say. It is, I believe, commonplace
enough. The only originality is in offering it in plain
English on a platform to a meeting of working men. And
here some of my friends differ from me. They say, Leave
them alone ; you will unsettle more than you will help.
You will shake the not very intelligent faith of believers,
and not convert the sceptics. Well, I don't think so ; and
it is for you to say whether I am mistaken. I think that
believers will find ground for stronger and more intelligent
faith : I believe that some doubting minds are getting new
light ; and as for unsettlement, I believe its chief cause is
the widespread conviction that old faiths and new lights
are hopelessly at variance ; and I believe that its cure, if
cure there is to be, will come from seeing the old faiths *in*
new lights.

The moral difficulties of the Bible may be summed up

briefly as follows :—The Bible is so unlike what you would expect; it does not consist of golden sayings and rules of life; give explanations of the philosophical and social problems of the past, the present, and the future; contain teachings immeasurably unlike those of any other book: but it contains history, ritual, legislation, poetry, dialogue, prophecy, memoirs, and letters: it contains much that is foreign to your idea of what a revelation ought to be. But this is not all. There is not only much that is foreign, but much that is opposed, to your preconceptions. The Jews tolerated slavery, polygamy, and other customs and cruelties of imperfect civilisation. There are the vindictive psalms, too, with their bitter hatred against enemies—psalms which we chant in our churches. How can we do so? There are stories of immorality, of treachery, of crime. How can we read them? These are representative of the moral difficulties you find in the Old Testament. You ask, Does the theory of the inspiration of the Bible compel me to believe that the God whom I am told to worship, the unchanging, eternal God, did, three thousand years ago, command or even tolerate actions which we now regard as crimes? If these were prejudices of the human mind at that semi-barbarous stage, ought not a revelation to have eradicated them at once, instead of seeming to tolerate and approve them?

An answer cannot be given in a word. You must be patient, and follow a train of reasoning; and even then it will require time and thought to lift yourself to a new point of view.

Let us be clear as to what we mean by difficulties in a book. We mean inconsistencies; not, however, between two facts. Facts are never inconsistent. It is theories that are inconsistent. Now in this case what are the theories that are inconsistent? They are the theory that the Bible tells us one thing about God, and the theory that it ought to tell us another. We understand the Bible to tell us that God is cruel, revengeful, and unjust; we think it ought to tell us that He is merciful, forgiving, and just. The moral difficulties of the Bible at the bottom come to this clash of two theories—what we think it does teach, and what we think it ought to teach.

Now in both these theories we are liable to mistake. What the Bible really teaches is plainly a question of interpretation, and not easy interpretation. This is shown by the vast variety of comment and opinion on it, and by the changes of interpretation the world has witnessed.

At the same time we may be equally certain that, if it is God's Word to all, it does not need human learning and critical insight, which is out of the reach of most ages and most individuals in this and every age, in order to get from it what it is intended we should get. "The wayfaring man, though simple, shall not err therein." [1] But mistakes of interpretation we may make. We may be mistaken in reading as prose what is meant for poetry; mistaken in reading as fact what is really parable; as logic what is really rhetoric. We may read in European literalness what is written in Oriental imagery.

I am saying that difficulties arise from the clash of interpretation with our preconceptions; from the difference between what we think is said, and what we think ought to be said; and that in what we think is said we may be mistaken. We must, therefore, most carefully re-examine our interpretation, and examine not only carefully, but modestly, allowing for the change which may take place in our own minds as our knowledge increases, for the growth of germs of truth that lie hidden in the soil; allowing also for the possibility,—shall I not say probability? —which so many men when thinking on this subject never seem to contemplate—the possibility, that is to say, that we may be wrong; and meanwhile suspending our judgment—a habit in which we ought to train ourselves. All great thinkers are patient thinkers.

The other possibility of error lies in our preconceptions as to what the Bible ought to be. We are apt to think that a revelation from God ought to be a sort of handbook to life—a perfect and complete "inquire within," with precise rules for all emergencies, suited for all ages, and

[1] Is. xxxv. 8.

countries, and capacities. We are apt to think its record ought to be guaranteed against the slightest mistake, and against even the suspicion of mistake ; that it ought to be vouched for by indisputable evidence. It ought, in fact, to satisfy and convince all. I will not stay to inquire whether such a revelation could be made, but I will ask why we say it *ought* to do all this. Not on scientific analogy. God has not made the laws of matter and motion, of health and food, the laws of trade and society, of politics or legislation, perfectly clear : in all these subjects light emerges out of obscurity by the steady and continued application of the power God has given us. If science teaches us any lesson, it is the slow preparation of the world before the appearance on it of man ; the extreme slowness with which races have been formed and ideas grown up. Science does verily teach us, like the Psalmist, that a thousand years are but as one day. It is not easy to see why we say that revelation ought to be in such and such a form. Who are we that we should decide ? Further, it needs but small acquaintance with the history of science to know that this talking of what *ought to be* always leads men wrong. " It stands to reason that the planets ought to move in circles," said these *à priori* philosophers, these men who decide beforehand ; but the fact turned out that they move in ellipses. " It stands to reason that there ought to be only five of them," [1] and there are more than a hundred. " It stands to reason that the sun ought to have no spots, that there ought to be no antipodes," and so on. In fact, you may pretty safely conclude that when a man argues " it stands to reason " that so and so must be the case, he means it stands to *his* reason ; he is saying what he thinks facts ought to be, instead of looking to see what they are. This was why so many ages passed without progress in the real knowledge of external nature ; and the method is still haunting all such discussions as the present. Let us try and look at what *is*.

The moral difficulties arise then from a collision between

---

[1] *I.e.* besides the sun and moon, to complete the perfect number seven.

what we think the Bible says, and what we think it ought
to say. I have pointed out, first, that we may be wrong
in our thoughts as to what it says; secondly, wrong in our
thoughts as to what it ought to say; and that from getting
right on these points the difficulties vanish.

Let us try and look at what *is*.

The Bible professes to be historical: it contains passages
from the history of a selected nation.   It is, in one sense,
a most important one, a single book, to be judged by its
end, not only by its beginning; it professes to lead up to
and culminate in the teaching and life of Jesus Christ, and
to give a remedy for evil in His death.   In another sense,
not less important, it is many books; each intended,
primarily at least, for the age in which it was written, with
the evident marks of the knowledge and feelings of that
age and that nation.

It professes to be passages from the history of a very
primitive nation, emerging from the impenetrable darkness
of prehistoric times, before the dawn of what we should
call arts and sciences and philosophy and literature.

Further, it is not an ordinary history.   It is the history
of the working out of an idea; of the development of the
idea of the kingdom of God.   All the history is regarded
in that light.   Events ordinarily attributed to human
motives are here referred to a more remote cause—the
will of God.

It is, further, the training of a typical nation,—whose
free-will amounts to stubbornness,—whose history is told
us in the Bible.   And, as we trace this nation through its
long history, the most striking characteristic is the conflict
of the wilfulness of the nation with a voice that always
opposed its wilfulness, a voice that seems to belong not to
the nation itself, not evolved out of its own history, but to
be external, authoritative, professing to be divine.   There
was a succession of men claiming to be prophets, *i.e.* to
speak forth what God had taught them, and in successive
ages they were at war with the desires and the practices
of the nation.   There was a continual divine teaching
going on; when the people obeyed it they prospered;

when they disobeyed, judgments overtook them.   To
prove this at length would take a whole Lecture.

Let me give one passage from its history.   The surrounding races were given to human sacrifices: we see
how Israel was induced to abandon them; first, by the
substitution of animals; then by the teaching that "mercy
and not sacrifice" is what God requires; which is the
voice of the prophets and psalmists; finally, by the lesson
that the true sacrifice is the surrender of the heart to the
will of God.   Other surrounding nations remained in the
primitive condition, and went on with human sacrifices.
This startling difference between the Jewish race and the
nations around them — nations, moreover, of the same
blood with themselves—cannot be traced to any development of civilisation.   On the contrary, the nations immediately surrounding the Jews were much more highly
civilised in all that we call material civilisation.   Yet the
researches of ancient history prove that they were so un-
speakably corrupt, so given up to the most revolting vices,
that there is no accounting for the utterly different standard
of right and wrong among the tiny Jewish nation planted
in their midst, but by admitting that the Hebrew prophets
were, as they professed to be, taught of God.   Thus this
contrast presented by the Jews was no mere development
of civilisation; it was the result of an opposing influence.
What was this opposing influence, so alien to their habits
of thought? so far-reaching in its grasp of the future?
The explanation given in the book itself is that it was the
Spirit striving with men.

There is a profound truth in St. Paul's words, "first,
that which is natural, afterward that which is spiritual." [1]
In the life of each one of us there spring up first natural
motives — self-preservation, hunger, passion, ambition;
then that which is spiritual—thought, awe of the unseen,
love, humility, worship.   So it was with the Jews.   The
Old Testament contains fragments of the record of their
education from the natural to the spiritual: fragments,
indeed, and yet revealing on study a singular unity, frag-

[1] 1 Cor. xv. 46.

ments of surpassing interest and value as the key to the history of man.

The account of the creation, for instance, may not be an anticipation by direct revelation of the discoveries which God has given man the power to make by his own intellect. It is misunderstood if it is regarded as a narrative to be used for purposes of science. It is a revelation, made through Moses or some early seer, of the fundamental hypothesis of religion, put in a form that could be grasped by the popular imagination and handed down by memory; the revelation that all this wonderful world of nature and life and mind had an origin, and an origin in a Power we cannot comprehend, which we call God. This deep spiritual truth, deeper than any science and quite uncontradicted by science, is conveyed in narrative form.[1] The spiritual truth was always felt in it, and may still be felt even by those who do not need the garment of narrative to put the truth into a form that could be apprehended. In calling this an inspired account of the creation, I mean that it surpasses far the similar cosmogonies of kindred nations; that it did actually, and does actually, teach the great truth of One Personal God, and that God is good, and the Creator at once of matter and life and mind, One that may love and be loved; and that these were truths beyond the experience and reach of man. It is surely the fault of our dull apprehension to read such a narrative as if it were science. I said it surpasses far the similar cosmogonies of kindred nations. Even now men are digging up in the valley of the Euphrates, and deciphering in the British Museum, records on earthenware of the beliefs of Chaldæa contemporary with Moses. They bring out into startling relief the purity, the depth of the truth conveyed in the early chapters of Genesis. As to the form of those chapters wise men will suspend their judgment; that is a matter of third or fourth rate importance; and for the truth conveyed in them they will thank God.

The Bible next relates the fall of man in such form as

[1] What St. Ambrose called " in specie historiæ."

children and simple folk can comprehend. It is a narrative that teaches both the unquestioning mind and the questioning mind; both that which accepts the story as it stands and the truth that underlies the story, and that which accepts only the truth that underlies the story. But there is a stage of mind between the two. It is the stage that rebels against such narratives. "Isn't it quite true?" the child says after hearing a story, and doesn't care to wait for the moral. So it is with some of us. The literal truth is for some of us gone from the narrative: the serpent, the apple, the garden, and the flaming sword—this is gone; and the religious truth is not discovered, not even looked for by some of us; nay, listened to with impatience. But this is only a passing frame of mind. Turn to it once more, and ask what is the truth it tells; and then you will see that the story of the Fall teaches us neither more nor less than what it has always taught the world—in the only way in which hitherto men could learn —that man has a free-will of his own, that he has an inner voice of right and wrong, that terrible voice of conscience, the voice of God in man; that he can disobey it, and that suffering is the sure consequence of disobedience. The book tells us that at a certain stage sin began. That is the lesson of the Fall. The book tells us a truth that no heathen nation ever fully attained to, that there is such a thing as sin—the yielding of the spirit to the flesh: and moreover the wonderful narrative of Genesis looks forward from the very beginning to a conquest over evil, and a redemption from sin. Did some one invent this in those ages? Must it not have been given him? What should we have been thinking now but for this revelation about God?

But I cannot go through the Bible with you in one Lecture. The story of the Flood has doubtless a historical foundation, as its counterpart is found among the traditions of almost all nations. The later history tells us of growing light, and struggles against the light; of mixed human characters like Abraham, Jacob, and David, in whom good struggled with evil and overcame; of the lofty words of the prophets; until at last the final revelation was made which gave goodness fresh power, and which shall, we believe, one day make holiness supreme on earth.

If you ask why was the revelation so wrapped in narrative and history and action, ask yourself how could any philosophy, any abstract truth, have been handed down and impressed itself on all ages.   How would the sort of Bible we might write in the nineteenth century have suited either past or future ages?   If we were to write it, it would be forgotten in a few years, or if remembered, would be remembered for its mistakes.

You cannot, then, read the Bible intelligently except as a progressive revelation.   You must not look at it as if it was all on one plane.   There is a moral perspective. The morality of one age was not the morality of another.

Did, then, God leave a low morality uncorrected?   Yes, for a time, "for the hardness of their hearts."[1]   So Christ says.   The stubborn free-will of man had so to be trained, and so it was trained.   I do not find this hard to believe. But the teaching was always above the people.   The teaching was not a mere outcome of Semitic character. There was a high Purpose leading them by paths that they knew not.[2]   They were intensely idolatrous, always lapsing into idolatry: what power was it that not only thought the second commandment, but gave it a moral weight which at last overcame their stubborn idolatry?   Surely it was a power not of the people themselves.   They were selfish, tribal: whence sprang up the antagonistic conception of devotion to a far distant end?   We trace the growth, against a resisting pressure, of a purer morality, of personal responsibility,[3] of the spirituality of God, of the thought of a future life.   But the thought of the prophet in each age is far in advance of the nation, and is often highly antagonistic, dragging a reluctant people after them.   This is no case of natural evolution of morality.   They stoned their prophets; and it was not till long after that they built their sepulchres.

Is not the education of the individual the same?   The

---

[1] Matt. xix. 8 ; Acts xvii. 30.

[2] Is. xlii. 16.   [3] See especially Ezek. xviii.

child is not born full-grown, with full-grown conscience and intellect. You cannot press on him full Christian principles. The law of the universe is continuous growth : the early principles were not false, they were imperfect; they were adapted to their age, not ours. The great law of continuity prevails in revelation and in history, as in physics and biology. All alike are the expression of God's laws.

The way adopted in the Bible of giving progressive instruction in morality is the only way in which the human conscience ever is or ever can be educated. God wants of us not our deeds but ourselves. He does not want our outer life to square with right, but our inner, which will then carry the outer with it. It is not enough to tell men what is right; it is far higher and more divine to train them to see for themselves what is right. And this can only be done by providing that the precepts, while above the conduct of the day and in some respects above the conscience of the day, shall yet not be so far above the latter as to be beyond the possibility of appreciation.

It is natural to press the question, Wherein does the Jewish history differ essentially from any other? Why do you believe in any special divine influence on the Jews? I should reply, in brief, that while I cannot think any nation to be not under God's training for some purpose or other, because I cannot think of the world of man apart from God; while I think that the philosophy and art of the Greeks, the law-making and organising power of the Romans, the power of self-government and mechanical skill of the Anglo-Saxon race, were the result, broadly speaking, of the influence of God on man, and may be said in one sense, not without Biblical sanction, to be inspired,[1]—yet facts do point unmistakably to the Jews as the nation that formed the chief channel for divine influence in religion. Through them came the fundamental idea of the one God ; the idea of sin—that deep mysterious truth which other nations never reached ; of forgiveness ; of righteousness ; of holiness. Through them, too, came

[1] Exodus xxxi. 1-6 ; 2 Chron. ii. 12 ; 1 Cor. xii. 6-11 ; James i. 17.

the idea of the equality of all men, the rights of the individual, and the teaching that duties are higher than rights; that self-sacrifice is above self-seeking. There is a want of spiritual teaching in the highest heathen writers : they do not speak with a voice which touches the soul ; they educate intellect, but the spirit does not bow before them.

My Lecture is on the moral difficulties of the Bible. If with this view—surely an extremely simple and natural one—that the Bible is exactly what it seems to be, fragments of the history of a nation which has contributed, as no one would deny, the most important factors in the history of the religions of the world,—if with this view we turn to it, what difficulty is there to us in reading the Old Testament ? It is the gradual revelation of God made through human hearts and minds. It is at once natural and supernatural. It is both because it is the continuous operation of God on man. Ridicule of it is out of place. It is a record of the ancient life and religious thought of this selected nation. Trace it in its course right to the end, and see it culminate in the person of Jesus Christ. The morality of the Old Testament is no pattern for us, except so far as our conscience, enlightened by the completed revelation, approves. Certain rules were given to them of old time, rules adapted to their condition ; but Christ has superseded these by higher principles,[1] and bidden us look forward to still further enlightenment.[2]

Believers in Christ cannot but expect the fulfilment of His promise and hope for further enlightenment, though they may well be cautious. "I am verily persuaded," as the pastor of the Pilgrim Fathers said to them as they embarked in the *Mayflower*,—"I am verily persuaded that the Lord has more truth yet to break forth out of His Word." "It is not incredible," says the great Bishop of Bristol, with characteristic caution, "that a book which has been so long in the possession of mankind should contain many truths as yet undiscovered."[3]

---

[1] Matt. v.   [2] John xv. xvi.

[3] Butler's *Analogy*, Part ii. c. 3.

I do not know whether this Lecture strikes you as difficult and obscure; but I cannot put the same thoughts into plainer language without extending the Lecture to still greater length. It is intended for the thoughtful and intelligent, and that there are such among you the letters that I have received bear witness. I do not think I am lecturing, as the saying is, "over your heads." I want you to see what the leaders of thought in all parties see, that this view of the Bible as it professes to be—may I not say as it is?—as fragments of a record of a progressive revelation of God and morality made through a selected nation, removes altogether and at once most of the so-called moral difficulties that seem, taken singly, to be so perplexing, nay, "even turns many of them into valuable instructions."[1]

At each age those truths are supplied which men assimilate. Who are we, to look back with scorn and ridicule at the form in which truth sufficed our fathers? It is by those truths that we have risen to our present point of view. It is not ungrateful, it is simply silly, to scoff at the ladder by which our generation has climbed. We are judging the moral law given through Moses by the light into which it has itself developed. The beginnings of mathematics and physics, the dawning truths of astronomy and geography, the earliest classification of animals and plants, interest us profoundly and excite no scorn. If they do excite scorn, it is only in ill-trained and foolish minds. For the fact is that it is not at all uncommon to vaunt our progress in science, and sometimes to talk as if the superiority of the Copernican to the Ptolemaic astronomy indicated a great intellectual superiority in the present over the past astronomers. The truth of course is that those who made the beginnings must have been intellectual giants of the loftiest stature. What geometer can ever be ranked above the man, whoever he was, who first saw the universal in the individual geometrical figure? Surely the sole records of the early growth of religious ideas, of the truths which now have such a grip on the human mind, are not to be sneered at.

[1] Stanley's *Life of Dr. Arnold*, vol. i. p. 288.

Do you think that by saying this I am reducing the
Bible to the level of any other book? Indeed I am not.
You will come to see that it contains not only the upward
struggles of man, but the gradual revelation of God : that
there is a human element in it of history and dialogue and
poetry, but that there is a divine element too. It speaks
with authority to the soul, with a voice that man, woman,
and child can recognise as akin to the voice of conscience.
Through it all we see a purpose and unity : we feel a divine
influence acting through men and on men. This divine
element cannot be separated by the critical faculty. We
cannot say, This is human, this divine. It is a spirit per-
meating the whole. It may be that in some men the
spiritual faculty is in so incipient a condition that they
cannot for a time feel this Spirit. But as they cannot feel
it, so they cannot persuade others contrary to the evidence
of their hearts that it is not there : and no one need
acquiesce in a state of doubt as final.

The book is its own testimony; we need claim nothing
for it; it needs not our defence. It has comforted,
strengthened, inspired men and women, learned and unlearned, in sorrows and perils. We need formulate no
theory of inspiration in its defence or explanation.
"Theories of inspiration," as the Bishop of Gloucester
and Bristol says, "may be most profitably dismissed from
our thoughts. The Holy Volume itself shall explain to us
the nature of that influence by which it is pervaded and
quickened." [1]   Or to quote the words of another thinker,
James Hinton, "I find the Bible the secret of all truth ;
all I truly know I derive from it ; and yet I would say to
every man, Don't believe the Bible if you cannot see clearly
that it is true. Deal freely, boldly by it. Don't be afraid.
'Tis a friend, not an enemy. If you don't treat it straight-
forwardly it cannot do its service to you." [2]

But a few more words of explanation may be useful.
It is, I think, commonly fancied by men who have not
closely thought on the question of inspiration, and it is
continually stated or assumed in Secularist literature, that

---

[1] *Aids to Faith.*   [2] Hinton's *Life,* p. 214.

there are really only two alternative views of the Bible. Either the book is literally the words of God, as much as if it had been written by the finger of God on the rock or the sky; or it is simply the work of men like other books; it has survived by a process of natural selection; and our reverence for it is due simply to its antiquity and the associations that have gathered round it. I say it is commonly thought that one of these two alternatives must be chosen. But to make an imaginary dilemma is the commonest artifice by which we deceive ourselves. It is the vulgarest fallacy of logic. Let us see if there is no third path.

There are, indeed, compromises in plenty: that it is human in matters of fact, and divine in matters of faith; human where it could be human, and can be tested; divine where it could not be human, and cannot be tested;— theories of dynamical, plenary, supervisory, suggestive inspiration without end. All these are of the nature of compromises between what we may describe in single words as the purely miraculous and the purely rationalistic theories of the Bible. They are fine edges on which a man may balance himself between the abysses of miracle on the one hand, and of rationalism on the other. There are doubtless men present who hold the purely miraculous theory, with or without some abatements; others who hold the purely rationalistic, with or without some sense that it does not explain the marvellous power the book has had, and still has, on the hearts and souls of men; and there are probably some who balance themselves precariously between the two. But there is a third view of inspiration to which thoughtful men of all shades of opinion are tending, happily entirely open to us of the Church of England, no narrow edge, but a broad ground, on which men of science and scholars and men of simple faith can meet and are meeting.

This is a view which I cannot yet define by a single word, which requires thought to familiarise ourselves with it. For want of a better definition, however, we will call it at present *an illumination in all that concerns Religious*

Truth.[1] It accepts the broad assumption that the progress of human thought, like Nature itself, is at once under the guiding control of a Providence, as well as subject to uniform laws. It assumes that Purpose and Design are not inconsistent with such laws; that they may be providential without being miraculous: it assumes that there is a human and divine element to be traced in the progress of humanity, an element of freedom and an element of control. The marks of the divine are permanence, continuity, and silence; of the human, they are variability, and intermittence, and clamour. It assumes that we are not merely cunning beasts, but men with souls and longings far beyond our surroundings, with aspirations which witness to truth, and goodness, and God. It assumes that the Power which created the human mind has followed up its action by continuous guidance. It accepts broadly the fact of God's providence over all nations, though we cannot read all His purposes. It does not hesitate to speak of a universal influence of God on the hearts of men ignorant alike of the name of Jehovah and of Christ; an influence which we may, if we like, call an inspiration, though we cannot define it or assign its limits. It is so great as to be illimitable. It asserts, on historical evidence, that the nation which has contributed incomparably the most important and most luminous elements to the religious thought of the world, by deed and life as well as word, is the Jewish nation; and that its books show a progressive advance from lower to higher, the effect of immutable truth on the growing range of human knowledge and experience; that they have a wonderful unity and purpose; and finally culminate in the revelation of Christ; that "God spake at sundry times and in divers manners by the prophets, until at last He spake by His Son."[2] It asserts that the Bible is unique: that whereas other books show an inspiration of intellect, and other men show an inspiration of inventiveness or skill or imagination, this book has shown a

---

[1] This paragraph is suggested by the book *Catholic Thoughts on the Bible* (Strahan).

[2] Hebrews i. 1.

unique insight into morality and into the spiritual needs of man; that it is at once educational and redemptive. In a special and distinctive sense then it is inspired with profound insight into spiritual truth; it has been and is God's chosen instrument for guiding and educating the world. So explained, we may call this the theory of continuous divine inspiration; an illumination in all that concerns Religious Truth.

This view of the book makes it clear in what sense we all must read it. We must read it as it is. It is meant for learned and unlearned, for uncritical and critical. The humble cottager, spelling over the Bible, finds in its pages much that he cannot comprehend, but much also that tells him the main truths of human existence, in the form in which the experience of all ages and all countries has shown that such truths can be conveyed to the uninstructed, uncritical mind. It tells him of God above, of providence, of sin, of the redeeming love of Christ, of the hope and glories of heaven: it is literally a beacon-light to him over the stormy waves of this clouded world. Neither intellectual nor moral difficulties come home to him at all; if they suggest themselves they are but a trial of his faith, and he puts them aside. He is almost in the stage, so far as abstract ideas are concerned, of the men of the ages in which it was written. He does not misinterpret, because he passes by so much without interpretation at all. It is thoughtless cruelty to put into such a man's hand a Secularist leaflet, and perplex him with a stage of thought with which he is wholly unfamiliar. It makes his life neither better, nor happier, nor truer; it destroys his peace, shakes the foundation of his life, gives him no substitute, and plunges him into unhappiness, and sometimes into sin. It extinguishes his light and wrecks his hopes. It destroys the old truth, and he is not ready for the new. It is cruel and it is senseless.

The thinking artisan of our cities is often now in a somewhat different stage. The results of criticism and science have penetrated his ranks. He has begun to eat of the tree of knowledge. The old world-wide, world-felt

problems are discussed in workshops and at clubs.   How
shall you read your Bible?   The Word of God is written
for you also.   Cast away preconception and read it as it
is; with the wish to penetrate the mystery of the power
this wonderful book has exercised, not with the wish to
pervert it, but to see it truly.   Look below the surface
for permanent truth, not temporary accommodation.   You
are not required to believe it till you have read it; but let
me beg of you to read it with a sense of its being, at any
rate possibly, an historical revelation.   Read it with a
humble sense of ignorance, and of reverent thankfulness.
Even in interest and beauty alone there is no book that
comes near it.   Select from it the parts that profit you
most.   Do not condemn those who select other parts.
We all select.   Few of you, I suppose, have read the whole
Bible through.   I cannot profess to have studied it all
through.   That is the work of a lifetime, devoted to it
alone.

And do not imagine that this study of the Bible from a
literary, critical, historical point of view is incompatible
with its use as the book of practical devotion, which
enlightens the soul with its humble, prayerful, devotional
study.   It is this combination of submission of the spirit
to the authority of God's Word, with the vindication of
the right of the intellect to criticise and understand its
form, this use both for spiritual and intellectual enlightenment, that you find hard to conceive.   Yet that is the
true use of the Bible.   Criticism and religion are compatible.   I can assure you that while I welcome broadly the
whole range of historical and critical and scientific investigation, and while I use it as an auxiliary to the growing comprehension of the book, yet I feel all the while the
positive supernatural revelation made by God to man, the
true inspiration of the Spirit of God speaking through the
writers and through the writings, so profoundly as to be
unshaken by any rationalistic arguments whatever.

And how are we clergy, who are familiar enough with
the humble faith of some, and with the doubts and dawning scepticism of others,—how are we clergy to preach to

men and women coexisting in such diverse stages of thought as there are and ever will be, I suppose, in our congregations? There is the practical difficulty for which perhaps you make little or no allowance. Some people need absolute direction, and shrink from nothing so much as the exercise of judgment. "Tell us what to believe," they cry, "and we will believe it, be it Pope, or Church, or Bible, or the inner Mystic Light." Others demand freedom and reasoning, and the right to think for themselves: they want facts, and instruction how to reason. You say our sermons are different from our lectures. So they ought to be, for the audience is different, and the object is different.

What ought our sermons to be? You will see that it is no easy problem. They must not unnecessarily startle and distress those whose faith clings round the letter of the sacred book, and yet they must not be untrue to the highest truth we see. They must show the inner meaning under the ancient forms, and so help all alike. They must convey primarily the great message with which we are charged as ministers, God's love revealed in Christ, the indwelling Spirit, the eternal difference between right and wrong, the exclusion even now from God of one who persists in sin. Of the future they will say little, since little is revealed. Neither the Bible nor the Church defines the condition of the soul after death. This is an unknown and awful mystery. They will tell more of a God whose tender mercies are over all His works, who punishes only to redeem from the power of sin ; of a God whom we know only as Incarnate in Christ, and a Christ whom we commemorate in the Sacrament of His love. Those of us clergy who feel this difficulty most will build less on individual phrases in the Bible, and more on its general spirit: we shall not balance pyramids of doctrine on the apex of a single text: we shall consider more the circumstances under which the words were spoken, and judge, with a deep sense of responsibility for our judgment, as to the application in our own day. We shall more and more feel the need of prayer, and of study, and of mixing with men in all stages of thought. We shall learn more and more to practise what Lord Bacon called "an adult suspension of judgment." We shall grow more tolerant of those who differ in opinion; more convinced that intellectual differences do not separate men, that no particular views have a monopoly of God's love.

To return then to the moral difficulties which we have left far below and behind us.

We must judge of a divine command in the Old Testament by the following considerations. The voice spoke in the heart, not outside it, and was but the voice of the conscience enlightened up to its then standard, and receiving from the ever-present, ever-acting Spirit of God such fresh enlightenment or inspiration as it could bear. Did the voice seem wrong to them? Was it not in general a call to something higher, to some fresh duty? Could it have been intelligible if given in the modes of thought of this century, so widely separate as they are? and why of this century rather than of any other, past or to come? To my mind the only imaginable revelation is the gradual, historical, accommodated revelation. Such commands or permissions are only so far given to us as they are applicable to our condition of society and morals; and here is the function of intellect, an ample sphere for our keenest moral judgment and most trained insight.

Take the well-known case of the command to Abraham, "Take now thy son, thine only son Isaac, whom thou lovest, and offer him for a burnt-offering." [1]   I for one can only interpret this as in any sense a command from God by the help that I get from the historical view of revelation that I have been setting forth. The inner voice of God in our hearts, and later revelation, tell us this command is wrong to us: if the outer voice tells us that it is right to us, the contradiction is intolerable and even maddening. But the question is not what the voice in *our* hearts *now* says, but what it said in Abraham's nearly four thousand years ago. And to understand this we have only to reflect that, strange as it may seem, the offering of the first-born

[1] Gen. xxii. 2.

was then common; that it was no moral shock, only a sorrow and trial to Abraham ; and that the command was used,—its importance is that it was used,—not to sanction but to abolish human sacrifices, and to look forward by a long series of types to the perfect sacrifice of will and life that Christ made on the cross. Our reverence for the character of one who was called the Friend of God must not remove him from his place in the historic series, assign to him an insight into truths which had not dawned on the world, or even assign to him a perfect mastery over the truths which had so dawned.

The moral and theological difficulties arising out of the New Testament doctrine cannot be here considered, for lack of time. I will make one remark only. It is plain that men differ, and probably will differ, widely in opinion ; let us accept this fact: let us further be certain that we are all "God's creatures and the sheep of His pasture." It is not our opinions for which He will judge us, but our lives. And there is within the Church of Christ, nay, even within the Church of England, room for widest differences of opinion to coexist in peace. There may be and are in the Church of Christ sects and parties composed of men more or less like - minded. Let us accept this as God's will, and while we strive to enlighten ourselves, and modestly submit to one another our views of truth, "let wrath and clamour and evil-speaking be put away from us, with all malice." This is not unfaithfulness to truth. Truth is wider than the opinions of any man or any party. This is not indifference ; it is to combine charity and zeal, knowledge and faith.

The moral difficulties of the Bible, like its intellectual diffi-culties, rest, then, on misconceptions, and are removable by patient thought and a candid submission to facts. And now you may begin to see the answer to the question why men *do* believe the Bible. They believe it to be the in-spired Word of God (1) because it shows the characteristics of God as shown in Nature. If, indeed, there were no God ; if matter created itself, and life sprang out of matter ; if our thoughts are but motions of molecules in the brain, and right and wrong a widespread delusion; then the Bible is no more the Word of God than is the world His work. But if this is not so—if to most men, though not quite to all, the existence of a God, even though a God unknown, is certain, then they may see in the Bible, intelligently studied, the work of the same God. There is in both Nature and the Book the same far-reaching purpose, beyond the grasp of us creatures of a day, the same continuity, the same silence, and the same subtle harmony amid infinite variety. And (2) they believe it because of its wonderful history: not merely that it has survived such efforts to annihilate it, but that it has done such a work in the world. Who can attempt to recount its triumphs? And (3) chiefly, they believe it because it is its own witness. See what it is to myriads now. If you try to make its principles the rule of your life; if you read it daily, in times of sorrow and of joy; read it humbly; read it with prayer, and with a strong wish directed heavenwards, it does at last so touch and master the soul that you are obliged to say with the blind man, "Whether it be of God or no, I know not; one thing I know, that, whereas I was blind, now I see."[1] Other reasonings do but remove difficulties; this compels conviction.

But as I said in the last Lecture, this is an internal question, not an external one. It will not convince those who do not study it; it will not convince those who study it without the desire both to attain truth, and to quicken their perceptions of right and wrong, and further to purify and deepen their lives. Truth compels me to add that the Bible does not convince all who study it, or at least begin to study it, even with that professed desire, which I dare not say is not genuine and deep. No man should venture to say or hint that this is due to moral faults from which believers are free. Every one must, however, be conscious that there are in his mind conditions predisposing him towards belief, and others towards unbelief, and that his will is capable of exercising some control over those conditions. I can only say with our Bishop that I

[1] John ix. 25.

am certain that those who seek will at last find, on this or
the other side of the stream of death.

Finally, let me say that you must judge this history of
revelation in the light of its consummation, to which all
its lines converge.   And what is that ?   Put together your
ideal of true greatness of soul ; power combined with
gentleness ; dignity with no pride ; benevolence with no
weakness ; sympathy and love for humanity as it is, and
especially for the poor, the sad, the suffering.   Let your
ideal be stainless, and even unsuspected of stain ; and let
him cheerfully and patiently live and die for men who misunderstood and even hated him.   This is what you will
see in the history of Christ—the Messiah of humanity as
well as of the Jews.   That sight melted the heart of the
stern Roman soldier who stood by the cross ; it has melted
many a heart since.   This taught us that God is love :
taught us that on that God, whom Christ revealed, we can
lean in life and death.   What to us is it that ages before,
when the world was not ripe for such a sight as this, the
lessons of morality, the teachings about God, were simpler ?
that His sternness was revealed before His mercy, His
hatred of sin before His forgiveness of the sinner ?   These
moral difficulties are absorbed in the consummation of
revelation in Christ.

Do not let any perplexities about the dawn of revelation hide from you its daylight sun.   This earth itself was
once a chaos of fiery elements, but it became the glorious
and wondrous globe we dwell on, with its infinite har-
monies and beauties in sky and earth and sea.   Even man
himself may once have risen from lower forms, and at any
rate from savage life ; but now intellect and conscience
and love stamp him as divine, as made in the image of
God ; and we rank him as he is, not as he was in a bygone
age.   In like manner judge of revelation by its end, not
its beginning.   To Christ it all pointed, and in Him it
culminated, and from Him still flows a power that shall
mould the world.

There are abuses of Christianity, there are ignorances
and bitternesses and follies almost innumerable, and it is

these that alienate and shock you. You are scourging us for these. Christian ministers and Christian laymen are not as Christlike as they should be; not with hearts so full of love and truth; setting the letter above the spirit, desiring our own way, trampling on one another, not without bitterness; yes, I accept for myself, and many of my brethren will also accept, with all humility, some part of Christ's stern denunciation of the Pharisees—"Ye make burdens grievous to be borne—ye have left undone the weightier matters of the law—ye shut the kingdom of heaven against men—ye have made the Word of God of none effect through your traditions." May God enlighten and fill us with more love! But our faults of interpretation and of spirit do not destroy the truth of revelation or of the Bible. The clouds and dust we raise eclipse, but do not annihilate, the sun. Who shall separate you from the love of God? Surely not our shortcomings. How can virtue and true godliness progress in England without your aid? We cannot do without you. God needs your help.

When I recall that second speaker[1] on our first evening, I think how well he could speak in this new light: how his earnestness and warmth and courage would shine out if he were to tell us how he began to see God revealing Himself in perfect love and perfect self-sacrifice; and how he saw that all earlier revelation was but the rod of the schoolmaster that brought men to Christ. How he could tell you—better than I—in homelier, stronger language, that the great miracle of Christianity was Christ Himself, the great surprise in human history, neither Jew nor Gentile, that unique figure in the long gallery of the portraits of humanity, round whom centre the love, the hopes, the tears, the joys of so many ages. God grant that his and many voices may yet be heard, as brave and clear as ever they were, teaching the old faiths in the new light which is bursting on their souls!

[1] A working man, a fine specimen of an honest Secularist, who had suffered deeply from the perverted Christianity which had been put before him, and had abandoned it for what seemed higher though unchristian teaching.

V

LETTER TO A BRISTOL ARTISAN[1]

My DEAR SIR—You are probably aware that a friend of yours, who saw the note in which I acknowledged the receipt of your pamphlet, *Why Men do not Believe in the Bible*,[2] wrote promptly to me to express the eager anxiety with which he looked forward to my reply; declaring that if I did not reply, I should be taken "to have lowered my arms in submission," and adding a good deal more in the same brisk tone. I mention this because I wish to explain to you at once why I do not reply by a published pamphlet, but prefer the form of a letter to you, and why I mark that letter "*private.*" And I mean by marking it private, that neither you nor others, into whose hands it may fall, have a right to quote it in public or in print, and that no one but yourself has a right to address me by letter respecting it. Under these conditions, you may show it to whomsoever you please, and I can send you as many more copies as you are likely to ask for.

I reply, because your pamphlet has deeply interested me, not only from its singular directness and lucidity and general moderation of tone—qualities which are too often wanting in controversial writings, and chiefly in those on religion—but also because it is full of misconceptions and

[1] A Bristol artisan, to whom I alluded on p. 101, had published a pamphlet in which he stated, with modesty and ability, the ordinary grounds urged by Secularists of the *National Reformer* type for their entire rejection of the Bible.

[2] Published by W. H. Morrish, 18 Narrow Wine Street, Bristol. Price Twopence.

confusions which appear to me to be removable, and because I have real hopes of putting you into a more advanced and more intelligent point of view; of helping you, and possibly others, to see things in what appear to me a truer light and better proportion; in a word, of adding to your mental happiness.

But I do not reply in a pamphlet, because I could not give you an honest exchange of opinion if I were writing for publication. It may be my personal weakness—some of your friends will probably say it is the weakness of my position—but it is a fact that I could not, under those conditions, write simply and solely to you and for you. I should find myself writing with one eye on you and the other on the public. I should endeavour to make my answer pointed, perhaps even clever. If I got into a controversy—and a published reply is a controversy—I could not feel sure that I should not behave as other men do in a controversy—forget truth, and aim at victory; try to *score*; point out errors and inconsistencies in your pamphlet; slur over weak points in my own argument; perhaps try a little rhetoric when reasoning fails. And even if I did not do so, some kind friend would assume that I did.

But this is not all. I should have to enlarge still further the scope of my reply. The subject of my original lectures, you will remember, was not chosen by myself: I merely stopped a gap at the request of some of the clergy; I was merely completing a course which had been begun by some one else. Those lectures were on "The Theory of Inspiration; or, Why men do not believe the Bible"; the object of the lectures being limited to the one point—to state the theory of Inspiration, so far as any theory is held by the Church of England, and to show how its distortion has led to a mechanical and unintelligent use of the Bible by some Christians; to a somewhat widespread doubt as to the nature of its authority among others; and, finally, to a mistaken rejection of it by some Secularists—mistaken rejection, I say, because some of you seem to be unable to regard the Bible except under

the popular and crude theories respecting it. Now your
reply points out very truly that a defective and false theory
of inspiration is not the only reason (though it is, I feel
more sure than ever, the chief reason) why men do not
believe the Bible, but that there are other reasons as well.
It is open to me to reply now, before I go further, that
the subject of my lectures was chosen for me, and that
beyond it I had no power to go; and this answer is
complete. But if in a published paper I were voluntarily
to enter on the whole question and all the questions which
you now open, I should have to consider, in my turn, how
far *your* treatment of these questions is adequate and
representative and philosophical, even from your own
point of view. For otherwise, if I merely took up your
points—and that would be a large business by itself—you,
or some philosophical friend of yours with a talent for
correspondence, would not be long in discovering that
there were deeper questions still, which neither you nor I
had touched, and which it was very wrong of me to shirk;
and so the area of controversy would widen indefinitely in
illimitable circles, and I should have to go on replying to
you or to any of your friends, anonymous or otherwise,
in pamphlets, letters, or journals, on every conceivable
religious topic, or "be held," by some of your friends, "to
have lowered my arms in submission," and promptly be
taunted for my silence. He who got the last word would
be held to have won the dialectic victory, and would make
a fine cackle over it, as your friend was considerate
enough to warn me. Now I put it to you that to expose
myself to all this would be not only foolish, but wrong.
It would be foolish, because it would be going out of my
way to pull a nest of hornets about my ears. It would be
foolish, because my object in the original lectures was, as
you may easily see, not controversial, but to remove misconceptions, to help the anxious, the doubting, the devout.
And of all these imaginary hornets, how many, think you,
would be anxious, or doubting, or devout? They would
be anxious about nothing but how best to sting. All my
correspondents are not like yourself. I have felt their

stings. It would be foolish, because the vast majority of the Secularists into whose hands my reply might fall are not on the level of thought or education which would enable them to understand my reply. It would be foolish, because it would be pure controversy, which never helped a human soul.

But it would also be wrong; and for this I care a great deal more. It would be wrong, because any complete reply which I might attempt to publish, if adapted for a man in your advanced stage of thought, would contain statements and views wholly unsuitable to very many in a less advanced stage of thought, into whose hands it might fall, and might do positive harm. This you will understand better when you have read my letter to the end. It would be wrong, because I have a great deal of necessary duty to perform day by day, which taxes my energies to the full; and I have no right to incur voluntarily a boundless addition to the demands upon me.

It would be wrong, moreover, because I should be putting myself forward as a champion of Theistic and Christian faith against all comers, when I am wholly unworthy of such an office. I did not do so in my former lectures. If it were a mere matter of intellectual fencing, I should not so much shrink from undertaking it, not because I think myself specially qualified, but because I should not so much mind a defeat; I should not mind it more than I mind losing a game of chess, or failing in a mathematical problem. But Theistic and Christian faith are not matters for intellectual fencing; they are matters much more of feeling and conscience; the results of a life devoted to holiness and service, and not the results of literary study or scientific training; and in these qualifications how do I stand equipped?—I confess myself wholly unworthy.

I do not know whether you will quite understand me; but the point is important, and, at the risk of still further extending these introductory remarks, I will explain.

I look up to certain intellectual giants, and feel that their powers altogether surpass mine. I know just enough

mathematics to compare my ability and knowledge with
those of the great mathematicians of the day—men like
Thomson and Cayley and Stokes.   I know enough of
literature and thought to feel the greatness of men like
Browning and Lightfoot and Max Müller.   In comparison
with them I feel like an untrained child.   I know enough
of science to appreciate the genius of men like Huxley
and Helmholtz.   But I look up no less to spiritual giants
and spiritual genius.   I wonder whether you do the same.
There are men and women whom I know, and have
known, who have a genius for godliness ; who are quite as
vastly my superiors in that insight into godliness which
comes of lives of sweetness and unworldliness and prayer,
as are any of the great men I have named my superiors in
intellect.   I am not speaking of the magnates of the
religious world, though among such magnates are men at
whose feet I humbly sit, but of persons, quite unknown to
the great world, whom I reverence, knowing that their
minds are finer, their love of God and man—or, if you
prefer it, of duty and man—their feeling for the Infinite
that lies behind Nature, the Highest that lies before man,
is stronger and keener than ever mine can be.   And it is
men of this finer clay, these gifted souls, to whose words
I would fain listen.   Who am I that I should speak ?
Silence becomes me.   I must repeat that I do not feel
sure that you will understand me here without an effort.
"One man is as good as another," you may say ; or, at
any rate, "I have nothing to depend on, in the last resort,
but my own reason ; my own mind must ultimately decide
for me what to think."   But is one man as good as
another ?   One man is not as good a linguist, or doctor,
or mathematician as another ; one man is not as good a
workman as another.   To get light on science we defer to
the men of genius, to the Darwins and Maxwells.   Is
there nothing like this deference in religious, ethical,
spiritual truths—call them by what name you will ?   You
do not deny that there is such a sphere for reason ; you
yourself exercise your reason much therein.   Are there
no gifted souls, as well as gifted intellects ?   or, if you

prefer the expression, no intellects specially gifted in this direction? I think there are; and I am deeply grateful that education has enabled me to recognise men of genius and insight in the spiritual as in the intellectual world. I do not know whether you equally feel the incomparable genius for what I have called godliness shown by some of the great names of the past. I feel it deeply; and, therefore, it is no affectation of humility to decline controversy on such subject. It may still seem to you as if every man ought to be able to defend his faith at every point. I do not at all agree with you in this view. A man's faith is not an intellectual fortress; his attitude towards it is not, and ought not to be, that of armed and watchful defence. My attitude towards my religious belief is not at all that of defence, nor towards yours that of attack. This is the attitude of the half-educated, and of the glib controversialist. To me, the attitude of mind towards religious belief is rather that of a child gazing out on the stars, or watching the flow of some mighty river.

Let me now turn to your pamphlet. I have sufficiently explained why I do not publish a pamphlet in reply.

I think your pamphlet may be summed up in three theses: First, that the observation of Nature and the use of your reason do not disclose to you any God—or, rather, any Power or Providence which you can identify with that which you suppose Christians to worship under the name of God; secondly, that you see no authority in or for the Bible which shall compel your reason to accept it as an infallible revelation given by God; thirdly, that you, on these grounds, refuse to accept Christianity, or even Theism, as you understand them.

It is, of course, impossible to condense into so small a space as this short paragraph the whole of what you have said; but I think you will agree with me that all you say is intended to establish these three main theses or propositions.

Now, I would ask you at once not to imagine that I am going to attempt to prove the contrary of your theses: that would be to enter on controversy, which, as I said before, is unprofitable. My aim is a different one. I wish you to see that religion, rightly understood, is not the defined and hard thing which you are attacking, and which, from the way in which it has been presented to you, you naturally suppose it to be ; and that there is no such discrepancy as you suppose between the results of your observation of Nature and your reason, and the best results at which philosophical Christians arrive, and have always arrived. And, further, that the view which you take of the Bible, and its statements about God, is still a very narrow and mistaken view. It is, or was, a very common view ; but it is characteristic of an early and immature stage of religious education and thought, and it is strangely out of keeping with your profounder mind and insight in other directions. Your view of the Bible is scarcely more intelligent than that of Ingersoll or the *National Reformer ;* and I expected from you something better than this. Such writers are very clever and very shallow, and they have no notion how shallow they are. But when you suppose that your way of reading the Bible—which is, I admit, that of the religious non-educated class, and, to a considerable extent, that of the teachers of that class—is also the only way ; that Christian scholars and men of science—men of mature intellects—necessarily read the Bible in exactly the way you read it, this is a mistake ; natural enough, perhaps, but one which you really must correct, if you wish to understand what intelligent Christian faith is.

It is absolutely necessary for you to grasp the conception of religion as being, not a system of dogmas about the Being of God and His relation to man, revealed by some external and supernatural machinery, but as being an education, an evolution, a growth of the spirit of man towards something higher by means of a gradual revelation. Pause here, and consider well how much is implied in this statement. You cannot see it all at once. It implies the indwelling of a spirit ever aspiring towards the Divine, of a supra-evolutionary force incessantly guiding

the growth, of immense impulse to growth such as came
with the coming of Christ. It involves, perhaps, a revolution in your views about religion, and the thoughts of
religious men : it is perhaps, in your eyes, an abandonment
on my part of all that you thought I and other Christians
held as the very essence of religion. You will, perhaps,
even call it a "concession." I can scarcely tell, indeed,
how you will regard it ; for you must feel how difficult it is
for me to see things from your point of view. Still, I give
it you as so much information ; it is the philosophic view
of religion held by thoughtful Christians.

Let me explain this more fully, perhaps even at considerable length ; and then, perhaps, you will see your
theses in a very different light : you will see that they
crush, not the reality, but the shadow of Christianity.

We cannot be said to know anything until we know
how it has come to be what it is. All study runs back to
the study of origins. We do not really know the meaning
of the very words we use until we know something of their
origin and history. This is quite as true of religion as it
is of anything else. We do not understand religion as it
is till we know how it arose, and through what changes it
has passed. You may reply, "Then how can the wayfaring man—one who lives by the labour of his hands—
understand religion ? " And the answer is, that religion
is, primarily, principles of life and conduct, and an attitude
of mind ; and that it is no more necessary for most men
to *understand* religion (that is, the origin of religion) than
it is for them to *understand* the words they use, or the
stones they tread on. But there are in all classes and in
all ages a few philosophic minds, to whom it is necessary
to understand religion. Yours is one of those minds : and
when such philosophic minds are found in men who, by
their circumstances, are unable to get this genesis or
explanation of religion, then we find such phenomena as
your pamphlet and similar writings of leading Secularists.
And we find, besides, a good deal of Secularist writing
which is scarcely philosophic even in semblance : we find
such a phenomenon as the *National Reformer*, perplexing

us by the combination of cleverness and a good deal of knowledge with a hopelessly limited, mechanical, and erroneous conception of the subject, incurable except by some transforming light of education. It is this that makes any reply to you so difficult. You have escaped, by the natural growth of your mind and the influence of other writers, from the popular, childish, mediæval, and very inadequate views of Christian doctrine and of God. Had you been so placed as to have free access not only to writers below you, but to the best thought of the age, it is easy to see that you would have grown to the perception that what you had escaped from was but an elementary stage of religion, and you would have straightway seen that it was not God you were denying, but the adequacy for the philosopher of the conception of God held in childhood and by the common folk round you. You would have found many of like mind with yourself; you would have sprung to the conception of religious evolution; you would have seen that you were passing from a lower to a higher stage of religious thought; you would have taken your natural place with philosophical Christians; and you would have seen the immense educational value of the more elementary stages of religion; and, perhaps, even taken part in educating others in those stages.

But as it is—you must pardon my saying so—it is plain that you have not had access to the best thought of the age; you have thought that the religion formulated as you first learnt it, and as it is held by the uninstructed people round you, crudely presented in its bare elements, and even then distorted and imperfectly grasped—you have thought that this is the absolute, defined, and rigid Creed of all Christians, from the child to the man, from the peasant to the philosopher; and seeing that this form of Christianity, which is all you know of, is childish and imperfect and erroneous, you feel straightway called on to denounce the whole Christian religion, and even belief in God, as misleading and damaging and irrational.

Believe me, there is a more excellent way than this. There are stages beyond you, as there are many stages behind. I shall do you a great service, if I can convince you of this.

The history of religious thought reveals an incessant progress. It always tends to keep pace with knowledge. If, for example, you traced the evolution of religious thought in India, you would see how, stage by stage, the conceptions of Deity and of religion advanced, from the elementary feeling of the mystery of things as shown in mountains and rivers, and the unknown and infinite which they suggested, to a reverence for Sun and Sky, as still higher powers. You would see in some detail how, from the operations of Nature, they first formed the conception of an Operator—a Power that produced the rain and the thunder—an Unseen, known only by imagination and by faith. Far back in the old world of our forefathers— farther back than any one can say; back in times before written history, deciphered only by the traces that thought has left on language—arose the conception of faith in an Unseen Power, and, along with Faith, its inseparable sister, Unfaith. You would see how the same principle of evolution of religious thought went on working, how crude conceptions were spiritualised into higher forms, and how men were, after all, dissatisfied with the highest conceptions they could attain. The infinite for which they were striving was not river, nor mountain, nor sun, nor sky, nor even Heaven-Father Himself; it was something greater than all these. They were yearning after a purer and higher conception of God than that which had satisfied their forefathers. Doubtless, the long-ago forerunners of such free thought were looked at askance: perhaps some of them were put to death as Jewish prophets were put to death, as Socrates was put to death, as Jesus Christ, and St. Paul, and many another since. Others were called hard names—and in our own day men are called hard names still—heretics, agnostics, atheists. But such an atheism, that longs for a higher conception of God, is not atheism, or, if it is atheism, it is the root of all true belief; it is the atheism which confesses itself unable to formulate in words the infinite Power behind Nature and man.

Or if you turn from the evolution of religion in India, which in its later course seems to have been stopped, and turn to the more familiar history of Jewish and Christian thought, which is still progressing, you will see, if you can but throw your mind into an historical frame—and you cannot understand religion otherwise—how the crude, early conception of a national Deity to be propitiated by human sacrifices, and a cosmogony derived from Assyrian or still older myths, formed the early religion of the Jews. You will watch how, under Mosaism and the prophets, they slowly outgrew that imperfect and erroneous religion; how human sacrifices were abolished, and loftier thoughts about that High and Holy One that inhabiteth Eternity were attained. And then you will see how the nation sank into practical disbelief, and substituted ritual observances in the place of the reverence that inspires men to holiness and righteousness and charity; and then you will see the one unique phenomenon in religion that the world has witnessed—the coming of a Teacher whose words have partially transformed, and are still slowly transforming, the religions of the world; whose life is still guiding the evolution of religion. He came not to destroy but to fulfil. We have no contemporary records of His life, not a fragment written by Him : He appears to have taught for not more than three years, and to have died, at thirty-three, the death of a slave, in an obscure province of the Roman Empire, without having made a single distinguished convert. His influence during His life was not great, as men count greatness. But those who had lived with Him were themselves transformed by His influence, and far and wide they spread His name. The world took a new departure in religious thought. The Greek and Roman religions were dead or dying : dead as ethical forces ; dying or dead as speculations. Here sprang up an offshoot and development of the best Semitic thought—a self-devotion to goodness. The work of Christ was the popularisation of the ideal of personal holiness. You quote a very shallow saying of Renan, that "if all moral truths taught by philosophers who lived before the time of Jesus were eliminated from the teachings of Jesus, there would be little indeed left." It is one thing to state a moral truth ; it is a totally different thing to move the world to live by it. The distinctive work of Christ, from this point of view, was not the revelation of new ethical truths, but the popularisation of the ideal of personal holiness, and of self-consecration to the service of God and man. Never, surely—you do not doubt it—was such an addition made to the religious thought, or to the humane impulses and the morality of the world !

And just consider to what a world it was added. To one strewn with old, dying, and dead forms of faith ; to one teeming with new and subtle philosophies that were almost powerless against licentiousness and cruelty ; a scene of such disorder and despair as has never been witnessed since. Into such a world was thrown this new ideal of life, personal holiness and devotion to the service of God through the service of man—the new religion of Christ. This is the leaven which is to transform the mass. I am not asking you now to say that Jesus Christ is therefore the Son of God ; I am asking you to look at history with fairness and with intelligence. I am asking you, not to approach this history with any *à priori* conception how revelation ought to have been made, but to study how Christ's life has acted on the world.

To trace this, even in outline, is too great a work for a letter. But I can briefly remind you that the action of the Church on the world was accompanied by a reaction of the world on the Church ; and, therefore, the new religion had to undergo the inevitable processes of degeneration as well as growth. The Christian Church and the Christian creed soon became other than they were. The history of Christianity did not stop when the Canon of the New Testament was closed. It did not stand still through the Middle Ages. The Reformation was not a mere return to ancient simplicity ; the centuries since the Reformation have not been ages of stagnation. They have been and are ages of continuous growth. No one will deny, on the one hand, that the Church—and by the

I

Church I mean that permanent association of men whose
object it is to educate mankind in the faith and spirit of
Christ—no one will deny that the Church has been slow
to recognise light and truth when from other sources it has
dawned on the world. This is on the whole right, because
her sympathies and her mind have rightly been with the
unphilosophical many, and not with the philosophical few.
She has been slow to see that her formulæ were but quasi-
scientific, approximate, even temporary; and that growth
would of necessity bring an alteration of them, in one way
or other. I say in one way or other, because such an
expansion takes place in two ways: either by the gradual
modification of authorised documents which define the
faith, such as has frequently taken place and may be traced
in the history of the Creeds, or by a change in the interpretation of them. And the latter for various reasons is
the more important of the two: it is quite insensible, unconscious, and involves no revolution. It may be doubted
whether any one now reads our Creeds in the same sense
in which they were drawn up. It is certain that we do
not read our Bibles exactly in the sense in which our forefathers read them. Growth, evolution, change are inevitable in everything that is alive: and Christianity is alive.
But on the other hand, no well-informed person will deny
how truly the parables of the leaven and the mustard seed
are fulfilling themselves in the history of the Christian
Church. Christianity is more widely spread, and it is
more like the Christianity of Christ now than it has been
in any age since the Apostolic. The Christianity of Christ
was so immeasurably above the level of the people to
whom the Apostles preached that they could not, even
under that inspiring influence, spring up to grasp it. It is
a very, very long way above us still, both in theory and in
practice. Nevertheless our duty is to press forward to that
which is before; to aim at the perfection of the Christian
spirit and life in our whole community; and, thank God,
some progress towards this has been made.

Now to what is all this tending—all these illustrations
from the history of the Indian, Jewish, and Christian

religions? To this: I want you to see that your pamphlet is very largely beside the mark. I want you to see that the conception of God which you find in the Old Testament, and so indignantly repudiate—the attributing to Him of human form, or imperfection, or passion, and so on—is but the record of an early stage in the evolution of religious thought. It is not the revelation of God as He is, but the representation of God as He was once thought to be by men who confounded their own passions with His revelation, and misunderstood the latter. You are quite wrong in supposing that the Jehovah, as conceived in any one age by the Jews, resembles in all points the God the Father as conceived by Christians now. "The God of the Christians," you say, "is that of the Bible." To suppose this is to be guilty of an impossible anachronism. The conception of Jehovah of the Jews in any age—and it was by no means the same in all ages, or to all men in any age—did perhaps represent the highest thought of that age and that nation: there was a point beyond which neither the science, nor the legislation, nor the religious conceptions of the nation could go. It is a mere quibble, as you will see, to say that because we receive the Bible as containing the record of the progressive revelation or evolution of the knowledge of God, we therefore receive as our ideal of God the Jehovah of the Jews in all or any of the evolutionary stages of that ideal. But it is worse than a quibble—it is surely a sort of shutting your eyes to the truth, to collect from various stages of this evolving idea all the elementary images and inconsistencies you can find, all the crudest thoughts of various ages, omitting all that is noblest and best, the revelation of Him as "just and righteous altogether," hating iniquity and loving every man; and then—when you have by such a process of selection of the unfittest, selection of all that was transient and has long perished from religion, made an impossible picture—to turn and ask me whether this is the God I expect you to worship, and the Bible I expect you to accept as authoritative. This is to sink to the level of the worst writers in the *National Reformer*, a level quite

unworthy of you. In you, as in the *National Reformer*, I am
sure it is no mere rhetorical artifice; it is *bona-fide* mistake.
You really do so read your Bible. You do so because you
have not grasped the idea that religion is itself an evolved
and evolving conception.   There are pages after pages of
your pamphlet which are devoted to proving what all
educated Christians have almost always known, that the
early conceptions of the Jews, whether of the nature of
God or of scientific fact, and of the relation of God to
Nature, were very inadequate; and to be inadequate
means in some cases to be erroneous.

The reply is already on your lips: "But this is what
the Christians about me believe—indeed, belief in this is
their religion.   This is what fills the tracts and religious
books I used to see, and the sermons I once heard."
And to some extent this is so; but what of that?   The
great majority of people are still in an elementary condition of religious knowledge, as were the Jews of old.   But
I ought to add that probably no Christians, or very few,
hold such crude beliefs as you seem to attribute to them;
and, on the other hand, that we think far more of God as
the ideal of holiness and goodness, and of Christ as a
Saviour, and of the Holy Spirit as a sanctifying influence,
and of all this as an impulse to duty and love, than you
probably imagine.

The fact obviously is, that most of us are wholly unfitted
to deal with philosophical questions, with abstractions, with
conceptions that we find it difficult to define precisely;
and yet we all equally need a guide to life, an impulse to
right conduct, and a sustaining power in it.   Religion is a
necessity of men.   The clear, visual image, so to speak, of
a God the Father is as much a necessity to one man as
your dissolving of that image into an abstraction—into, as
you say, nothing—is to you, and to many a good man
beside you.   And what then?   Is your conception true
and his false?   No; both are but attempts at the expression of what lies equally beyond your grasp and his.   Your
state of mind is not the final one.   You, too, are but in a
stage of the evolution of religious thought; one which is

for the moment negative, and may seem at first sight to some people to be atheistical and irreligious, but which seems to me, as I look back on it—for I do look back on it—as but one step towards a purer and truer faith, in which most of what you have said will strike you as very elementary, as well as being ill weighed.

You will ask, "How long have you clergy known this? You and your predecessors have for the last three hundred years taught me and my fathers to reverence the Bible as infallible. If you have not all used this word you have at any rate allowed this impression to prevail. Some of us Secularists and Sceptics have, in spite of odium, and authority, and petty persecutions, and inferiority of position, by our own unaided studies come to the conclusion and dared to publish it, that the Bible is not infallible. You now tell us you knew all this before. How long have you known it? Do you all know it? Why did you not tell us before?"

You see that I do not wish to shirk the strongest point in your case against us. I feel how it must perplex you. It will perplex you less when you have read the whole of what I intend to say. But the fact is that the knowledge is not old. To trace the effect of the Reformation on the theory of inspiration, and the way in which the growth of knowledge, historical, critical, philosophical, scientific, has slowly modified the popular—which was never the authoritatively adopted—theory of inspiration, would take me far from my present subject. It is a matter of history; and to these influences the writings of those who are commonly called Secularists have not made, as far as I can judge, any appreciable contribution. And I do not think we are to blame for extreme slowness in changing the language in which we speak of the Bible in ordinary teaching. To inquirers we are bound to speak most frankly; but we have no right to disturb the ordinary worshipper, if the familiar but imperfect way of presenting truth is a guide to conduct, and satisfies his heart and his intellect.

Another remark which may be on your lips is, "If this

teaching of the Old Testament is so elementary, why should
we study it? Of what value are these old-world notions to
us?" Here is another very large question, which merits
very full handling, and admits of a most complete answer.
But in this letter I can but sketch the answer, and I must
leave it to you to fill up the outline.

The end and aim of all religion is righteousness and
holiness, the true happiness of men and of man. Now
there is no nation which so made righteousness and
holiness its aim as the Jews. This does penetrate their
literature. Their words do, as a fact, move men as nothing
else moves them. That the supreme aim of their religion
was more or less associated with imperfect theories of
theology and cosmogony is of comparatively slight importance. Again, the Bible is interwoven with our national
history and national mind and literature. The worst misuse that has been made of it will plainly never occur again.
Biblical texts will not be quoted again in defence of burning people. Blasphemy prosecutions are defended on the
ground of the annoyance and pain and insult such blasphemy inflicts on society as a whole. You are well aware
that this is true, and all that is said on the other side is
mere rhetoric. The Bible is one of the heirlooms of the
world, and of England in particular, and it is destructive
madness to try and befoul it. The man of sense and of
patriotism will try to secure for posterity this precious
link to the past. Let us learn to use it better by all
means; but to hold it up to ridicule, as some of you do,
is like bespattering with mud the mother that gave you
birth. .

One inference that I want you to draw from all that I
have said is, that when you write you must make up your
mind to whom you are addressing yourself, and with what
object. Are you addressing the educated or the uneducated—the Christian or the Secularist? To the educated
Christian you have nothing to say with which he is not
familiar. You can shock him, but you cannot teach him.
Nor, I imagine, can you teach the educated Secularist.
Is it for the uneducated Christian, to disturb and perplex

him ? or for the uneducated Secularist, to confirm him in an essentially mistaken and uncultured way of regarding the Bible ? Who is to be benefited by what you write, or by the *National Reformer?* Have you at all realised the fact, that just as the long history of religion shows that the highest thought of one age is not the highest thought of another, but that there is an evolution and progress from age to age, so also that almost all these stages are actually coexisting before your eyes in this country ? To which of these stages are you addressing yourself ? Are you trying to educate to a higher and nobler faith any particular class or stage ? Perhaps you are. Perhaps you think that it would be better for the poor folk who live in Totterdown, and go to church or chapel, to believe in nothing, rather than to have the imperfect and elementary faith which is all you think they possess. But think again. Are you right, or philosophical, or kind in this ? I think you are not any of these. I say "which is all *you think* they possess," because you probably do not know how the simple faith of a good man purges itself of crudities, how it gathers round a few great truths, the selection made by a life. This you cannot know. A man's religion is not the same thing as the collection of statements which he would not deny, or which are contained in the formularies of the religious body to which he belongs. It is small game for you to be ridiculing the elementary forms of faith of the uneducated, and attributing to them beliefs which they do not hold, though you think they logically ought to hold them. There are writers in the *National Reformer* of confirmed narrowness, who appear, week after week, to find a pleasure in ridiculing what they think uninstructed Christians hold. I think better of you than to class you with these. But what are you doing ?

If you ask why Christian preachers and writers are not more explicit, why they are so timid, I would ask you to remember that they are in an especial sense the teachers of the young, and the unphilosophical and the semi-educated ; and that to attempt to teach them a religion based on such abstractions as yours would be an absolute

failure.   The individual learns by the same stages as the
world has learnt.   It might succeed with the units; it
would fail with the thousands.   The thousands would
relapse into superstition and immoralities.   I hold it as
certain that the premature acquaintance with advanced,
cold, and critical writings will drive, by their purely negative
character, a fraction—a small fraction—of the people into
superstitions resembling Romanism, and into wild eccen-
tricities of religion; and another fraction, perhaps a considerable one, into selfish worldliness—every one knows
how constantly this accompanies loss of Christian faith—
and even into heartless licentiousness.   The history of
Rome and France, and of the effects of the Reformation
on Southern Germany, ought not to be in vain.   Think
again!   Are you right, or patriotic, or philosophic, or kind?
Religion to an uneducated people is a discipline, a law;
and as such it is of inestimable value.   Mere ritual observance, however superstitious, marks a great advance on the
absence of all religion.   It is "a taming process"; it is
the submission to law; an acknowledgment of spiritual
inferiority; it implies self-conquest; it is not religion in its
highest sense, but it is the preparation for it.

How little, moreover, do you seem to be aware that
you are, in every bone and fibre of your body and brain,
the product of Christian forefathers.   It is not only discoveries of coal and steam and movable type that make
you to differ from the barbarous Briton who roamed over
the site of Bristol two thousand years ago.   The human-
ising, softening influences of Christianity are traceable in
every sentence you pen.   You climb up a ladder, and then
kick it down: no one else shall climb up it, you say.   You
"eat of the pastures," as the prophet says, and then "foul
with your feet the residue thereof."   How little you seem
to know what Christianity has done for the world!

You will see that I am not defending the points you
assail in the representation of God in the Old Testament.
My reply is, that the whole attitude of our minds, yours
and mine, towards such representations ought not to be
one of attack and defence, but of historical appreciation—

docile sympathy: and till I can get you to see this, there is no use in writing more to you.

But perhaps you think,—Then for all practical purposes there is no God, even to Christians; that I too worship no God, and am exactly in the same case that you are, though I call myself by a different name. But you would be wrong. If anything is certain to my reason, it is that this world we see has some cause and purpose; and that the reason and conscience of man, being a part of Nature, and its highest part, are a proof that the Cause and Purpose of the world, the controlling principle of its development, is itself of the nature of Reason and Conscience. Science and history and personal experience also lend themselves to the one theory that this Cause and Purpose is working around us and in us, and that we find our highest selves when we raise our thoughts to that Purpose and work along with it. I may speak of it as the Eternal, or as the Power that makes for righteousness and justice; or by the oldest name of all, the Heaven-Father— our Father which art in heaven; by the name of God; or by the name of natural Law or moral Duty. We may conceive Him as the Jews did, as nearly all the ancients did, as a Transcendent Being, external to the world, acting in space and time; or we may conceive Him as the Indwelling God, in whom all things consist; whose voice is in the conscience, and whose supreme manifestation is in the human nature of Christ. It is not the name which signifies; it is the attitude of our own minds, whether or not they look up and out of themselves to the ideal and the infinite, and feel the eternal supremacy of right. This is what signifies, and not our various, more or less childish, representations of God. All language about God is metaphorical, whether we call Him a Father, or a Rock, or a House of Defence, or a Buckler, or a Tendency, or a Cause, or a Voice in the conscience of man. All that we can do is to choose the best metaphor, to remember that it is a metaphor, and that the spiritual reality is far better than anything that we can conceive; and I think that you will feel that the revelation of God as our Father resting on the stupendous authority of Christ must be attentively received and studied. It comes to us infinitely better attested than any other. "Nothing, however, is fitted," as Dean Colet says, "to denote God Himself: God, who is not only unutterable, but inconceivable." We come, in fact, to the teaching of Christ that "God is Spirit."

It is this thought of God which, because of its imperfection, you would ridicule and do your best to banish from the world ; and you think complacently of your work. Did you ever read Carlyle's *Past and Present*? He was not exactly a Christian of the orthodox type, and his words may carry weight with you. You may find scores of such passages scattered up and down his works, but here are a few. "Verily it was another world then, seven centuries ago. Their Missals have become incredible, a sheer platitude, sayest thou? Yes—a most poor platitude : and even, if thou wilt, an idolatry and blasphemy, should any one persuade *thee* to believe them, to pretend praying by them. But yet it is pity we had lost tidings of our souls : actually we shall have to go in quest of them again, or worse in all ways will befall." . . . "It is even so ; to speak in the ancient dialect, we have forgotten God." . . . "The infinite is more sure than any other fact. But only men can discern it." . . . "The faith in an Invisible, Unnameable, Godlike, present everywhere in all that we see and work and suffer, is the essence of all faith whatever."

Do passages like this strike a chord in your heart? Do they set you thinking how you too may help to restore a real and true *faith* to England, and not to kill it and substitute a no-faith, to replace its present too doubting and too elementary a faith? This is the duty of all of us, "To strengthen that which remains which is ready to die." This is the work which I should like to see you and others helping in, instead of standing aloof, or even playing the part of Shimei.

I try to picture to myself how you will receive all this. Will you still say—Why then do you value the Bible if it is so elementary, so erroneous? What is its inspiration if it be not literally true and infallible? If you ask these

questions, I have only to say, that did you read the Bible
as I read it, and as I have been describing it, you could
not ask them.   I value the Old Testament because it contains the record of the growth of religious conceptions,
and in that record along with mistakes, with much that is
elementary and irrelevant, are such thoughts, such true
inspiration-flashes as herald the coming day.   It is the
beginning of the one fruitful and permanent line of the
religious education of the world, and it is therefore the
one sure guide to the early religious education of each
individual.   Its inspiration is not its accuracy, nor its
finality; but the fact that it is instinct with God, and that
it is effective, as no other book is effective, to turn men to
righteousness and to God.

Or will you turn to the later pages of your pamphlet,
confident that here, at any rate, you are on firm ground?
But it is not so.   Here, too, you are entangled with your
old elementary conceptions of the Bible.   Literally true or
false—is still the dilemma you make.   If literally true,
then—contradictions in the teaching and conception of
Christ; if false, then—in both cases equally valueless.
Such a dilemma, imaginary as it is, is no mere artifice on
your part; it is the result of your position.   You have
struggled yourself free from one false view of the Bible;
you have not yet attained to the true.   Yet perhaps you
should reflect that as in the case of the Old Testament,
so the New Testament contains the record by men of the
life and words of Christ; and it does not really detract
from its value, though it wholly removes the ground of
your argument, to recognise to the full its human character.
The writers do but tell us what they remember, or have
heard, or think of Christ and God, and the way of righteousness and peace, and the fruits of the Spirit, and the
social and personal ideal taught by Christ so far as they
could understand it.   Their inspiration is not a guarantee
of accuracy.   Their narrative of Christ's life and words
does but contain their estimate and their tradition of Him.
It is for us to see the Christ behind the veil of the memoirs
that we have of Him, and for us to see the gradual

development of Christian thought. It is for us too, I must
add, to see what perhaps the writers themselves felt, but
could scarcely have formulated, that they were the instruments of the great Divine purpose in the education of the
world, and marvellously endowed with wisdom and spiritual
insight. You may express this endowment in any way you
think truest to the fact : it seems to me truest to the fact
to call it an inspiration of the Holy Spirit, that is of God
Himself.

Why does God so educate man ? It is not for man to
say; but he can see that man is so educated.

Now, to take this view of the Bible that I have been
describing requires "the historic sense"; it requires some
sympathetic and literary insight. To say a thing is true
or false requires none. And I must ask you to believe
that I approach the subject as honestly as you do, and
that I see behind the veil of the Gospels, behind the fragmentary, and often prosaic and literal, perhaps even in
some respects mistaken, but always honest narratives of
the Evangelists, and in the Christ whom Paul preached,
One whom I revere as the highest manifestation of God
that has ever been seen on this earth of ours.

What do I mean by "God"? I mean something not
so very unlike what you imply in your last paragraph on
page 35. I mean that which underlies the highest conception that man has yet attained, or perhaps can ever
attain, of power and holiness and righteousness. And I
mean what the heathen were feeling after when they called
Him the Heaven-Father, or even the Unknown God. I
mean by the highest manifestation of God, One who first
taught this conception to mankind effectively; One who
alone "popularised" the ideas which you proclaim as
your principles—the self-culture, self-government, and self-
respect, as means for contributing to the good of the community; One who did far more than this; who found in
love to God our Father the one unfailing source for love
to man our brother; and thus made a life devoted to the
good of mankind, not a dream of Utopia, but a fact realised
in myriads of homes; One who taught us that our own

hearts and consciences are the voice of God in us; One who redeemed the world from sin; One whose Spirit is still a power in the world. I count you to be His follower at heart, though all unconscious that you are so, and though you know not His voice.

Such unbelief as yours is not immoral. In essence and origin it is easy to see that it is born of a love of truth. Some of the forms it has taken are unattractive, but they are so only from an inevitable want of knowledge and culture. But it is no more immoral than is bad spelling or bad logic. Such ridicule as yours also is not criminal; it also is plainly *bona-fide*, and, compared to the language used by some Secularists, it is moderate and gentle.

How to bridge across the chasm that separates the old non-critical acceptance of an infallible Bible from the new critical belief in it as a record of the development of religion, is a problem which taxes our generation. My lectures were a contribution to the solution of that problem. We get no help from the uninstructed Secularist, and none from the uninstructed Christian. They misunderstand and revile one another. The wise are for the most part silent. In all ages the cry has been, "Our religion or none;" and so it is now—"Our Christianity—our Secularism—or none." And therefore the wise are silent; or if one ventures to speak with some sympathy for both, he is straightway pelted by each for having sympathy with the other, for "making concessions" to the other. Warfare of opinion is what the less educated part of the community rejoices in. We may bridge over the chasm for our individual selves; but we can scarcely make the way so broad and plain that the wayfaring man shall not err therein.

I do not think that you and I shall see this bridge built. That is the work of the next Reformation, to which in our degree you and I ought to contribute. But greater chasms than this have been spanned, and the development of Christianity will not be long retarded by this.

There are a few more considerations I should like you to weigh well.

One is the very great value to a nation of settled axioms of faith, even if to the philosopher these axioms seem questionable, and the intellectual deductions from them inadequate or erroneous. If they are true relatively to the capacities of those who hold them, this is all that can be attained in the present condition, or in any immediate future of society. Such settled axioms are of exceedingly slow growth. It would be a great mistake to suppose that they are built up afresh in each succeeding generation. They are rooted in our language and customs, and are doubtless inherited as are instincts and national character. And none but the thoughtless will regard them otherwise than as an invaluable part of national character and national discipline. Some of you Secularists are unwittingly doing what you can to destroy one of the slowly-won and most valuable traits of English national character, the faith in God's providence and the sense of duty to Him. We may change Goldsmith's well-known lines and say:

> A pious peasantry, their country's pride,
> When once destroyed can never be supplied.

To disturb the settled order of religion, to provoke discussion of accepted axioms among the uneducated, to ridicule the faith of childhood, and the books which the nation reveres, this is the destruction of piety. You may think it is not piety, but superstition and error, you are attacking. You are wrong, because you fail to notice how the piety of the early stages of religion is involved with forms of faith and modes of representation which, to the later stages, appear erroneous, and by the unsympathetic and hard are dismissed as superstition. The God-fearing Puritan element is the backbone of England. You perhaps know the story of Lord Clyde (if I remember right) asking his officers to pick him the bravest men from his small army before Delhi, to form the forlorn hope in a desperate attack. It was on a Sunday evening. "There is a prayer meeting going on now," they said, "in the camp. If you go there, you will find all the bravest men!" That story tells a tale. Ponder it again and again.

Once more: In holding up to contempt the early representations of God, you are doing an injury not only to the less talented and less educated men than yourself, but also to all children. You cannot teach children the reverence for an abstract law. I have known men and women quite as conscious as you are of the inadequacy of the popular faith, and as clearly resolved at the time of marriage as you could be that they would not bring up their children in any belief which they deemed a superstition; and yet, when the children came, their innocent and direct questions—the exigencies of moral education—very unexpectedly necessitated a recurrence to the elementary forms of teaching which they themselves had got past. It is one thing for a man like yourself to have had such teaching, and grown out of it; it will be quite a different thing for another generation, if they have never had such teaching at all. The Board Schools—which you speak of almost as if they were a new revelation—if they did not teach the elements of religion and reverence for the Bible, and were not supplemented by other agencies, would unquestionably be the heralds of new and extravagant and degraded sects of religion, both Christian and semi-Pagan. There are indications enough that this is so, if men will but look about them. But if, on the other hand, the elementary schools teach the elements of religion and deep intelligent reverence for the Bible, and if they are, as they ought to be, supplemented by the teaching and example of mother and father at home, and by the continued and higher teaching of a Christian Church, then they will not spread an anti-Christian spirit. But how some of you are throwing difficulties in the way of doing this! If you could but survey the conditions, past and present, of this and other countries, you would hesitate long before taking the line you do. You plunge into war with a light heart! Ah! think again, and yet again.

But it is not only children and the uneducated that need elementary and accommodated views of God and religion: to say this would savour of a stupid pride. We all need them. We are not, and cannot make ourselves independent of them, or of forms and discipline in religion. I can sympathise for a time with the Pantheist, who loses himself in the contemplation of Nature, and worships in her temple alone; or with the Mystic, who guides himself solely by the inner light; or with the Sceptic, who finds the evidence complete for no theory, and, therefore, holds none; but not for a permanence, not even for long, with any of them. I must fall veritably on my knees by my bedside, and must pray to my Father in heaven, for I know no better name. I must pray for forgiveness, for growth in grace; pray for my children, for my country and the Church. And at such a time I do not perplex [myself with representations of God; I only know that God is, and that prayer is a necessity, and that it is the upward and not the downward look that helps me. I do not know whether my prayer alters God's will. I do not wish it to do so; I cannot conceive its doing so when the laws of Nature are concerned, except through the laws of Nature; and yet prayer is all the more a necessity. Prayer is not begging: on the contrary, it is self-surrender, a giving up of all we hold most dear. I am quite sure that the various stages of religion through which I have, with more or less of help, struggled up—the condition you are now in of impatient disbelief being one of them—have all helped me to a fuller and deeper view of the world, to greater happiness and charity; and, therefore, I love even the earliest stages and the simplest conceptions, and I can honestly take part in teaching them. I look at their beauty and truth and their educational value, more than at their inadequacy or their mistakes. I am writing this in Switzerland. The other day I went into a church in one of the Catholic cantons, and there watched the good, simple folk telling their beads and muttering their prayers, while the priest performed a mass inaudibly. Then they touched themselves with holy water, and went out into the early morning sun to their work. "Gross superstition!" say you and some fierce Protestants; say rather, the material steps by which they are being led to the thought of their Father in heaven. Superstition it would be to us if some one were to hold up this as religion to you or me, or to Englishmen in general; but to them it was religion, and true religion, in an elementary form.

It seems, therefore, to me a most poor performance on your part to cry out, when you are part way up the ladder, "Look at the poor fools below me!" It is not calculated to win the respect of those above, or the love of those below; it can only be applauded by the ignorant or frivolous or cold-hearted. By the good it will be received in silence, or with the half-spoken prayer, "Father, forgive them; for they know not what they do."

But if you ask me whether nothing ought to be done to help forward this evolution of religious thought, and to prevent thoughtful men of the next and later generations from feeling the contradictions you feel, and to help them to see things more justly than the past generations saw them, I say at once that we, educated Christian men, have a distinct duty to perform in this direction—always remembering the great law of charity. I think that the Church ought to provide meat for her strong men, as well as secure that her babes shall get milk. One of our failures is in this duty. I do not think it can be denied that the popular Christianity of the day, whether among priests or people, in church or chapel, is for the most part far less tolerant than is the spirit of Christ, or of St. Paul, or of the great minds among Christians of all ages. That it should be so among the people is for the present unavoidable. It ought not to be so, and it need not be so, among the educated laity and clergy, and they ought not to permit the intolerance of ignorance to pass unchecked, as it too often does. We clergy ought to stem the tide more bravely than we do, and we ought to have done so in time past. We, as a rule, regard differences of opinion on speculative questions, and even on the terms in which we choose to present them, as very serious matters; and expect old and young, philosophers and simple, men and women, to accept unquestioningly the same terms. I think this is wrong. I do not at all think that this is the mind of Christ. Much may be done to claim for more

K

abstract and philosophic views, and especially for all views that profess to rise directly from the study of facts and promote rightness of conduct, a place within the recognised boundaries of the Christian Church. We should, however, highly value the discipline of established forms. We should hold fast with the utmost tenacity the conquests of religion, and especially the conquests of Christianity, in the regions of humanity and morality. Such laws are the observance of days of rest, the laws of purity, the protection of the weak, the sanctity of human life and property. But I wish to go further than this, and I have no doubt that here you will agree with me. I have spoken of the childhood of the individual being like the childhood of the race, and said that, therefore, the education of the one will follow the lines of education of the other. And this is true, but with some important qualifications. The child of the present century is not in all respects like the man of a bygone century. And the child may pass very rapidly through the elementary stages; and we do him a positive injury—we dispose him to reject religion—if we prolong these stages artificially, for in that case we make him identify religion with that which he will grow out of. Further: As education advances this transition will inevitably become more rapid. It is more rapid now than most people think. My little boy of nine was reading the first chapter of Genesis to his mother the other day, and she explained to him that the days were long periods of time. "Why, mamma, I should think I knew that," was his remark. I cannot conjecture how he should have learnt this. I feel quite sure that, as a rule, religious teachers postpone the higher teaching too long. It has already come upon their people from many sides; and this discredits the sincerity, and therefore diminishes the weight of their teaching. No doubt there are grave reasons for the delay. The unwillingness of the majority of people to permit any growth in their minds, or make any intellectual effort in religion, and their readiness to suspect unsoundness in anything that is not quite literal, are very discouraging to the teacher. And the inherent difficulties of

the question—the right use of the diversified contents of
the Bible, and of established forms, in religious education
—are very great.   Still, that is the problem before us.
Your solution is—reject them altogether.   That is not
mine.   That is an impossibility.   The experience of other
religions is not encouraging to your view.   Buddhism was
an attempt to anticipate the final stage of Brahmanism;
it was a noble attempt, and it did noble work, but it has
ended in many parts of the world in being vulgarised by
the masses into the most debased religion on the earth.
The true solution is in another application of the words of
Christ, " I come not to destroy, but to fulfil."

I have already alluded more than once to India as affording
a field of singular interest for the historical study of religion.[1]
India has a great lesson to teach us on the subject of toleration.   The Brahmans pass through three or four stages of
life: the student, the householder, the two stages of the
philosopher.   The student is rigorously brought up on the
Vedas, their sacred books; and in this faith, as householder, he believes and prays and sacrifices.   But in the
third stages, when his children are grown up and his hair
is gray, he is emancipated from all these fetters, and con-
centrates his thoughts on the Eternal Self.   The *Vedas*
now become lower knowledge to him: the gods Agni and
Indra become as mere names.   " For thousands of years,"
to quote Max Müller, "there have been Brahmanic families
in which the son learns by heart the ancient hymns, and
the father performs day by day his sacred duties and
sacrifices; while the grandfather looks upon all ceremonies
and sacrifices as vanity, sees even in the Vedic gods
nothing but the names of what he knows to be beyond all
names, and seeks rest in the highest knowledge only.
The three generations have learnt to live together in
peace.   The grandfather, though more enlightened, does
not look down with contempt on his son or his grandson;
least of all does he suspect them of hypocrisy.   Nor does
the son—though bound by the formulas of his faith, and

---

[1] See Max Müller's *Hibbert Lectures* and *What we have to learn from
India.*

strictly performing the minutest rules of the old ritual—
speak unkindly of his father. He knows that he has
passed through the narrower path, and he does not grudge
him the freedom and the wider horizon of his views."
And further: Not only is the grandfather permitted to
pass into this more philosophic stage: he would be considered as not performing his duty, as not passing rightly
through his education if he did not do so. This philosophic stage is as authoritatively prescribed in the *Upani-
shads*, or later sacred books, as are the earlier stages in the
Vedas. It is as much a part of the religion of the Brahmans to rise in old age above the forms of religion, as it is
in youth and manhood to adopt them. Religion is, in
fact, avowedly regarded as a discipline, and as an introduction through symbols to higher truth. But at last the
discipline has done its work: the symbols are exchanged
for realities, and the aged Brahman enters as a freeman
the temple of philosophic truth. Well indeed may Max
Müller say, "Is not here, too, one of the many lessons
which a historical study of religion teaches us?" Why
should we fail to recognise the fact that man ought to
grow, and does grow, not only in stature and favour with
God and man but in wisdom also? No church is honest
which does not recognise that fact, and which is not
anxious to secure a place of safety, nay, of honour, to those
who have grown in goodness and wisdom and understanding, in the gifts of the Spirit, and have thus attained to a
truer insight into the nature of religion than can, for the
present at least, be reached by the majority even of educated people. A church which declines to recognise the
right of the Few, who are "fond of wisdom," not only to
be tolerated, but to be respected, must become stagnant;
and if it actually encourages the ignorant intolerance of
the multitude, if it identifies itself with the narrowness and
exclusiveness of the uneducated or half-educated masses,
it will drive its best champions into silence, and many who
under proper guidance might have fought a good fight,
and done noble work for the Church, into atheism, or
what is still worse, into hypocrisy.

In spite of all the prejudices against everything which in our enlightened times calls itself *Esoteric*, we must not forget that Christ Himself spake often in parables to the people, and in plain words to His twelve disciples only. Christ sanctioned a degree of accommodation in His teaching. No army will conquer which dismisses its pioneers, and no church will conquer which not only deprives itself wilfully of the services of those who are most anxious to serve it in cutting new paths and letting in new light through the wilderness of ignorance and superstition, but stones " its prophets, wise men and scribes." When the Few cease to differ from the Many, we may have uniformity and peace, but we may also have dishonesty and death. When the Few are respected by the Many, we may hope to have again in the Church a true spiritual, that is, intellectual aristocracy—a small heart throbbing *within*, but giving life and strength to the large body of Christian people *without*.

But I am digressing into reflections suggested by the reading of these *Hibbert Lectures*, rather than replying to your pamphlet. I wish, however, you would read the lectures from which I am quoting. It would be of the highest value for you to see what has been said by a wise and true Christian like Max Müller in the Chapter House of Westminster Abbey.

But I will copy out a few more passages for you, to tempt you to read the whole. After urging us to learn this lesson of toleration, of human sympathy, of love—lessons worthy of the sage who knows what man is, and what life is, and has learnt to keep silence in the presence of the Eternal and the Infinite—he continues thus: "It is no doubt easy to find names for condemning such a state of mind. Some call it shallow indifference, others call it dishonesty, to tolerate a difference of religion for the different stages of life, for our childhood, our manhood, and our old age; still more, to allow any such difference between the educated and the uneducated classes of our society.

" But let us look at the facts such as they are around

us and within us, such as they are and always must be.
Is the religion of Bishop Berkeley, or even of Newton, the
same as that of a ploughboy? In some points yes: in all
points no. . . . Bishop Berkeley would not have declined
to worship in the same place with the most obtuse and
illiterate of ploughboys; but the ideas which that great
philosopher connected with such words as God the Father,
God the Son, and God the Holy Ghost were surely as
different from those of the ploughboy by his side as two
ideas can well be that are expressed by the same words.

"And let us not think of others only, but of ourselves;
not of the different phases of society, but of the different
phases through which we ourselves pass in our journey
from childhood to old age. Who, if he is honest towards
himself, could say that the religion of his manhood was the
same as that of his childhood; or the religion of his old
age the same as that of his manhood? It is easy to
deceive ourselves, or to say that the most perfect faith is a
childlike faith. Nothing can be more true, and the older
we grow, the more we learn to understand the wisdom of a
childlike faith. But before we can learn that, we have
first to learn another lesson, viz. to put away childish
things. . . .

"The Divine, if it is to reveal itself at all to us, will
best reveal itself in our own human form. However far
the human may be from the Divine, nothing on earth is
nearer to God than man, nothing on earth more Godlike
than man. And as man grows from the cradle to old age,
the idea of the Divine must grow with us from the cradle
to the grave, from grace to grace."

These passages illustrate excellently what I wish to
impress on you, that Christianity recognises the relativity
of religious dogma to the condition of mind of the individual. But I am tempted to give you another quotation,
to show how even the most inflexible of Christian churches,
the Roman Catholic Church, admits the evolution of religious dogma from age to age. "We have to account,"
says Cardinal Newman in his *Essay on Development*, "for
that apparent variation and growth of doctrine which

embarrasses us when we would consult history for the true idea of Christianity. The increase and expansion of the Christian creed and ritual, and the variations which have attended the process in the case of individual writers and churches, are the necessary attendants on any philosophy or polity which takes possession of the intellect and heart, and has had any wide or extended dominion. From the nature of the human mind, time is necessary for the full comprehension and perfection of great ideas. The highest and most wonderful truths, though communicated to the world once for all by inspired teachers, could not be comprehended all at once by the recipient; but as admitted and transmitted by minds not inspired and through media that were human, have required only the longer time and deeper thought for their full elucidation. . . . The more claim an idea has to be considered living, the more various will be its aspects; and the more social and political is its nature, the more complicated and subtle will be its developments, and the longer and the more eventful will be its course. Such is Christianity."[1]

No doubt the view I am putting before you is not an easy one. You find it difficult, as do thousands of intelligent men and women, to use the Bible now that you have ceased to regard it as an infallible and mechanical authority. Neither Bible nor Church is infallible; and if they are not this, what are they? you ask. Is there any foundation for positive dogmatic beliefs about God and Christ and the future world? I feel as strongly as you feel that the fallibility of all written records, and of all that bears the impress of man's mind, carries with it the conclusion that there is no theological doctrine, not even the existence of God Himself, which can be so demonstrated to the intellect that its denial is impossible, or to the conscience that the refusal to accept it is sin. And, therefore, when doubts arise from the intellect and not from the blinding of the soul through selfishness and sin, I utterly refuse to blame any man for doubting, or exclude him from Christian Communion. And, further, there

[1] Quoted by M. Arnold, *St. Paul and Protestantism*, p. 145.

have been and still are quasi-scientific dogmas about God,
our attitude towards which ought, on proper occasions, to
be rather that of denial and repudiation than that of doubt.
And yet I should like to help you to something positive:
and this letter is but preliminary; it is clearing the ground
and making more positive teaching possible.　For along
with this I have an entire conviction, which penetrates my
whole being—a conviction which has steadily grown in
intensity since I abandoned untenable views of the infallibility of the Bible and of the Church—that there is a
Highest, be it Mind, or Person, or Law, or Tendency, or
none of these things, an Infinite which human thoughts
and human words cannot reach, an indwelling Spirit of
God, and that the self-surrender to this, and the identifica-
tion of this with the God to whom the Bible raises our
thoughts and of whom Christ spoke, is the highest education of man's spirit.　Christianity, as it came from its
Founder, was a society which, starting from the intense
Jewish consciousness of the God who loves righteousness
and justice, learned from Christ that that God was a God
of love to all men and all nations, and was inspired by
Christ to a passion of love for God and man.　Hopes for
an after life, but above all holiness and charity in this:
these were their watchwords; this was "the Way of Life."
It is not the first step in Christianity as contained in the
Gospels to make assertions respecting the nature of Christ,
and to denounce contrary assertions; it is the first step in
Christianity to recognise His divine leadership, to believe
that there is a Highest yet unattained by man, and that
fidelity to Christ's principles will lead men towards that
Highest.　Sincerity in the endeavour to live in Christ's
Spirit, the habitual attitude of reverence to God and love
to man, these are the essentials of Christianity.　He who
begins with these, or arrives at these, finds fresh depths
and heights of truth as years go on, and he knows, by a
conviction which cannot be shaken, that he is standing on
a rock.　We may not know much of God: indeed we
know but an infinitesimal fraction of His nature, His purpose, His methods, and yet this little that we do know is

all-important to us. A dog knows but a small fragment of a man's mind, and yet that small fragment is everything to the dog.

But my letter is becoming unreasonably long, and I must draw to an end.

The world has in it a considerable party, who think that Christianity is exploded equally as a practical rule of life, and as an intellectual system. They think that life must be led on other principles, chiefly self-interest, tempered by as little humanitarianism as will serve to satisfy public opinion, and not injure self-respect, or incommode an inconvenient conscience.

There is another considerable party who think that no fresh light, or growth, or purity can come into religion, and that either their favourite dogmas selected from the creed of their Church or sect, or the literal infallibility of the Bible, or both, must be retained for all Christians of all ages and educations alike. It seems to me that both alike have lost something of Christianity, and that the old root of heathenism in our human nature is showing itself equally in both.

But there are others, and I hope that you and I are among them, who see that the religion of Christ admits of endless growth; they adhere to the old forms and expressions, for the sake of the deep truths they have taught, and are teaching, and can still be made to teach; forms and expressions fitted by use to the human mind. They do so because they know that it is better to fulfil than to destroy. But they do not fetter themselves from the freest investigation and the freest thought. It is possible to combine the most fearless study and the widest knowledge of the laws of Nature and history and criticism with a profound faith in God. The most profound minds of the present day recognise, on scientific grounds alone, the very high probability of something more than evolution, as commonly understood, being necessary to account for facts as we see them. The examination of physical laws and systems, of biology, and most of all of the intellectual and spiritual faculties of man, all lead to the belief in some-

thing ultra-scientific, ultra-evolutional. The theory of an
interference of something not strictly evolutional is more
in accordance with actual knowledge than the negation of
such interference. How to express that something—what
its nature is, what the method of its working—is the
almost final problem to which science and theology are
converging. But you should well weigh the fact that in
working at this problem they are friends and not foes. It
is not the reconciliation of science and religion that is
occupying the thoughts of the best men; it is their
alliance, it is their convergence, it is their continuity, nay,
it is their identity. I cannot but believe that the more
we know on all subjects, the more we shall approach
towards a unity of conception and of knowledge. It is
ignorance that divides men, not knowledge.

And now I must conclude, not without an apology if I
have said anything which may have hurt your feelings, or
may have looked like the pride of a so-called better education. Nothing can have been further from my thoughts,
as I trust you will see; but the fact of our different educations explains why we look at some things differently. I
have not taken up all your points in detail, and I know
that there are some large questions which you open to
which I have scarcely alluded. But if you master the
principles of this letter, and I have stated them as clearly
as I can, you will not find great difficulty in applying them
to all the points which you raise. If, however, on specific
points you wish to write privately to me, I will gladly do
my best, as far as other duties and engagements permit,
to satisfy you.

I will only add one word more. You speak of the
shadows and superstitions of a supernatural creed. It is
possible to be a Christian, and be as free as light itself
from any such superstitions. You speak of loving virtue
for its own sake, and of rescuing humanity from its present
evils. He is the truest follower of Christ who most truly
lives and acts in this spirit, and with the ever-present
thought of God. Here is the Christianity of Christ, and
that of many and many a Christian, and I trust it will be

the Christianity in which I, not less than you, shall live and die.

And now, with sincere respect for you, and with prayers that God's blessing may rest on you here and hereafter, I remain, yours very faithfully,   J. M. WILSON.

CLIFTON COLLEGE,
Sept. 14, 1885.

THE LIMITS OF AUTHORITY AND
FREE THOUGHT[1]

FROM the wording of this question it would seem as if the discussion were intended to be an attempt to determine the limits which bound Free Thought—and, from the fact that it is a Church Congress at which it is proposed, the subject would seem to be limited to Religious Free Thought—in other words, that our object is to say to Free Thought, "Thus far shalt thou come, and no farther." But I would venture to suggest that this phrase *limit* is based on a fundamentally wrong conception of the question really before us, and we are in much danger of being misled by it, and of giving the discussion a wrong turn. It is, of course, a geographical metaphor; but it is an inappropriate metaphor. It conveys a wrong impression of the relation between Authority and Free Thought, and one which may quite vitiate our reasoning upon them. It brings up in our minds the idea of two territories, conterminous, but with disputed boundaries; and we picture the past and future histories of opinion as the records of one territory growing at the expense of another. The age of mediævalism, we say, witnessed the territory of Authority growing at the expense of Free Thought; that of the Reformation, the territory of Free Thought growing at the expense of Authority. The present, we hear on all hands, is an age of "encroachment of Free Thought" on the "time-honoured boundaries of Authority"; or, to use a

<hr>

[1] A paper read at the Church Congress, Derby, October 1882.

kindred metaphor, "the advancing tide of scepticism" is swallowing up "the fertile land of faith," and we know not where "the final barrier" will be placed. It is important that we should see how profoundly this metaphor has affected our thoughts on the subject. It is difficult now even to think of the relation of Authority and Free Thought under any other metaphor.

Now, I venture to say that no limits exist either to Free Thought or Authority; that the relation between them is not one of mutual exclusion and encroachment.

It is, perhaps, a commonplace, but it must be repeated, that it is a mistake even to talk of Free Thought. Thought cannot be free. All thought is conditioned by the past, the product of antecedent thought, the result of influences. The question is not whether Free Thought shall exist, for it certainly cannot exist; but whether there shall be imposed on thought additional and artificial restraints, besides those imposed by the nature of things.

This is very far indeed from being a quibble about words. All thought grows or is evolved out of the past. The question is whether this growth and evolution of thought in certain directions ought to be artificially repressed by Authority. At any rate the *onus probandi* lies on those who would repress it. For it is obvious to ask, Why should such thought be always suspected of leading men wrong? We train men of acutest minds by the best propædia we can devise to make them truth-loving and courageous. Why then should we say that on certain subjects they must not think, or think with foregone conclusions?

And the question arises, Who can repress the growth and evolution of thought? Let us never forget the illustration of Plato's cave. The limit there imposed on Free Thought was imposed by the men who remained in the cave with their backs to the light, contemplating the shadows of passing objects—imposed on the one man who had unfettered himself and had gone up to the upper air, and seen the realities themselves. In all our discussion let us remember that we may be "cave-men."

Nor can it be said that it is not we who impose a limit
on human thought, and that the limit exists independently
of our will.   For where and what is the limit?   It is not
a man.   The first so-called freethinkers, whose spiritual
descendants we are, the Protestants, got rid of the Pope
at any rate.

It is not the Church.   The Church—any Church—has,
of course, power to impose on itself, on its teachers and
its members, a test and a creed.   It "has Authority in
matters of faith."   But to suppose that this is the same
thing as to define the limits of thought to the world, to
embrace all truth, and exclude all errors, is to confuse
eternal verities with that imperfect vision and expression
of them which it is given to any one age or race to obtain.
There must be many who accept such tests and Authority,
not as absolute and final, but as demanding all respect, as
containing much truth, and as helping to the acquisition
of more.

Nor is the limit to be assumed to be a book, still less a
particular interpretation of a book, without the free and
continual examination of the book.   We all want to know
the truth about the book; no one desires anything else;
but the world can never be persuaded that the truth can
have been attained if examination is barred.   There is an
enormous gain in thus desiring, and not precluding, discussion and research.   A man can then breathe freely.
When we clergy can stand up like other men and say, "I
believe this because it holds its ground in face of free
investigation in which we have played a fair part; because
it is historically true, or historically probable;" when we
use words in the same sense that other people do, we
shall be infinitely stronger.   But to do this we must
differentiate our evidence.   We must venture to say out
loud, and not with bated breath, I believe in the Resurrection of Christ, because it seems to rest on sufficient
historical evidence to prove even so great a miracle,
while there are articles in our current belief which are
speculative and rest on less evidence, but which I do not
necessarily think untrue.

There is, then, no artificial limit, no limit other than the limitation of our faculties and the law of continuity of human thought, that can be imposed on the mind of man; whatever tests or creeds a church may from time to time think best to impose on itself: tests and creeds which must be, as they have been, from time to time interpreted and revised by its supreme Authority, and, as we trust, under God's guidance, so as to bring them into accordance with progressive knowledge. Nor again is there any limit to authority. Heredity, education, the weight given instinctively to established beliefs, the vast momentum of long-standing habits and institutions, give to the past an influence on the present which secures continuity amid change, and makes progress steady. In other words, there exists a natural authority, subtle, boundless, far stronger than any artificial authority, and resented by none. We are held by the past, not to our harm, but our good; nursed by it, trained by it, for growth and for the right use of freedom.

The relation then between Authority and Free Thought is not that of rival forces occupying conterminous territories, but may be compared to that of the forces in a living organism which determine growth, but limit the rate of growth; they are not antagonistic; they are essentially the same. One is the force regarded as securing growth; the other the same force as securing continuity. Individuals will incline to one or the other according to bias and early influences, and thus co-operate to the great end —continuity in growth.

Our true reply to freethinkers is, that according to our ability we are freethinkers too. If they point out prejudices, errors, one-sidedness in us, let us be thankful. Perhaps they, too, have something to learn. But their methods must be our methods, when we deal *in pari materiâ*, in history and criticism. Every assertion about objective facts must be capable of verification and proof.

Besides these facts of history and criticism, there are, as we must point out to them, other facts which cannot be traced to their ultimate origin; the result of the evolution of human nature under the influence, as we believe, of God's Holy Spirit; the facts of conscience and consciousness, of hope and aspirations and worship, spiritual facts, which have no verification but themselves. With these lies most of our concern. They contain the germ of the spiritual life and progress of every man, the inner life which Christian teaching fosters and trains till it is supreme. These facts lie in a region equally beyond Authority and Free Thought.

It may be further remarked that when we once accept this relation between Free Thought and Authority, and regard them as the manifestation of one quasi-vital force, we shall see that the weight to be assigned to a great consensus of opinion in the past depends on the subject. In objective fact it is *nil*. All the world having thought that the earth was flat, is inadmissible, even as an argument that it is so. All the world having held a view on the antiquity of man, or on spontaneous generation, has no weight in deciding the question whether the fact is thus or thus. In criticism the weight is very small. The question of the antiquity of the Levitical legislation we all feel must be decided, not by quoting authorities, but by an examination of the evidence. In theology, as a speculative science, it is far higher, for the genius of the great theologians of the past seems to have deserted the present. In ethics it is highest of all, because the axioms of ethics, honesty, justice, patriotism, filial obedience, monogamy, purity, rest on such an enormous mass of observed facts and experience in human nature. In these subjects it is so high that we are right in treating Free Thought, or rather its consequence, free action, as a crime.

Lastly, as the rate of growth of opinion and knowledge in a nation is dependent on the aggregate of human wills and judgments, it becomes an individual duty to exercise that judgment and will. It may be in the highest interest of a nation at one time to do our best to repress growth and emphasise continuity with the past; at another to demand that repression shall be removed, and that growth shall be more rapid. At this point the discussion of principles passes into practical application ; but the principles themselves cannot vary.

On the extremes on both sides, as is usual, are the ignorant and the bigoted. Between the two are those who, claiming absolute freedom to think on all subjects, yet attach great weight to any belief, any custom, any institution, which has proved its value, as our Church has done, by its profound and lofty influence on man, has stood the test of time, is polished by the friction of ages, and fitted to man's use—a Church which, we may say with all reverence and humility, seems to have God's blessing on it, and that in increasing measure. These are the men who endeavour humbly to carry out the apostolic injunction to "prove all things, and hold fast that which is good." In these words lies the true relation of Free Thought and Authority.

CHURCH AUTHORITY:
ITS MEANING AND VALUE[1]

LET us try and clear the ground a little. We will therefore first ask: "The Authority of the Church on what
subjects?"

Setting aside exploded ideas, such as the authority of
the Church to enforce discipline or moral laws on the
world, these subjects may be divided, as a first approxima-
tion, into three classes.

There may (or may not) be an authority which deals
with (1) disputed questions relating to the history of the
Bible and Christianity—*i.e.* the criticism and historical
veracity of the Bible; the history of the Canon; the study
of the remains of Christian antiquity; in a word, the
nature of the materials for the history of our religion.

(2) Disputed questions relating to what we may call
the more or less formulated doctrines of Christianity,
inferred from, rather than explicitly stated in, the Bible.

(3) All that relates to Church government and
discipline, and ritual and finance.

We will briefly refer to these divisions as *criticism*,
theology, business. It is plain that these subjects are so
different that it is mere confusion of thought to class them
together.

Next, "What do we mean by authority?" Here there
is an obvious ambiguity.

[1] A paper read at a Clerical Meeting in Bristol, 6th July 1885. (Reprinted from *Macmillan's Magazine.*)

There is (1) the preponderant weight we assign to the learning and judgment of men whose veracity and impartiality we trust. We speak of the authority of a scholar like Lightfoot. It is not, however, an authority in the sense that it demands obedience; it only demands respect and consideration.

There is (2) another sort of authority. There are men with an unrivalled genius for holiness; men refined by prayer and unflinching devotion to duty, and therefore gifted with a singular delicacy of touch and insight, with a true inspiration of God's Holy Spirit. We feel in them our best selves: we feel that they are nearer to God than we are; their words have an authority. Still, this is not an authority which commands obedience: it silently appeals for respect and love. It is compatible with error.

There is (3) yet another authority which does command obedience, which has the power of enforcing itself. The Church, acting through its defined powers, has authority. The Bishop may suspend for defined offences in virtue of his "authority."

Once more, these kinds of authority are so different that they can only be taken together by confusion of thought.

Let us call them the authority of *learning*, of *holiness*, and of *law*.

Happily it is not necessary to define what we mean by the Church for the purposes of the present essay. One meaning we can point out in passing. The Church of England, "as by law established," has unquestioned authority in certain matters of discipline and ritual. The disciplinary functions of Church Courts and Bishops are not wholly suspended. The Church has the authority of *law* in matters of *discipline*.

So far is easy. The more difficult question is, "Has the Church, whatever the Church is, an authority of learning to decide matters of criticism; or of holiness and inspiration to pronounce authoritatively in matters of doctrine or of conduct?"

Pray do not let us confuse these two—the authorities of learning in criticism, and of holiness or inspiration in theology or conduct.

There are many questions before the world which are purely matters of learning. When was the Book of Deuteronomy written? By what route did Israel come out of Egypt? What is the authority of the Gospels? What was the relation of the agape and the Eucharist? What is the value of Codex B? These, and an infinite number of such questions, are questions of learning and criticism; they are questions as to matters of fact; they are not questions of religion or conduct.

Now, the question is an intelligible one, and admits of a positive answer: "Has the Church, in any sense of the word, authority to decide these questions? Is it possible that matters of fact can be decided by authority?" Now, it is a matter of fact, one way or the other, whether, for example, the Masoretic text of Samuel is as old as the LXX.; whether a whale swallowed Jonah; and whether St. Paul wrote the Epistle to the Hebrews. Could any past consensus of opinion on these points decide them? Might it not have been wrong? These are as much matters of fact as whether the earth is round or flat. Let us never forget that there was a time when it was pronounced to be "a shame in a Christian man even so much as to mention the antipodes." St. Ambrose and St. Basil were, I believe, exceptions among the fathers in the liberality of their views on this point. They were brave enough to defy public opinion, and to declare that a correct belief in the antipodes was not necessary to salvation. Men made the mistake then, which confused thinkers make now, of making assertions on authority about matters of fact. The Copernican theory, the Darwinian theory, the Straussian theory, most of our disputed questions, are questions as to matter of fact. Now, the result of the last four hundred years of growth of the human mind is that we now at last know that matters of fact are not decided by authority. They are settled by evidence, and by reason. Can this be seriously disputed?

The scientific mind is unable to conceive how a question as to a matter of fact can be settled by authority.

The Church, therefore, has no authority to decide questions of learning and criticism and matters of fact, other than the preponderant weight we assign to the learning and judgment of men, whose veracity and impartiality we trust, when they had full opportunities for exercising that judgment.

Now remains the other less explored region into which we must penetrate. What do we mean by saying that "the Church hath authority in controversies of faith"? Here we seem to be on solid ground, for this is one of the Thirty-nine Articles.

No doubt most of my hearers know the history of these famous words, as given by Bishop Browne. I suppose we owe them to no less profound a theologian than Queen Elizabeth herself. She is said to have refused to sign the Articles as drafted and signed by the two Houses of Convocation until these words were added. Convocation seems to have submitted to her will, and accepted the authority for the Church. Some may think it is a slightly Erastian origin for the power claimed; others may think it defines those powers. But we will not look a gift-horse in the mouth.

But the words are not free from ambiguities. There is not only the plain difference between the *fides quæ creditur* and the *fides qua creditur;* but even when we agree that it is the first of these that is intended, an ambiguity remains.

The words may mean, "There is a perennial association of men, in legitimate possession of the property bequeathed to the Church, charged with the duty of teaching and preaching God's Word, and of administering the Sacraments and other Christian rites. This association has, under certain limitations, the power of deciding from time to time on the qualifications for membership. These qualifications consist in the profession of certain beliefs, and the conformity to certain customs. This association or Church can define those beliefs and pre-

scribe those customs subject to the limitation that nothing
shall be contrary to God's Word written."

This is one meaning. The Church can declare, not
that this or that is true, but that to believe this or that, to
act thus or thus, is the condition of membership, and of
enjoying the emoluments and immunities it brings, or
professes to bring.

We will call this authority *declaratory of the terms of
membership*. The Church *has* this authority.

Now this is probably what Elizabeth meant, and what
Convocation accepted, if they did accept this clause; but
it is not the sense in which we ordinarily now quote the
words. We think of a Church older than the Thirty-nine
Articles; and we mean by its authority a power resident
somewhere, not to declare conditions of membership, but
to ascertain and declare theological truth. This is a
totally different thing.

The real question then at last is this. We believe—I
suppose we all believe—that there is disseminated among
all individuals, and all branches of the Church of Christ,
some illumination in spiritual truth, as the result of the
influence on us of the Holy Spirit. At any rate this is
my firm conviction. I have no belief more fundamental
than that God guides the reason and spirit of His faithful
servants.

Does there, then, exist—did there ever exist—any
means for so focussing this illumination as to produce a
perfect light? If any method existed for collecting, if I
may use the expression, the sparks of the Holy Spirit in
the hearts of all Christians, till they combined into a
perfect and heavenly flame; any celestial chemistry which
should separate the fragments of the divine in us from the
masses of the earthly, the result would be an "authority"
for ascertaining and declaring spiritual truth.

The ages have made several answers to this question.
They have said that Œcumenical Councils were such a
focussing, such a chemistry; that the Pope and his College
of Cardinals were so. They have said that it was possible
once before the great schism, but is impossible now.

If any one thinks that it was possible once, and is impossible now, let him read Church History in some detail; let him read the Acts of the Council of Chalcedon.

The truth is, that such a process is impossible. There exists no such method of focussing, no such celestial chemistry. We cannot separate the human from the divine in man.

It is the old fallacy. On *à priori* grounds, men think that God must govern the world and the Church as they themselves would govern it, by giving them an infallible Pope, a verbally inspired Bible, an authoritative voice of the Church. We had better study what is, instead of deciding what must and ought to be. There *are* spots on the sun, though it was declared to be impossible there should be: the earth *is* round: the earth *does* move. When a man argues that so and so must be the case—that it stands to reason it must be the case—it always means that he averts his eyes from facts. He prefers to tell us what he thinks God ought to do. I prefer patiently to try and find out what God has done and is doing. This is the method of science, and is adopted by those who desire, above all things, to see things as they are. I think it is the reverent method.

But perhaps some one will say, There *is* an authority; but it resides not in Pope, nor Councils, nor letter of the Bible: it resides in the consensus of Catholic antiquity; and he will quote the Vincentian rule, *quod semper, quod ubique, quod ab omnibus.* This is equally illusory, and specially so if applied only to the past. Not only did no such consensus ever exist; not only, if it did exist, would it fail to indicate more than the opinion that prevailed at the time; not only would all sorts of errors and crimes find in the Vincentian rule a strong support; but it is fundamentally opposed to the charter of the Church. That charter is, that the Church is alive, a living body with Christ as its head, and subject to the laws of life and growth. The Vincentian rule, limited to the past, unintentionally strangles that life. It says, You shall not be led into all truth; you shall not advance beyond such and such a century. Now, to one who, like myself, believes that the Holy Spirit is training and guiding and shining on the whole Church of Christ, that the whole world of man is growing and shall grow to the stature of the fulness of Christ, that the very best of us has but imperfectly grasped the meaning of Christ's words and life, and that the Spirit of God will make that life and those words better understood—to one who holds this faith, any such notion as that growth is to be strangled by an imaginary consensus of the past, the living heart stopped by the dead hand, is monstrous, and a falsehood to be repudiated with all his might.

But a belief widely held always has some truth in it. What is the truth in this?

The truth is that there exists a diffused and daily growing illumination in a Christian society; on the whole, the verdict of a Christian community is not far wrong—what they bind or loose on earth, is bound or loosed in heaven.

These verdicts are not only on questions of right and wrong. On these the Christian conscience, give it time enough, will pronounce right. It has pronounced against impurity, against slavery, against religious persecution; it is slowly making up its mind on other subjects. There *is* a slowly working divine chemistry which finally crystallises out the truth.

But even on questions of criticism and doctrine within certain limits, *securus judicat orbis.* The formation of the Canon—*i.e.* the selection from the fragments of early Christian writings of such as should be deemed Canonical—was such a popular judgment. The *vox populi* sifted the literature; the *vox concilii* did but confirm the verdict of the people. The real authority was the diffused voice of Christian men. Our Prayer-book is similarly the result of the verdict of a later Christendom: it is the concentrated essence of the devotion and the inspiration of fifteen Christian centuries.

The authority of an approximate consensus in the past is a real thing: it resides in the fact of some opinion having prevailed in the struggle. *It was the fittest for the human mind then;* it does not follow that it is the fittest now. The heterodoxy of one age sometimes becomes the orthodoxy of another. It may have been but the school-master to bring men to Christ. But the proved fitness of any opinion in the past, or in another level of thought in the present, will make us hesitate long before we abandon it, still longer before we denounce it. We can only abandon it for a wider application of the Vincentian rule. We can only denounce it when it poisons as well as weakens spiritual life.

I can now briefly sum up:

Authority, in the sense of *power to transact business,* is possessed by every Church.

Authority, in the sense of *declaring the tenets and other conditions of membership,* is possessed by every Church.

Authority to *decide questions of learning or of fact* in the past, there is none anywhere; and further, it may be added that such matters of fact and of learning are not and cannot be religion, though for a time men may think they are.

Authority to ascertain dogma—that is, to give an inspired and final decision on a speculative question, not as a condition of membership, but as an absolute truth—there is none, and has been none. The diffused illumination of the Christian world cannot be so focussed. The growth of pious thought cannot be anticipated. But there is a power resident in the Christian world as a whole to decide right at last. Misconceptions of God do not last for ever.

Authority on questions of right and wrong—absolute there is none, approximate there is, in the growing consensus of the total Christian society, and especially of those who have the gift of holiness and the grace of the Spirit. This absolutely adds to the known ethical and spiritual truths of the world.

Such seem to me to be the facts. Thus God sees fit to educate His Church. It is vain to wish it were otherwise, to dream that it is otherwise. We must look at the facts.

VIII

CHRISTIAN EVIDENCES[1]

I FIND it impossible to compose a twenty minutes' paper on Christian Evidences. I shall not attempt to state the evidences : but simply to show what is meant by the phrase, and what is the aim and benefit of the study.

The first point to make clear is, Evidences to whom ? Is the object of evidences to confirm the faith of the ordinary middle-class congregation; to confute professed unbelievers ; or to approach the cultivated and thoughtful layman who now conforms, if at all, with large reservations, and is unable to see how Christian faith is compatible with intellectual honesty.

To the first two classes, at any rate, the evidence that tells far beyond all others for conviction or conversion, is personal experience, and the character of people who profess that they are Christians. If we really desire that God would strengthen the faith of the Churches, and also "show to them that are in error the light of His truth, to the intent that they may return into the way of righteousness," then let us take care that "all we who are admitted into the fellowship of Christ's religion may eschew those things that are contrary to our profession, and follow all such things as are agreeable to the same." The witness of the Christian life is the standing witness to Christ—its unworthiness is, unhappily, a standing witness against Him.

But I say at once that I hope that our discussion will have chiefly in view that third type of person, who seems

[1] A paper read at the Wakefield Church Congress, October 1886.

to me most of all to need a new and strong presentation of Christian Evidences, purely from the intellectual side; one to whom the excellency of the life of Christian faith is no proof of freedom from great intellectual error, and who regards it a virtue of the highest order to aim at truthfulness of thought—to see things as they are. Such a man is compelled to study this complex historical phenomenon of Christianity, to trace to what elements in it these admitted results on character are due, to examine how far we rightly understand its narratives; he is accustomed to distinguish between idea and symbol, between truths which no words can define, and the quasi-scientific definitions of them which men have made. He brings to the study a mind enlarged by some acquaintance with scientific methods, and with other religions and philosophies, and comes in a spirit of humble docility, but also of resolute honesty. And he feels that while the teaching of the Church at present does much to satisfy his moral and sympathetic faculties, it does little to satisfy his desire for lucidity, and the need for a solid foundation for his faith. It is this type of man or woman, not an uncommon type, who is compelled to study the intellectual aspect of Christianity, that I hope we shall keep in view in our discussion and in our proposals.

The next point is, What do we mean by Evidences? By evidences—to such a type of person as this—we mean, in the first place, matters of historical testimony which go to establish certain facts and inferences; in a wider sense we include all grounds of belief, including the emotions, sympathies, and spiritual experiences, and all reasoning based on them. Whether or not a perfect demonstration can be given of any inference, even in physical science, we need not now discuss. All that is meant by evidences in connection with Christianity, is such grounds of belief as satisfy the spirit, and within certain limits satisfy the reason. More than this is certainly unattainable in any religion, or in any philosophy. It cannot be maintained for a moment that the Christian creed is a matter of logical proof. It is founded indeed on matters of testimony,

which may be established with a degree of conclusiveness
varying according to their nature; but the Christian creed
is built up by faith, and hope, and aspiration, and imagination, as well as by sight and reason, and its articles are
held with varying degrees of conviction.

A man of the type I contemplate, who dreads exaggera-
tion or an over-statement of the degree of his faith as he
would dread an untruth, is repelled by having to listen to,
much more is unable to speak with, tones of certainty
about such abstruse subjects as the relation of God to
humanity and the world, the methods or limits of Divine
revelation in the past, or man's destiny in the future.
Modest interpretations, modest inferences, modest hopes,
are the necessity of his nature.　His religion is at first one
of faith, and hope, and trust, rather than one of confident
assurance and insistence.　But it is not on that account
less a religion.　To such a man evidences of Christianity,
so far as they consist of testimony and reasoning, will fall,
for a long time, far short of absolute proof, and yet may
supply an assured basis for faith and for conduct.　They
will be a raft, to use Plato's image, not a rock; and yet
they may bear the weight of his life.　If assurance comes
to such a one, it comes from within rather than from
without; from indefinable experience rather than from
explicit testimony and reasoning.　And yet the testimony
and reasoning may be indispensable as an intellectual
justification for his accepting the experience as a ground
of assurance, that he has the βεβαιότερον ὄχημα λόγου θείου
τινος—"the more sure word" of a divine revelation.

This being the nature of Christian Evidences, let us
next ask, Evidences of what?　For what statements and
inferences is it that we ought to supply, to such a one as
I have contemplated, testimony and reasoning, though they
must fall short of proof?　This is a matter which requires
much thought.

Perhaps the answer may be given briefly as follows.
Christian Evidences consist in a philosophical verification
from history and individual experience of a correspondence
between man's rational and spiritual nature and the super-

natural person and character and divine revelation of Jesus Christ.

I think we have, therefore, first to supply testimony of the assertion that the distinct consciousness of a connection with a Higher Power has hitherto been the supreme elevating and purifying influence on men ; and, further, to show that in Christ this consciousness of union with that Higher Power, whom He taught men to regard as His Father and theirs, rose to a unique intensity ; that through His life and words this consciousness has been partially realised by men ever since ; and that nothing else has exercised so ennobling a power on man's spiritual nature. In brief, we have to bring testimony to the statement that the belief in God is the great uplifting influence on man, and that now, in this century, the belief in God as revealed in Christ is the most rational belief. Of course that a belief has been beneficial is by itself no proof that the thing believed is true. That further inference rests on a latent premiss that there is an order of the world, and that our spiritual faculties have a corresponding reality. If there is, and there is no proof of this hypothesis, except that it appears to be verified, then we become convinced that Christianity, with its unique power of affecting man's nature, by inducing trust in God and love of man, and of blending with all other agencies and philosophies, of assimilating, and vitalising, and leavening them, must be inseparably involved in this order of the world, and with all the final problems of history, social, political, economical, philosophical. The narratives of Christianity disclose the coming and life of the greatest Leader of men, and the working of His life-giving Spirit in the hearts and souls of sixty generations.

The Christian spirit has, as yet, been most imperfectly realised ; but so far as it has been realised it has worked well.

On this foundation of testimony rests the possibility of intellectual conviction that Christianity is of Divine origin, and is slowly working out a Divine purpose ; and it becomes possible, while we freely hold that our conception of this or that detail of Christianity which we have been accustomed to regard as marking it as Divine may be in error, yet, consistently with entire truthfulness and fearlessness, to accept the Christian creeds as an expression, even if not a perfect and final expression, of the truth on the subject with which they deal, and to embrace the cardinal truth of its supernatural origin.

That this should be the substance of Christian Evidences need not surprise us. What were the evidences that Christ gave, apart from those peculiar powers over the minds and bodies of men which we cannot exercise? The evidence was that His teaching supplied the deepest needs of the soul; He spoke of God as His Father, and of a kingdom of God on earth, and His life gave credibility to His words. He presented Himself to the world as the Son of Man, and when they knew the Son of Man, they learnt of themselves that He was the Son of God. This was the order, this the method, of His teaching. Essentially the evidence is the same now, except that it is stronger. It rests on facts, not on authority. The proof is still experimental and verificatory, and cannot be otherwise. The evidence lies in human experience. Where else can it be? It is true that whoever comes to Christ has life. He who willeth to do the will knows of the doctrine. There is no shadow of proof or probability that materialism will make a religion which will contribute to human progress. Christianity has done so, and does do so, in spite of all defects of its presentation. It is contained in very earthen vessels. Nevertheless it "works."

I said that our evidence was stronger now. It is so, because we can appeal to all history, and show the relation of Christianity to all philosophies and religions, ancient and modern, as the early apologists did, and show how Christianity has absorbed, or is absorbing, what is best in them; and how its wide creed has embodied what was needed from time to time of the great truths, seemingly so diverse, taught by them all. We have the commentary of all subsequent history on "The Parable of the Leaven." We can show how Christ came, not to destroy, but to fulfil. Christianity combines the natural and supernatural; it satisfies the intellectual demand for continuity and growth, while it has always had the spiritual witness I spoke of. This capacity for growth and life has been obscured at times by stationary and reactionary influences; but life cannot be bound, and history bears witness to the life of the Church of Christ.

Thus we can see that a philosophy of history, deeper than any yet written, will be an overpowering evidence for Christianity. It will show what is the secret of greatness, whether of the individual or of the nation. It will establish the great saying of Augustine, which epitomises the teaching of the Bible, *fecisti nos ad te Domine.*

It is under the image of a tree springing from a hidden seed, nourished by every element in the soil from which it springs, and by every breath of air that touches it, that we now more and more regard Christianity. The Church is a living organism, not a stereotyped institution. Every subject connected with its development is being re-examined by men who are familiar with the inductive and historic method and spirit. It is only lately that such treatment has become possible. To those who have confidence in truth, the prospect is most hopeful. I desire that Evidences should be treated in the same large and learned and candid spirit in which origins are being universally studied. It is, of course, true that just as the conception of law in the physical world seemed at first to exclude Providence, and, therefore, made its way slowly, so the conception of an organic and growing Christianity may, in spite of Christ's words, appear to exclude supernatural influences in its introduction or its development, and, therefore, be viewed with suspicion by the timid. But we must not close our eyes to facts because they seem inconsistent with our theories; and precisely as it is beginning to be seen, and will, I believe, soon be plain, that evolutionary theories of biology are inadequate to account for the existing order of nature without supra-evolutionary forces as well, the operation of which is yet undiscovered; so it may be made even more evident that, in the history of man, and in the development of religion, there are also elements which we may describe as supra-evolutionary, or supernatural, or divine, and that Christianity explains them.

The treatment of Christian Evidences which I am contemplating would, to express it differently, exhibit Christianity as the chief factor in the spiritual education of the divine element in man, and would thus be based on two leading ideas, the presence in man of a divine element, and a continuity in its development under the influence of Christ, and would aim at verifying these hypotheses, and thus establishing a faith in Christ as the truly Divine light of the world, and leader of men against the powers of evil.

But, it will be asked, Are the evidences of Christianity so philosophical as all this? If so, what is to become of plain men without a turn for philosophy? The answer is, that men need varying degrees of evidence. Religion is taught us all on authority, and we all verify it to a certain extent by experience and reasoning. Some need a wider verification—a more exhaustive analysis—than others. There are philosophers in all ranks, and for them evidences must be philosophical. No one can say, to philosophy, "thus far and no farther." And it must be remembered that very many men and women in our churches, and still more outside of them, are profoundly affected by philosophical considerations, who could yet give no intelligible account of them. They feel that their faith needs a sounder basis than mere authority. They adhere, more or less patiently, to established forms, dreading pure materialism, and hating the degradation of religion into superstition and ceremonial. These people are not few; they wait hungrily for spiritual and reasonable teaching; they welcome it when it is offered to them. They would be profoundly affected by a popularisation of Christian Evidences on the historic and philosophic method. And such popularisation can only come from men who are at once real students, and in real sympathy with the people, and of real devoutness, and faith, and modesty. The philosophical study of evidences is, then, for this large class, a pressing necessity.

Again, the study of evidences is as necessary to purify our own faith as it is to induce others to embrace it. It will help us who teach to distinguish between what is essential and what is temporary; between substance and form. It is an important element in the preparation for the ministry of our Church, and in the study of its ministers. For when the conviction of teachers is based, not on evidence, but on authority, it always tends towards hardness and fanaticism. It maintains itself artificially, and is restless and fidgety under criticism or indifference. It settles itself on trifles. It hurries the weak into superstition and the strong into infidelity. And along with superstition, or sometimes without it, comes what is worse —insincerity. The weak, as they become stronger, recognise the doubtful points of their teaching; they are unable either to strengthen them or to give them up; and thus arises the silent conforming faithlessness which is familiar to us all, the mechanical repetition of phrases. Different types of mind will be sensitive to different grounds of belief; but clergy, more than all others, need, to use Locke's phrase, to "bottom" their beliefs continually, or they will not help doubters in any stage.

I have thus briefly indicated the nature and importance of Christian Evidences, and the classes which need them. It remains to add a few words on what seems the duty of the Church in reference to this subject.

It has been pointed out recently in several quarters, and among others by "A Layman" in a pamphlet on "The Spiritual Education of the Laity" (Fabb and Tyler, Cambridge), that while our University Extension Lectures, local colleges, and other local institutions, are supplying in most of our towns some of the demands of the people for systematic higher teaching on science, history, economics, and literature, there is no similar supply of lectures on religious questions. Most men and women get no teaching whatever on religion after they leave school, except what they get from sermons and desultory reading. That there is a demand for such teaching is certain, as is shown by the large sale of books of real learning and thought on these subjects, and by the attendance on such few lectures as are given by competent persons. What a range of subjects, all included under the head of Christian Evidences, could be profitably dealt with in lectures and manuals, and are excluded from sermons! There is Christian ethics, and its relation to other ethical systems; there is the development of our theology and our creeds, the discussion of the miraculous element in Christianity, and the characteristics of Greek and Roman patristic writers; there is the history of philosophy, and its influence on Christian thought; there is the effect of Christianity on legislation and morality, on the ideal of personal character, on social and industrial progress; there is the history of our Church, and of English Christianity generally; the history of our liturgy; and the whole range of higher Biblical studies; and there is, above all, the powerful presentation of Christ as the Son of Man, and of the Spirit of Christian teaching as the sole conceivable remedy for the defects in human character which produce all our social miseries. It cannot be doubted that teaching on such subjects as these might form a powerful influence for Christianity among the intelligent classes. We abandon much of this territory, and it is in part occupied by Secularist literature of a very one-sided type. How are able men and women to be retained in the faith without some such effort on the part of the learned and thoughtful and fair among ourselves? I am advocating a mission to the educated.

Who are to give such teaching? I am not prepared to answer; but I can conceive our cathedral bodies, as representatives of the "Regulars" among the clergy, doing more than they have yet done to supplement the work of the "Seculars," and filling, in part, this great gap in our Church organisation. And I can conceive a Church syndicate, of clergy and laity, formed at the Universities for this purpose, and giving a noble and attractive sphere to men of learning and thought, and strong Christian conviction, who feel themselves unfitted for parochial work. The main matter for us to-day is distinctly to recognise and proclaim the need of such teaching of Evidences ; and that is the aim of my paper.

MIRACLES[1]

I HAVE selected the subject of Miracles for this afternoon's lecture and this evening's discussion for two reasons.

First because, in consequence, as I believe, of grave misconceptions both of fact and theory, Secularists are in the habit of treating any reference to miracles with contempt and incredulity; and therefore the miraculous element of Christianity forms an insuperable obstacle to their finding common intellectual ground with us even where such common ground exists. I wish, if possible, to remove some of these misconceptions.

I will quote two passages to illustrate what I mean. One is from Colonel Ingersoll's *The Christian Religion.* "With most of the teachings," he says, "of the Gospels of St. Matthew, St. Mark, and St. Luke, I most heartily agree. The miraculous facts must of course be thrown aside." "Miracles are the children of mendacity." The other is from a letter of Professor Huxley, a man of the highest ability and candour. He wrote to me early in the present year (1883), referring to my lectures on "Why men do not believe the Bible," as follows: "You say that to you the evidence for what is commonly called the miraculous element in Christianity is convincing. To me it is wholly worthless as proof, hardly sufficient to justify a

---

[1] This lecture was delivered on one of the Sundays in Advent, 1883, in the nave of St. Mary's Church, Nottingham, at the request of the Vicar, the Rev. Canon Morse, to a congregation chiefly of Secularists, and was followed by a discussion in the Mechanics' Hall, under the presidency of the town-clerk.

faint presumption in favour of the element in question even if it were not miraculous. You are a very honest man and clear-headed. I believe I am too. Why do we arrive at such different conclusions from the same premises? You must solve that riddle before the question you deal with, 'Why men do not believe the Bible,' can be answered."

I wish to try and make some contribution towards solving that riddle.

The second reason why I select this subject is because Christian apologists deal with this question, for the most part, in what is to me a confused and unconvincing way. That miracles are not impossible, if there is a God—that all operations of Nature are equally miraculous; that they are of the essence of Christianity; that the historical and scientific evidence for them is confessedly incomplete but not worthless; that the Christian miracles present no difficulty to one who believes in the Incarnation; that any natural explanation of them is a deathblow to the general character of the teacher; and, finally, that we need not refuse to believe in them, related as they are to a Christianity in which we do believe—is a summary of the somewhat indefinite, disorderly, and untenable line of defence by which believers in miracles, as far as I know, generally vindicate their belief to themselves. And it is plain that many men both find them an inconvenient and perplexing appendage to their own Christianity, and are unable to explain to unbelievers in any logical sequence the arguments given above for the purpose of justifying their own belief.

Now in one lecture I can neither write a treatise on miracles nor speak for others. But I can attempt to speak for myself. Every one of us, I suppose, has in himself something of the temper which submits uninquiringly to authority, and something of the temper which questions and examines every dictum. Every man is in himself both believer and sceptic by nature. Now I can endeavour to explain how these two elements coalesce in myself, so far as miracles are concerned: I am not at all pleading a cause : I hold no brief for or against miracles. I am merely an individual Christian trying to give a reason for the faith that is in him, trying to clear the thoughts of others, but not even dreaming that an entire agreement of opinion on this matter is possible.

In face, then, of the question of miracles I used to find myself in this dilemma, which it is worth while to state with some explicitness because it may represent the present position of others. If I believe in miracles I am compelled to examine on what grounds I believe them. I must satisfy my intellectual conscience on this point. It is plainly only shifting the difficulty to say I believe them because they are in the Bible. The next question is obvious, and is not easier to answer. Why do you believe the Bible : in what sense do you believe it ? For on examination I find that such questions as the verbal inspiration of the Bible, the historical veracity of the New Testament, and what is called, not without much confusion of ideas, the authority of the Church, are inextricably involved together with our views about miracles. If any one of these were granted perhaps the credibility of miracles might more or less logically follow. Now none of these are self-authenticating : they all, in so far as they are true, need proof. And three or four unproved and unself-authenticating hypotheses, however closely connected, do not establish one another. Nor can I see that it is a virtue to accept an unproved and unself-authenticating hypothesis, which concerns not the spiritual life, but matters of fact which may be tested by reason and evidence. If then I believe I must say why I believe.

But, on the other hand, if I doubted or disbelieved in all miracles, was I not bound to the same extent to doubt or disbelieve the whole narrative ? Must I not abandon my confidence in the very volume which contains the evidences of our religion ? Was I not driven to abandon Christianity entirely, except as a source which has formed a purifying tributary—alas ! often stained with blood—into the stream of human morality? And is not this sheer

Secularism? Surely this was not the sole residuum of Christianity!

Such appeared to me for some years to be the logical dilemma. And my attitude towards the question was to suspend my judgment. The intellectual difficulty of the belief in miracles, the conviction that there was no discontinuity in nature, grew greater and greater, and simultaneously my conviction of the fundamental truth of Christianity—that Christ revealed in perfection the spiritual life of which we are all partakers—this conviction also grew greater and greater. The two convictions had to lie side by side. Intellectually I was at that time a sceptic, spiritually a believer. But of late years the matter has seemed to me clearer. The way in which evidence for miracles now presents itself to me is, briefly, as follows :—

We possess certain letters, written by St. Paul to people among whom he had lived and worked—to the Corinthians, the Romans, the Galatians, for example. It is quite undisputed that these are his letters. It must be kept in mind that here at any rate we are on a firm historic basis. The most sweeping criticism of scholars has not discredited them. It is certain that they were written by St. Paul, and we know very accurately the circumstances. Now in these letters we read such passages as follow—"To each one is given the manifestation of the Spirit to profit withal." Again, "To one is given through the Spirit the word of wisdom ; and to another the word of knowledge according to the same Spirit ; to another faith in the same Spirit ; and to another gifts of healing in the one Spirit ; and to another workings of miracles ; and to another prophecy" (1 Cor. xii. 7-10).

Again, "Truly the signs of an apostle were wrought among you in all patience, by signs and wonders and mighty works" (2 Cor. xii. 12).

And again, "God hath set some in the Church, first apostles, secondly prophets, thirdly teachers, then miracles, then gifts of healing" (1 Cor. xii. 28).

These words were unquestionably written to a congregation which St. Paul had lately visited, and was soon

going to revisit. And I do not see how any man reading
these passages, and knowing the circumstances as we do,
can doubt that St. Paul had exercised in a high degree,
and others had exercised in a lower degree, certain powers,
here described as "miracles, gifts of healing, prophecy."
Observe I am attributing no inspiration to St. Paul's words.
The fact is to be believed not because a St. Paul said it,
but because, in strictly contemporary letters, the man who
claimed to have exercised those powers writes so naturally
and simply of them to the very men who, by his own
hypothesis, were witnesses of those powers, and were keen-
witted to discern false claims, and more disposed to dispute
than accept the Apostle's authority. No illusion was
possible, no deception can be conceived, and the incidental
way in which they are mentioned shows that no purpose
was being served by the mention, and no special importance attributed to the fact.

I cannot doubt that here we are on the basis of historic
fact. So far, I believe, all may well go with me. The
mere lapse of time does not impair the evidence. If in
an unquestioned letter of Plato to some Syracusan disciple,
written in the short interval between two visits, he had
spoken in the same way, I should put exactly the same
interpretation on his words.

But what is this interpretation? It is that certain highly
unusual phenomena repeatedly took place, which the agent
and the witnesses agreed in considering in some sense
supernatural. That these phenomena consisted in an
exalted spiritual condition, which developed extraordinary
spiritual and intellectual gifts, such as those of exposition,
admonition, speaking with tongues, or extraordinary physical power, such as that of healing certain unspecified
classes of disease.

Now, the chief distinction between a scientific and
educated mind or age, and one that is unscientific and
uneducated, is that the former cannot view facts like these
as isolated. The uneducated and the unscientific feel no
such impossibility. "I never thought about them," is their
true and natural remark. They are willing to admit an

entire discontinuity in nature. But I assume that you and I are compelled to examine these facts, and view them in their relation to other facts. We cannot get rid of them. We are compelled to explain them, if explanation is possible. By explanation I need scarcely say that I mean a reference to a class of similar phenomena. The ultimate explanation of these, as of all phenomena, is of course beyond our reach. We are said to explain the colours in a soap bubble, when we find other phenomena of the same class. When we find no phenomena of the same class, no explanation is possible. We are said to explain the motion of a comet or a meteor when we refer it to the general law of gravitation.

Now it appears that these phenomena of healing consist in the action of mind on mind, or mind on body; and the conditions include plainly a highly-exalted spiritual condition in both agent and patient. The class to which the phenomena alluded to in St. Paul's Epistle belong, is that obscure class of mental actions of whose existence we now have ample evidence; but of the details of which we are still at present very ignorant, from lack of a sufficiently wide and accurate observation of facts to serve as the basis of induction. Such phenomena need not be regarded as in any sense miraculous, nor evidential of anything else except of those highly-wrought spiritual conditions which an induction from experience may show are inseparable from such phenomena. Certain Patristic, Mediæval, and Modern "miracles," as they are commonly deemed, may safely be referred to the same class. So far as they are true they belong to the class of the obscure rather than of the supernatural. Of course some of the Mediæval and Modern miracles are merely more or less clumsy inventions or exaggerations to meet the demand of the credulous for the miraculous,—designed doubtless in some cases to promote, as the inventors thought, the glory of God,—but more frequently for very terrestrial reasons. In this sense I agree with Ingersoll that *some* "miracles are the children of mendacity." But there is probably, I think one may say certainly, even in these mediæval and modern "miracles," a considerable residuum of real "miracles," that is, of exceptional actions of mind on mind, or mind on body, or possibly mind on matter, depending on an exalted spiritual condition of agent or patient or both. Evidence which convinced Pascal has something to be said for it.

For example, not to mention any well-attested mediæval "miracles" (and such do exist), I do not doubt that some of the cures performed by the water of Lourdes are in this sense miraculous : that is, they really have taken place, and are due to an abnormal spiritual condition of the patient, and were not due to what are commonly called physical causes, and therefore could not be repeated at will. (See *Les Episodes Miraculeux de Lourdes*, Par Henri Lasserre. Paris, 1883.)

To resume then, I am compelled to refer the "miraculous" spiritual and healing powers thus spoken of by St. Paul, as possessed by himself and others, to a large class of obscure mental and physical phenomena, constantly reappearing in one shape or another, and not yet defined and classified by mental science.

That these powers would in such a society be often misunderstood, the limits of them unperceived, the exercise of them misreported and exaggerated, is certain. In St. Paul's letters, however, I think it will be admitted by any candid reader, there is no trace of their misrepresentation, he was himself an agent, and speaks of them without exaggerations, and without surprise. Let us repeat, therefore, that no doubt need hang over our minds that St. Paul possessed astonishing power over the minds, and through the minds over the bodies, of men : that such powers were regarded by himself and others as miraculous, so abnormal were they : and that we may regard them as exceptional powers produced by certain conditions of mind and will, primarily highly-exalted and intense spiritual conditions, and therefore evidential of those conditions.

Now these powers, it must be remembered, produced effects of at least two kinds : on the one hand they displayed themselves in what is called prophecy and preaching ; a strong moral and spiritual influence over men ; a clear insight into our spiritual nature ; a stimulating, purifying, ennobling influence on the heart and the feelings ; and on the other hand power over men's bodies through their minds and emotions ; in other words, gifts of healing. Both of these were appreciated by contemporaries ; but the gifts of healing were witnessed by them alone ; we cannot see them.

To us they are only indirectly evidential. They have long passed away. But the moral and spiritual miracles in part remain with us ; and I must very briefly remind you what these are. We have not the living voice, the contagious sympathy, the earnestness of the inspired man ; but we have still the letters of St. Paul and St. John, to name these alone. It would be far too little to say that no other writings can be placed on the same level. No writings have at all touched the minds and souls of men as these have. No writings do still touch men's hearts as these do. They are on a spiritual level by themselves. They have done much to raise men to their level, but they still tower above us. Other books, such as Aristotle and Thomas Aquinas, have dominated men's intellects. But these writings have educated their hearts. We never seem able to exhaust the delicacy and depth of insight that marks them. Each age, each state of culture, turns to them and finds fresh wealth. I am not exaggerating. I am speaking the words of truth and soberness. The purer and loftier our minds, the more do St. Paul and St. John seem to tower away above us. If you have not studied them word by word you cannot easily believe how pregnant they are with thought and insight and light and spiritual genius.

Now as I become acquainted, and more and more profoundly impressed with these " miracles " which still partly remain, *i.e.* the intensely exalted spiritual condition which gave such marvellous insight and nobleness and wisdom, it is not difficult to believe that the same spiritual condition acted indirectly even on men's bodies, and gave men the gifts of healing, that St. Paul speaks of as accompanying

an exalted spiritual condition: it would be indeed perplexing if I heard that these manifestations of their spiritual
powers were altogether wanting. If there were no direct
proof of physical powers in St. Paul's case I should still
judge that they probably existed. The moral miracles
which we can see would almost imply a certain class of
physical miracle which we can no longer see. But in St.
Paul's case, it must be borne in mind, both are *proved*.

And now, starting from this firm basis I must proceed
to another point, the importance of which will, I believe,
grow on you very much as you reflect, What was the relation of St. Paul to Christ? It was not that of pupil and
master, not that of servant and lord: it was one of entire
spiritual and intellectual subordination; it was one of
absolute nothingness. He was to Christ less than a planet
to its sun. The proof of this is to be found in almost
every chapter of the unquestioned Epistles of St. Paul.
How indignantly he asks, "Was Paul crucified for you?
Were ye baptized into the name of Paul?" Christ is
everywhere his Lord: with Him St. Paul "died and rose
again"; in Him he "lives"; "nothing can separate him
from the love of Christ"; all Christians are "one body in
Him." Christ's example is final. But it is needless to
continue such references. Read an Epistle, noting all the
references to Christ, and you will see what I mean. These
are not the words of a Plato about a Socrates. They
breathe the entire conviction that in Christ there was a
new spiritual life for all mankind, and that from henceforth
was revealed a new departure for the world. The gifts
that St. Paul possessed seemed to him quite trifling; they
were but witnesses to his apostleship, reflected lights. In
the blaze of Christ's light such powers are in St. Paul's
eyes less than nothing. Who is Paul, or who is Apollos?
Mere servants and dispensers of the truth which Christ had
revealed.

Now I say that when this consideration is allowed its
full weight we could infer from it alone, independently of
other evidences, with certainty, that Christ Himself possessed far more astonishing spiritual gifts than St. Paul.

St. Paul's powers were the signs of a servant only, not signs of the Master. I am not yet, you must observe, considering the Gospel narrative, but simply the inferences from St. Paul's undisputed Epistles. If we had nothing but these, we should know, from St. Paul's greatness, and yet his nothingness compared with Christ, that Christ was the most unique spiritual power that this world has ever witnessed. If we had nothing but these letters we should have an indistinct image of Christ as He appeared to St. Paul; indistinct, but one radiant with glory: we should see a Christ divine in origin, yet for our sakes becoming poor, dying and rising again; our Saviour and our Example, and filling the world of man with new spiritual life and higher aims. Consider only St. Paul's description of the charity, that "more excellent way," in 1 Cor. xiii., of which more than one man has said, "This is my religion." From what original is it drawn? It is the character of Jesus Christ. There is no other ideal. It is Christ who suffered long and was kind; Christ who envied not; Christ who thought no evil, was not puffed up, was not easily provoked; Christ who bore all things, hoped all things, believed all things. It was the knowledge of his Master that enabled St. Paul to sketch a character so human and so divine; so perfect that all mankind involuntarily pay to it their homage. They are paying their homage to the picture of Christ.

If we had nothing but St. Paul's unquestioned letters we should be certain that Christ was the most unique spiritual personage alike in power and in character that had ever appeared in history. We should have been certain that He possessed still greater powers than St. Paul; inasmuch as He was so much greater than St. Paul.

But we are not wholly left to inferences. For these powers would of course include the same two kinds, powers over the bodies, and over the minds of men : physical and spiritual powers. And of the latter, at any rate, we can still in some slight degree judge. The moral miracle of Jesus Christ, seen even through the haze of imperfect memoirs and fragmentary history (possibly not unmixed with legends, but unaffected in its moral characteristics by such a supposition), stands out in a blaze of glory.

This is the great miracle of Christianity: a miracle not in any rhetorical but in a strictly scientific sense. We cannot feel the power of His presence, but the spiritual power of Jesus Christ, tested not only by its effect on His immediate followers, which perhaps might be paralleled, but by the effect of His recorded life and words on generation after generation, and by its intrinsic greatness, with the most dispassionate and scientific judgment, was so absolutely unique and exceptional as to merit the name, in the sense used above, of miraculous.

And now we come to the question of the Gospels. We possess these records of Christ. It is possible to dispute their genuineness; their dates at which they assumed their present form are somewhat uncertain. And though the reaction of scientific critical opinion in favour of their genuineness and early date has set in some time ago, it will take some time for the result of this reaction to become popular. The doubt and uncertainty is a good deal over-estimated. I am unable, however, to base on any scientific ground an assertion that every detail and narrative is cor-rectly reported. That assertion is not demonstrated, and is not self-authenticating, at least to my mind; it is not claimed by the writers in question, and not in the least indispensable to their use. But that is not now the ques-tion under discussion. Nor is its decision in one sense or the other of supreme importance.

What I wish you to observe is that from what I have proved, there does not exist any *a priori* improbability that Christ should have worked such miracles, at least as are recorded of St. Paul. If St. Paul possessed gifts of healing, and even his Corinthian converts possessed the same, as a consequence of their highly-wrought spiritual power (and I see no way of evading the fact), how infinitely more, when we reflect on St. Paul's relation to Christ, must Christ have had such powers! We must treat it as a historical certainty that Christ possessed, whether He exer-cised or not, extraordinary powers over the minds and bodies of men, and therefore to throw aside the miraculous parts of these narratives, one and all, as of course incredible, and as "children of mendacity," is entirely unscientific and unsound criticism. If St. Paul possessed such powers, and I cannot doubt that he did, *a fortiori* Christ possessed them; and no cautious scientific man who has attempted to realise the immeasurable gap that separates St. Paul from Christ will, in our present entire ignorance of the effect of exalted spiritual power on the minds and bodies of men, and possibly even on matter, presume to set a defined limit to the powers that could have been exerted by one so vastly greater than St. Paul.

To try to do so is very tempting. I am sure, however, that no critical and scientific discrimination of the recorded miracles is as yet possible in the present condition of science; they cannot be divided into classes; one class containing those which may naturally have resulted from the presence of great spiritual power, and are merely examples of occurrences more or less familiar to us, another those manifestations which are more or less incorrectly reported. The basis for such discussions does not exist. On this we must simply keep our minds open for some time to come, and beware of hastily closing them. The fact may be accepted as certain that Christ performed works of the kind that are recorded, and no essential element of faith or Christian character is lost by regarding the entire accuracy of the reports of all the Gospel miracles as an open question. All theologians admit a human element in Scripture: and a human element means an element in which error may occur. We shall tend in one direction or another to accept generally or question generally, according to our bias, to our age, education, and character, and especially our study of the books in question. And no one can judge his brother on this point. Belief is the result of persuasion, and persuasion alone, whether the persuasion comes from authority or from reasoning; and no one ought to condemn his brother either for credulity or for scepticism, if he takes a somewhat different view of the evidence before him. And

after all the point is not vital. That Christ worked
"miracles" is certain : that He worked all and every of
the miracles exactly as recorded in the Gospels is not of
the highest importance. The fact that legend has become
mixed with fact is in itself a proof that it is not here we
are to look for the final evidence or the central doctrine of
our faith.

But one miracle is of the highest importance ; and that
is Christ's own resurrection from the dead. Sooner or
later every discussion on miracles leads to this. And
before I proceed to it let me ask you to note at what
stage we have now arrived in our argument, and to attend
to one or two other remarks. There is conclusive historical
evidence that St. Paul possessed extraordinary physical and
spiritual power ; and evidence for the latter, the spiritual
power, is to some slight extent still before our eyes. That
Christ was far greater, immeasurably greater, than St. Paul,
is also certain. We infer that Christ possessed still more
extraordinary physical and spiritual powers ; and the proofs
of the latter are evident. I have no space to dilate on
them. But they are overwhelming. We infer the existence of extraordinary physical powers in Christ. We
cannot define their limits, our knowledge is altogether
inadequate. He would be but a shallow professor of
science who would venture to separate the possible from
the impossible. And to support this inference we have
the Gospels, which are of extremely high though not unquestioned authenticity ; and these place Christ before us
very much as we might have imagined Him from the letters
of St. Paul. We do not assert their entire accuracy ;
legend may have become mixed with history. But we
assert their evident *bona fides*, their honest good faith,
and, in fact, it would never have been questioned except
for an imagined *a priori* impossibility of the occurrence of
the miracles related in them.

And now comes the question, "Were these powers
natural ? " that is, the result of certain spiritual conditions
which might again reappear with the same result, or were
they preternatural, an interference with, or violation of, the

uniform course of nature, as known to us, by an external Divine Power. This is perhaps the popular definition of miracle.

This question, precise as it seems at first sight, and admitting of being answered only in one way or the other, that these powers were natural or supernatural, is nevertheless surrounded with ambiguities which must be cleared before it can be answered. You have only to reflect that we are in entire ignorance of the relation of will to organisation, of the way in which mind acts on matter; and in entire ignorance of the nature of our spiritual life, our higher human nature, which makes us differ from the beasts, and by which we have relations, indefinable but real, to that source of all will and reason, the Father of Spirits, whom we call God. The ordinary laws of inorganic matter are interfered with by life, which has higher laws of its own. And so it would appear, from the facts in the case of St. Paul and other men, that the ordinary laws of life, as well as of matter, are interfered with by the presence of a highly-exalted spiritual life; which, in its turn, has doubtless laws of its own. In one sense this interference is natural, it obeys fixed laws; in another sense supernatural—the laws belong to the higher sphere. The occurrence may be a very rare instance, it may be the very first instance, known to us, of a fixed law in the spiritual world. It is not, therefore, by pressing this dilemma, natural or supernatural, that we shall come to any conclusion. Miracles are the natural action of powers of a higher or spiritual order, or, in a certain sense, supernatural order.

But we are still pressed with the question, Are they *Divine*? Are they evidential of anything? And this must not be shirked. But it must be noted that we are now passing beyond the region of demonstrated facts, and are entering on the region of inference and opinion, in which unanimity cannot be expected, and differences are not sins. I cannot even imagine a *demonstration* that miracles are worked by *Divine* power. All that I can imagine is, such a concurrence of circumstances attending

them as to make us feel that the spiritual power concerned
in working those miracles resembled in nature the noblest
and highest faculties in man, but immeasurably surpassed
them in perfection and purity.   And this spiritual power
is what we call God.   I can imagine and feel a conviction,
but not a demonstration.

We have, in other words, the fact of strange physical
consequences of this great spiritual power in Christ.   To
find out what is their origin I look at the spiritual consequences, the moral characteristics of the same power.   In
a word, I look at the character of Christ and His teaching,
as we have it preserved, and only incompletely preserved,
in the New Testament, and in the lives of holy men and
women since His death.   And a fair and candid examination convinces me that this spiritual power which was in
Jesus Christ, and which we can to some humble degree
test by comparison with ourselves, *was* akin to our noblest
and best powers, and immeasurably their superior; and
therefore if in any sense men are children of God, if there
is any God at all, any spiritual power of which our world
of spirits is part—if this is so in any sense, then Christ is
such that He may be described as in a unique sense the
Son of God, and His works are the works of God.   The
Spirit of God dwells in us in fragments; in Him it dwelt
with all its fulness.   He was Man, but Perfect Man, perfectly filled with the Spirit of God, and therefore was seen
to be the Son of God.   We decide the origin of His
physical miracles, therefore, by His sublime and perfect
moral and spiritual characteristics, which indicate a Divine
Personality.   And then from this point, a point not wholly
to be reached by sight, but dependent on reason and faith,
by processes of the higher spiritual life, we see all in order.
We see Christ, the perfect Spiritual and Eternal Life,
making it intelligible to men what their own unconscious
spiritual life had been.   He *manifested the life*, the spiritual
and eternal life.   And so it seems to me that Christ is at
once the fountain and the goal of all spiritual life on earth.
Before His manifestation men possessed as God's gift all
the marvellous characteristics of humanity; the heart

uplifted to God in prayer and praise; the tender sympathy with one another. They knew the fatherhood of God, but they did not know that this was but the stirring of the indwelling spiritual life of God in their souls, merely the seed, barely yet the blade. But Christ showed them the ear, and the ripe corn in the ear. He showed them spiritual life in perfection; He showed them eternal life begun on earth. This is what we mean by saying that He was the manifestation of God.

This is so vast and interesting and fruitful a subject that it is difficult to avoid digression, and passing from a lecture into a sermon. What I have hitherto said, however, is not a digression. It is not until we have really looked into that wonderful microcosm, our own souls, and seen the spiritual forces there at work; not till we have realised that the characteristics of Christ which we can test, which have been tested by the verdict of 2000 years, are so perfect, so vastly superior to precisely the holiest and highest characteristics in ourselves, that we must call them divine, if anything is to be called divine; not till we have realised that Christ must be in some indefinable sense the very presentation to us of the Highest—and by that we mean God Himself—that we can regard His "miracles," the special subject of this lecture, in their right light as the natural action of His intrinsic spiritual power. And then, too, the one miracle which is of supreme importance to our Christian faith becomes natural—I mean the resurrection of Christ. The nature of that resurrection we do not understand; it would seem to have been a fact partly in the spiritual and partly in the physical world (Westcott's *Gospel of the Resurrection*), and for it we have no parallels, and can offer no explanation; but to such of us as are convinced of the reality of Christ's extraordinary powers, and from the deep conviction of the divinity of His character, recognise Him as above our nature, to us the fact of the resurrection, though not explicable, and though unparalleled, is not unthinkable nor absurd. On the contrary, it is the natural termination of such a life on earth, and is the central point of His revelation. I cannot speak for

others, but without it I do not believe in Christ. For
Christianity is above all else the revelation of the existence
of a spiritual, eternal life in man, by showing it perfect in
Christ. And it does not seem possible that such a life
should be held in the grave. The "word of faith which
we preach," says St. Paul, "is to confess with thy mouth
the Lord Jesus, and to believe in thy heart that God raised
Him from the dead." This is the simple theological creed
of St. Paul; and to this simple creed, freed from the
refinements and additions of later ages, one may intelligently and faithfully adhere.

But though this is my personal belief about the
resurrection of Christ, that it was in part truly physical,
although accompanied with some phenomena not physical
in the ordinary sense, yet I do not think that those who
interpret the resurrection as purely spiritual are therefore
unchristian. We may be in danger of making the same
mistake in insisting on the physical resurrection of Christ,
that the early centuries made in insisting on the physical
resurrection of our own flesh, particle for particle. On
such a point those who know anything of the great
changes of opinion in the Church will be tolerant and
diffident.

It will be seen that the old standing difficulty of
miracles is passing into the background. The popular
view of them is being modified in a scientific sense.
They are not now regarded by theologians as contraven-
tions of the uniformities of nature; it has become
impossible to scientific and devout minds to conceive such
contravention: they are regarded as manifestations of
higher uniformities, arising from the interaction of the
little-known forces of will and mind in their higher
manifestations upon life and matter. We are not bound
to explain all the recorded miracles of Christ by these
principles for three reasons: (1) The extent of ordinary
possible actions of will and mind on life and matter is still
imperfectly ascertained; and that of the extraordinary
possible action is quite unknown: no conceivable limits
can be assigned to the power of Christ when we have once

risen to the point of view of regarding Christ as filled with the Spirit of God. (2) We have no reason for asserting that the narrative of the Gospels is so perfect, so complete, and so correct, that we need feel that it is vital to our faith to believe that every recorded miracle is recorded exactly as it happened; and (3) The subject becomes less and less important as time goes on. The whole tenor of modern thought is to wean the mind from the abnormal and the unusual, and to lead it to discover the unity and continuity underlying all nature.

It may seem to some who still cling to the old definition of a miracle as an interference with natural law, that I am claiming as explicable facts which are essentially discontinuous, and therefore inexplicable, whose very importance consists in the fact that they are so—claiming as within the province of reason, subjects that they would prefer to regard as within the realm of faith. They view with suspicion any use of reason; an explanation is regarded as rationalistic. This contrast of reason and faith is constantly made; but I cannot grasp it in this connection. I believe it to be equally unscriptural and unphilosophical. Faith may be and is contrasted with sight, but not with reason. To say that certain occurrences, such as miracles, ought to be believed in without questioning them, is not to employ faith, but to employ, after a fashion, reason. It is reason placing a limitation on herself. It is reason saying that she will not reason on certain points. And the grounds on which I think it is a mistaken application of reason are that it is a purely historical question, whether particular miracles did or did not occur; and history is a field for evidence of which reason is the sole judge. The province of faith is wholly other than this. It is the province of spiritual power and insight; it is the region in which we touch the infinite and the unknown. It concerns the inference to be drawn from the works and life and teaching of Christ as to the spiritual nature and destiny of man, and the relation of Christ both to us and to the Supreme Spiritual power of the universe.

This treatment is not rationalistic, however, in another ordinary sense of the word. It does not assume that the reason of individual men, or even of collective humanity, can understand the relations of God to the world, and the laws of matter and life and spirit. Besides these miracles of healing which appear to be more or less continuous with exceptional natural phenomena, there are interferences with the laws of nature themselves, and their combinations, which reason compels me to postulate as possessed and capable of being exercised by God, although reason is unable to explain and find parallels for their operation. And the more I study Christ the more certain does it seem to me that He possessed, or that God wrought through Him, such powers over nature. Such powers cease to be incredible or even perplexing when the moral and spiritual miracle of Christ has once filled our minds. That the God who was in Christ should have power to wield the forces of the world He made, by the laws of that world, is not only not a contradiction, it is an axiom to men who are overpowered with a belief in God.

We see the lower links of the chain of miracles in the exceptional action of mind and faith on organisation, and in the power of the human will to subdue nature to itself; we can trace higher links in the miracles of St. Paul, and the miracles of healing of Christ; glimpses of yet higher links are seen in the mysterious power of Christ over nature, and thus finally we trace an outline of continuity that reaches to the very throne of God.

I have now done with the subject of miracles, and need not recapitulate my conclusions. I think I have shown that miracles cannot be summarily disposed of as universally "children of mendacity." But I should like to add a very few words on their relation to our faith and spiritual life. I have shown that there does not exist, to me at any rate, any intellectual difficulty in accepting the fact of many occurrences having taken place at the origin of Christianity, which were regarded then, and would probably be generally regarded now, as miraculous; nor in believing that they were so far miraculous as is implied by saying that they were caused by the presence of a Spiritual Power, partially akin to that exercised by ordinary men, but immeasurably superior to it, and therefore only partly explicable. Further, since this same Spiritual Power in its moral manifestations, which still exist for us to test, does, after my studying it, so absolutely and so uniquely command my homage, I am compelled to regard it as far the highest guide yet given to man's spiritual development,—as a sort of unveiling of the nature of the Supreme and Holy Spiritual force in the universe. Hence I feel that the general theory of Christianity, viz. that Christ was a perfect Man, a manifestation of God, is not antagonistic to reason. But it is little to show that Christianity is not unreasonable : there is no real power in faith until a man comes to feel that it is absolutely reasonable. Faith and reason come from the same source, and their lines must be convergent, even if in our present very imperfect intellectual and spiritual condition they do not yet meet. It is the convergence and the continuity of the purer faith and reason that is coming to light in this renascence of Christianity that is already beginning.

Do you find it difficult to grasp some of the thoughts I have brought before you? Is the phrase "spiritual life" unfamiliar? Do you doubt whether you possess it? You know it very well under another name. In every man who hears these words, pressed and wearied as he may be with wrongs, the discomforts and disappointments, the slow self-conquest of life, unworthy though he judge his own life to be, yet there remains the fact that he *judges ;* there remains the inextinguishable sense of right and wrong, the sense of truth and justice and duty and love, an ineffaceable tenderness and compassion for the suffering and the young, an aspiring consciousness of something better and holier. What is this judgment and aspiration, and in some cases a passionate enthusiasm for humanity, and whence and whither? This is the question of questions, and this is the question Christ answered. For He taught us that it is this, this conscience, this devotion, this love, this spiritual life; that it is this capacity for Eternal life, and not our bones and body, that make the man, the man that speaks with our voice and looks out of our eyes.

We may say we do not know what, whence, and whither we are, and give ourselves the name of Agnostics. Or we may say that it does not concern us to know, and call ourselves Secularists—men of one world at a time. But the fact of spiritual life remains, and we cannot get rid of it. No nation long continues Agnostic or Secularist. The facts of spiritual life are too obvious, too universal, too pressing, to be long ignored. "What must I do to be saved?"—saved from self-reproach, from sin, from despair, —will ever be man's cry; and some answer, right or wrong, will command his assent. Rely on self-help, good sanitation, and good laws is one answer. But the testimony of sixty generations is not to be lightly set aside when it replies, "Believe on the Lord Jesus Christ, and thou shalt be saved." Yes; but what is faith in Christ?

Faith in Christ, my Secularist friends, is an infinitely wider thing than you yet know. More shame to us Christians and teachers that it is so. It does not mean assent to articles or creeds; it does not mean comprehension of systems of theology or doctrines elaborated by man; it does not mean reliance on the Church or the clergy as an infallible guardian of the truth; nor on the Bible as an infallible book dictated by God. It does not mean helpless inaction in the present world, in hope of a better world hereafter. These may or may not coexist with faith in Christ, but they are not faith. But it does mean the hopeful and strong conviction that universal as is the sin and sorrow and weakness of human nature, so universal shall be and is the goodness, the joy, the strength of human nature; that "as in Adam all die, even so in Christ shall all be made alive." It means faith that the eternal Spiritual life, of which we are at this moment conscious, is as universal as our sinfulness; and that Christ is the Light and Guide and Giver of it; that He is "the life-giving Spirit." And we may verify this for ourselves every day. If we lived in His Spirit we know that earth would be a sort of heaven. But we know no one in whom the Spirit of Christ is perfectly seen; few, perhaps, in whom it is seen in large measure; many, probably, who are Christians in name and not conscious hypocrites, and are yet honeycombed with worldliness and cant and selfishness. Amid many shams what wonder if some of you fail to see the reality? But the reality does exist, and when seen it is altogether lovely.

The fact is the subject of miracles is not a very important one. I have taken the subject, not because of its importance to us individually, but because, being unimportant, it has had an accidental and factitious importance attributed to it from the fact that when the inspiration of the Bible was supposed to imply—which it does not—a divine guarantee of accuracy in detail, it was necessary to some men to do violence to their understanding or to abandon what seemed to be the faith.

Of what importance really is the subject of miracles to you and me, when we have once satisfied ourselves that they were but the natural outcome of the great Spiritual Power then manifested on earth, the spiritual effects of which we still see?

Let me say, therefore, a very few words before I close on what *is* important to us. It is important to us to have a theory and an aim of life; and it is very important to have such a theory and such an aim as shall lead us to the highest perfection of which we are capable. Up to a certain point we shall all agree what this aim is. We all agree that while physical perfection of the body, good health, good conditions of life, and all that this implies, is a great and worthy aim; that while education and all that *it* implies, sound intellectual judgment, wide and accurate knowledge, freedom from prejudice, genuine love of truth, is a still greater and worthier aim; there is yet another set of powers of the human spirit; there is its brotherliness, its sympathy, its care for the weak and the suffering, its love of justice, its yearning after perfection, its shrinking from acknowledged sins, its need of forgiveness of sins, its admiration for what is noble and self-sacrificing, its craving

after something above itself, some revelation of the meaning of existence, the origin of our spiritual powers; in a
word there is the conscience and the infinite soul which is
"athirst for the living God." And we all agree that these
powers last mentioned are the highest; for they demand
our love, as well as our respect. If there is a God at all—
and whence comes this world, whence the soul of man, if
there is no God? — these spiritual powers must come
from Him, and must in Him be in their perfection. That
is our conception of God, the Father of our Spirits, the
origin of all good.

Now we Christians think that the theory and aim of
life which we can learn from Jesus Christ is at once the
highest and truest. It brings out the best in us, it drives
out the worst, and it best satisfies our intellects. The
theory of life we get is in brief this : that in spite of all
appearances to the contrary, mankind is being educated
into a perfection yet unattained. That "at sundry times
and in divers manners," through nature, and through the
minds and words of men, God has taught and teaches the
world; but that the most complete manifestation of God's
ideal for men was shown in the person of Jesus Christ. He
seems so incomparably above all others, the more so the
more we study Him, that it is the truest expression of our
thoughts about Him to speak of Him as the Son of God;
and to say that our spiritual life is in some way touched
by God, the universal spiritual life : that at this moment,
and at all moments, we are under the influence of His
Spirit. In Christ is deliverance from the sin and evil
which oppress mankind and destroy the good of life. And
we do not see deliverance in any other. Such is the
Christian theory of life.

The aim, then, of life for every one of us is to use such
powers as we have in the service of Christ, to carry out in
our outer and inner life what seem to be His principles :
to make purity, love, holiness, and above all brotherliness
and charity the virtues at which we aim. He has taught
us that the best expression, and the immediate consequence, of our loyalty to God is the service of man, and

that the only pure ritual and expression of our service of God is in brotherliness and charity and purity. That is our aim. We have an example; we have principles; we have a hope: for we believe that the spiritual life in us is nothing less than eternal life now begun; that we and you are in some sense members of Christ.

Hasten forward the Kingdom of Christ, O clergy and scholars, by rightly interpreting to the world your Lord and Master; hasten it, O artisans of Nottingham and of England, by your lives of duty, of love, of self-restraint. The light that burns in us all is the same. He who follows this light, he who gives full play to the best impulses of his highest nature, is far nearer to God than he who professes all the articles of the Christian creed and lets them have no effect on his conduct. It is not I that say this. It is my Master. He said, "Not every one that saith unto me, Lord! Lord! shall enter into the kingdom of heaven, but he that doeth the will of my Father which is in heaven." We need a modern Luther to nail this on his Church door, and say this is his religion and the religion of Christ!

And thus, too, we become convinced of the reality of Christ's revelation of the spiritual life, and of God. This, too, Christ has taught us. "He that willeth to do God's will shall know of the doctrine whether it be of God." He and he alone. Not clever disputants, but he who lives the life. Let our Luther nail up this thesis also. "What will you do for the Christ in whom you believe?" shall be the question asked on admission to that Church; not, How do you define what you think you believe about Christ?

We have to learn Christianity not only in Schools and Churches and the Bible, but in our homes, and workshops, and offices, and in the streets, by being more Christlike. Let us try this. To do God's will is the first step towards knowing of the doctrine. Let us try this; and then by whatever name we call ourselves we are brothers in Christ, and I have no fear but that He will acknowledge us. "Lord, when saw we Thee?" you will say; and He will reply, "Inasmuch as ye did it unto the least of these my brethren, ye did it unto me." Yes, it was to Him, though you knew it not.

And now I must conclude with a prayer from one of our own collects in which we may all heartily join :—

"Almighty God, who showest to them that be in error the light of Thy truth, to the intent that they may return into the way of righteousness: Grant unto all them that are admitted into the fellowship of Christ's religion that they may eschew those things that are contrary to their profession, and follow all such things as are agreeable to the same." Grant unto all Christians that they may avoid the sins of uncharitableness, and avarice, and selfishness, and lusts of the flesh, and ever grow in likeness to Christ in all humility and charity and purity, and thus win the doubters by these gentle but irresistible arguments to the love and service of Jesus Christ our Lord and Master.

X

EVOLUTION :

AN ELEMENTARY LECTURE [1]

I HAVE called this an "elementary" lecture because I wish it to be understood at the outset that I am not professing to bring forward new views or new facts bearing on the theory of Evolution. My aim is different. I am not speaking to experts and specialists, but to intelligent people who are not experts, and who wish to know somewhat more fully what is meant by Evolution? What is the extent and range of it? Within what spheres of knowledge does it seem to hold? What is the value of the evidence for it? How far are its processes understood? and other similar questions; and I will add, if there is time, some remarks on its relation to Christian Faith.

It is obvious, then, that we have a large subject before us, and I shall not waste a minute in any prefatory remarks.

For a preliminary definition of Evolution, just to give some definiteness to our language, let us take the following. It is the theory that the condition of things at any moment is the result of the condition of things at the previous moment; it is implied that the interaction of the forces of nature is incessantly producing changes in the condition of things; and it is further implied that it is possible, at any rate to some extent, by studying these laws of nature and their interaction, and the changes now going on, to trace

---

[1] Delivered in the Theatre of the Bristol Library and Museum, February 1885.

far backward in outline the past history of things; in other words, to sketch the development or growth of the system of nature as we find it. The "forces" are spoken of merely as machines; no theory is assumed, or denied, as to a Purpose or Will directing the forces. That is a different and subsequent question.

This definition will become more intelligible when we see how it is applied in different fields of knowledge, what are "the things" spoken of in the definition.

Let me illustrate it first by astronomy; and we will begin with the sidereal system. There is, of course, in the sidereal system a "condition of things," geometrical and physical, at the present moment; and changes are going on. What we call the fixed stars are apparently all in motion, in every possible direction, and with vast velocities; there are systems of stars revolving round one another; there is the law of gravitation by which nebulous stars must be condensing, and clusters undergoing change; there are the same chemical elements and apparently the same laws of physics as on the earth, and therefore chemical and physical changes steadily in progress; and though these changes are so excessively slow, and our observation of the phenomena is so recent and so incomplete that no great continuous physical changes have been actually watched, yet the fact that stellar material exists in so many different forms, as nebula, nebulous star, cluster, and the like, suggests to us inevitably that we are seeing the different stages of progress simultaneously existing. In other words, we are certain that a change which we may call an evolution is going on, and has been going on for long ages. Hitherto it has been quite impossible to get more than an outline of the nature of this evolution. There are difficulties as yet unexplained in the processes of transition from nebula to stellar system. But this does not affect our general belief that there exist such processes. With the general problem, indeed, the construction of a theory of the sidereal universe that shall exhibit all the motions of the stars as necessarily following from it, not even a beginning has yet been made. This will need the accumulation for many an age to come of exact observation, probably also of new instruments of investigation yet undreamed of by us, and certainly new methods of mathematics as unknown to us as was the Calculus to Euclid.

In sidereal conditions, then, there is an evolution, a series of orderly changes, the condition of things at any moment being the result of the condition at the previous moment; but it is impossible as yet to trace their history far back into the past, or far forward into the future.

When we come to the solar system, there the case is somewhat different. Here we cannot only witness, but we can measure with some accuracy the changes going on. The hot springs that come to the surface of the earth, the molten lava that pours out, are phenomena that continue the great process, the secular cooling of the earth. The lava radiates its heat ultimately into space, and that heat is lost to the earth. And this loss is not compensated. The earth is still losing heat at a measurable rate. So again the meteors that fall into our air, whose dust can be collected on Greenland snows or in mid-Atlantic, are daily adding a measurable mass to the earth's bulk. The earth is growing while we speak. The earth and the other planets sweep round in their vast orbits, and collect on their surface the still remaining interplanetary or interstellar matter. Every now and then, moreover, a comet seems to be drawn into the system from external space, and is gradually transformed into meteors, or absorbed by the great planets. Here is an evolution going on, at a measurable rate, before our eyes. Our earth is cooling and it is growing, and so, doubtless, in past ages it cooled and it grew.

Now you will see at once that this is not a barren fact, to be mentioned and then set aside. It opens up all sorts of other questions. We have to ask how the form of the earth, its rate of rotation, its density, its temperature, its relation to its satellite, its atmosphere, its tides, are being affected by these changes, and thence to infer what they may have been in past ages. And so we are carried back farther and farther, and compelled to speculate—always checking our speculation by sound physical reasoning, and when possible, by quantitative calculation—on the gradual growth of our earth and our whole solar system from some nebulous origin.

If you ask whether any such speculation has been consistently worked out in accordance with physical and mathematical laws, the answer is that at present it has not. No detailed nebular hypothesis has yet reached the rank of a doctrine of science. It is an affair for physicists and mathematicians alone, and they exercise a wise reserve; and when others attempt it they fall into absurdities. But though no detailed and complete theory of the evolution of the solar system from a nebulous condition has yet been given, it may fairly be said that such an evolution is an established doctrine of science, and that the points under discussion are comparatively of minor importance.

Let us next glance at geology. This is a still more familiar subject. It may be assumed that every one present is more or less familiar with the elements of geology. It is now established and witnessed by universal experience that the surface of the earth is at this moment undergoing continuous change. Continents are slowly rising or sinking; coast lines altered by the action of tides and waves, or the deposit of rivers; the whole mass of a continent diminished by the incessant denudation of water. These changes are too plain not to strike even a casual observer, though he may not reflect on their significance. But if he will reflect on what he sees, on the quantities, for example, of suspended or dissolved matter swept annually by our rivers into the sea or carried off on its coasts, he will perforce come to the conclusion that in a finite number of years hence, no matter what, if no other causes intervene, all the British Isles, nay, all the existing continents, will be brought to the sea-level; and that a finite number of years ago, no matter what, our hills stood higher, our escarpments extended farther, our rivers ran on higher levels, our shores were other than they are. This is familiar knowledge. The geologist does but investigate

this subject closely and in detail and quantitatively, and
carries back into far ages the application of these principles.
He studies the records of the rocks for the past history
written so legibly on them.   The Avon gorge, the cap of
Dundry Hill, the conglomerate on the slopes of the Ob-
servatory Hill, the coal-fields of Bristol, the tilted and
water-worn limestones of Durdham Down, the meadows
by the Frome, the cliffs of Nightingale Valley, every feature
and every rock in other familiar scenes, bears its history
written in more or less plainly decipherable language ; and
all tell us that our earth has come to its present condition
through a very long series of gradual changes. Geology has
thus become typical of what Whewell called the Palætio-
logical Sciences,—sciences that deal with ancient causes
of change.   It is now quite impossible for any one to suppose that the earth was created as we see it.   All admit
an evolution ; but only the geologist, with his familiarity
with detail, can realise how vast, how ancient, how universal
this evolution of the earth has been.

   A shrewd questioner will here ask, Must a geologist
necessarily be a Uniformitarian ? must he believe, that is
to say, that to existing causes, acting with their present
intensity, is due all that one now sees ? And the answer
is, " Certainly not."   In the first place, part of the complex
problem of geology is to determine the departure from
uniformity, the variation of intensity of processes in the
past ; and this part of the problem has hardly yet even
been faced.   It is probable that there was a time when
the cooling had not progressed so far, when eruptive
phenomena were more violent, when the mass of the earth
was less, its rotation more rapid, its moon nearer, its tides
more violent, its sun hotter, its precipitation more intense,
its surface more uneven.   But to grasp the combined
effect, and the interaction of these and similar causes, on
such an action as that of aqueous denudation, is very difficult.   It is necessary to reason out fully the dependence
of the present intensity of aqueous denudation on the
present circumstances, and then infer what it was under
other circumstances : to put it mathematically,—forces and

circumstances being functions of one another,—it is to express both forces and circumstances as functions of time. And this has not been done. No geologist, however, can be a Uniformitarian as above defined. He knows that the laws of the forces are the same as ever, but that the forces vary in intensity with the circumstances. And he sees that when this great problem can really be grappled with, and not till then, shall we fully understand many geological phenomena; such phenomena, for example, as the widespread similarity of the Silurian rocks, the vast denudation and conglomerates of the Devonian age, the great subsidences and contortions of the Carboniferous age, the great upheavals and faults of subsequent epochs, and the formation of our older hill and valley systems.

And further, there is another sense in which he cannot be a Uniformitarian. He knows that at successive stages of development new laws come into operation and others cease. For example, when the earth's crust began to harden by cooling, convection ceased and conduction began; when the surface cooled so that water could exist as liquid, aqueous denudation began, and stratified rocks were made; and when it cooled still further, vital action began and limestones were formed; and then, after a still further cooling, glacial action began, and not till then: he must keep room, therefore, in his theories of the past for forces which are dormant in the present. It is like the mathematical process known as Extrapolation, continuing a curve of which a portion is given; and this is not a very satisfactory process.

Hence in physical geology, too, we see absolute proofs of an evolution, the outlines of it clearly and perfectly intelligible, and the details of it more and more obscure the farther back we go. No one can doubt an evolution, or the general plan of its processes; and no one professes to master every detail, or to be able to reproduce in imagination the earth as it was in every previous age.

We will now pass from Physical to Biological, or rather Zoological Evolution. And it is no easy matter to compress into a single lecture all that I want to say; but I must attempt in this part of the subject, as in the former part, to give not only the theory, but some outline sketch of the evidence on which the theory rests. Of course the subject cannot be fully appreciated except by experts and specialists, for the evidence is in a high degree technical, and in a very high degree is cumulative ; that is, it depends on the vast number as well as the individual cogency of its verifications. Still an intelligent person without much technical knowledge can understand the broad lines on which the argument proceeds ; and as in the case of all great truths, it is on broad familiar facts, which all can understand when their meaning has once been explained and appreciated, and not on minute details, that the truth and acceptance of the theory depends. It is not on the discovery of the skeleton of an archæopteryx or hipparion that everything hangs for its general acceptance. It is from what could never have been got except from a vast knowledge of detail, an intelligent view of the great patent facts of classification in the present, of the relation of present creatures to the past, of the similarity of structure in animals apparently most dissimilar, and of the growth of the individual, and the progress of a species, that the theory of Zoological Evolution spontaneously and necessarily arises.

First let us consider what is meant by classification, and what is the legitimate inference from it.

The number of species, whether of plants or animals, that an average educated man knows is relatively very small. It may be doubted whether he could name fifty birds, fifty insects, fifty plants, and fifty quadrupeds ; and that out of a total to be counted by the hundred thousand. If you doubt it, try when you get home in your own case. But he has seen a friend's collection of butterflies or beetles, and has been through a museum or two of stuffed birds, and has heard of Kew ; and perhaps he once collected ferns or grasses or shells ; or is perhaps a fancier of pigeons or pelargoniums or pears ; and so in some way or other we do most of us get a conception, very inadequate no doubt, but still a conception, of the wealth of species in the world, and what is more, of the existence of varieties and species, and genera and orders, and kingdoms.   Everybody knows what is meant by varieties of roses and strawberries ; by the assemblage of characteristics which enables us to call a plant a buttercup or a daisy ; he knows that buttercups and anemones resemble one another more than they resemble fir-trees or grasses ; but that they resemble fir-trees and grasses more than they resemble beetles or birds. Every one, therefore, has the familiar knowledge which forms the basis of classification by resemblance.

Further, every one is an Evolutionist to some extent. No one supposes that the present breed of dogs and pigeons and horses and sheep existed very long ago, or that our garden roses and cauliflowers are to be found wild.   He need not go far back in botanical history to discover the appearance, a sudden appearance, of the first weeping ash and the first nectarine.   It is a matter, therefore, of common knowledge that by the slow process of intentional selection, or by the accident of a sudden sport, certain true-breeding varieties or species have come into being.   Every one is a Zoological Evolutionist to some extent, even without knowing it.

Now the student of Natural History differs from us, partly in his having acquired a vastly more extensive knowledge of species ; mainly in his more accurate appreciation of what constitutes likeness.   It would be impossible for him to class bats with birds, or worms with snakes, or whales and shrimps with fishes.   The superficial resemblances are entirely outweighed by structural differences. It is the distinguishing between the sorts of differences, ascertaining the grounds on which very different weight must be assigned to them, in fact, laying down the principles of rational classification, that constitute one great work of the naturalist.   But when he has done this he finds, first, that the difficulty of defining his species and genera amounts in many cases to an impossibility, from the fact that increased knowledge breaks down all definition ; and, next, he finds that he has unconsciously treated as superficial all points in which the descendant may differ from

the parent, and fundamental those in which not the
slightest variation is observable.   In a word, he finds that
in studying classification he has been studying relationship.
A classification of plants and animals into species, genera,
and orders resembles a classification of men into families
and tribes and nations; it is not an arbitrary classification by resemblances; and it is a scientific and correct
classification in so far as it approaches a genealogical
classification.

This point must be firmly grasped, for it shows us what
classification is, and why it is so important, and what it implies.   The first classification of plants was the Linnæan or
descriptive, by resemblances often superficial and numeri-
cal only; then came the "natural"; and now comes the
explanation why it is natural, viz. that it is approximately
genealogical.   To classify words in a language by the
number of letters or syllables they contain would be a sort
of Linnæan or descriptive classification; to classify them
by their derivation is "natural" and genealogical.

A world might be imagined as wealthy in organisms as
ours, and yet one in which no classification would be
possible; in which there were no groups of organisms
possessing permanent and transmitted resemblances; in
which the number of teeth or eyes or ears in animals
varied as much as the number of hairs in our eyebrows;
and the number of floral whorls in a plant was as variable
as the number of branches of a tree.   Such a world is not
ours.   The grand and universal fact of classification is, to
one who will duly reflect on it, a witness to the great theory
of Zoological Evolution.

To trace out this great idea of relationship among allied
species, to discover the processes by which general permanence is secured, and yet varieties are introduced,—in
a word, to trace the growth of this wonderful family of
terrestrial life,—this is the study of the Evolutionist in
Zoology.   This point is so important that I shall add an
illustration in order to make it still plainer how the mere
fact of classification being possible suggests a theory of
Evolution.

Imagine a great tree of Life, the closely-packed leaves on its surface representing the species now existing on the earth. The leaves on the same twig are different in some minute respects; those on the same branchlet differ somewhat more; while those that spring from different main branches are widely different. If we were like humming-birds, flitting outside such a tree, but unable to enter into its interior, we might notice the general resemblance of adjacent leaves, and we might speculate on the origin of their resemblances. Very ingenious humming-birds might, in fact, construct an imaginary system of trunk and branches and twigs merely as a framework for their theory, to account for the observed resemblances by relationship; and the more perfect their theory, the more their imaginary framework would approximate to the actual framework of branches—the more would their natural but hypothetical classification be identical with the genealogical classification. That is exactly the work of the naturalist and the classifier.

And this illustration lends itself to the first of the great confirmations of the theory of Relationship.

Imagine an adventurous humming-bird penetrating a little way into the interior and returning to his scientific friends with some withered leaves that he had found still adhering to the twigs and branches; and suppose that these leaves resembled those which were still growing on those branches in certain important respects. They would see in these withered leaves a great confirmation of their hypothesis; they would correct their framework by them, and might finally obtain a very accurate conception of the unseen branches and twigs, and thus of the real affinities of the leaves. Their classification, in fact, if they got sufficient materials, might at last become perfectly genealogical.

Now this again is exactly what is being done by geologists to assist zoological classification. Our geological museums are being stored with the remains of species that once lived on the earth, and were the ancestors of species now living. Those which are found in recent strata differ slightly, or not at all, from existing species ; and those in older strata, representing more ancient forms of life, differ more widely. And the palæontologist, as the student of these ancient forms of life is called, has ascertained that they do serve to connect widely-diverse species and even orders. At present, for example, the horse, the deer, and the tapir are widely separated, forming well-marked kinds ; but an examination of the extinct animals resembling these kinds leads to the conclusion that they have a common ancestry, and have diverged from one another. In the same way the reptile and bird form now remote divisions of the great vertebrate class. But fossil remains carry both back to a common ancestral type, and show the ever-diverging lines of progenitors, successively more birdlike or more reptilian, till the present types are reached which seem to have so little in common.

This is the first verification of the theory of Zoological Evolution ; and it is of the very highest importance. There are others also which, however, I can do no more than briefly indicate.

The second is the fact that animals and plants are constructed on well-defined types. Take the vertebrata existing and extinct—What is the significance of their being all constructed on the same general plan ? Why should such different-looking organs as our arm, the fin of a whale, the wing of a bat, and the foreleg of a horse so closely resemble one another in the number and arrange-ment of bones ? Why should it be possible, out of the mere varieties of four floral whorls, with diversities of adhesion and cohesion and suppression, to produce all the types of flowers ? It cannot be an accident. This homology of structure is the second great and universal fact that verifies the theory of Evolution.

The third is the existence of rudimentary organs, dwarfed members of the body which are of no use under present conditions, which merely *represent* the organs which in other animals are of use. There are multitudes of these in all parts of the zoological world. Why should whales have rudimentary teeth which they do not use, snakes rudimentary hind-legs under their skins, and birds that cannot fly have rudimentary wings? The explanation on the theory of Evolution is obvious : they are organs disused and dwarfed by disuse. Some organs dwindle from disuse, as people's brains do, till they disappear, or nearly disappear. Others grow stronger, and so the infinite variety amid essential unity of the animal kingdom is arrived at. Shall we take as an illustration the human being alone, and one set of rudimentary organs alone that exist in him? Of what use to us are some of the surface muscles which we so seldom use, and most of us have not even the power of using? I wonder whether a certain exalted personage —so exalted that I dare not refer to him by name—recollects how, "when he was comparatively a fellow-creature," at a table round which some friends were assembled, he beat time, as well as laughing would permit him to beat time, while others of a family more gifted than his own, with control over rudimentary surface muscles, went through a performance! Does he remember how one moved the skin of his scalp, like a horse shaking off flies ; and another wagged both ears together like a dog ; a third wagged them alternately like a donkey ; and a fourth set the skin of his nose into rapid vibration,—a power exercised, I am told, in still greater perfection during the time of courtship by the blue-nosed monkey? Why do these rudimentary muscles still exist in some of our species? They are visibly of use in other species. They are not to us. They unquestionably verify the doctrine of a Zoological Evolution.

The fourth and last verification I shall allude to is that derived from embryology,—the study of the animal before birth. This is a highly technical study, and one on which it is necessary simply to accept the testimony of experts, and judge of the general bearing of the result. It is not, perhaps, possible to convey to non-experts the significance of the discovery of an "embryonic notochord in the tunicata" ; but expressed in general language, the result of embryology appears to be as follows. The evolution of the individual of every species can be traced from the first appearance of life in the microscopic speck, till the full-grown individual is reached; and the individual is seen to pass through stages in which it resembles widely-diverse families or orders. The embryos of widely-diverse creatures are indistinguishable : they start alike, and diverge, one on one path, another on another. But this is the very doctrine of Evolution shown in small before our eyes. It is only explicable on the hypothesis of a really existing relationship among organised beings of widely-differing classes. "Ontogeny," as Häckel says, "is a short and quick repetition or recapitulation of phylogeny." The growth of the individual is a specimen of the growth of the race.

Another very important and closely-connected subject, indeed, an obvious part of Zoological Evolution, is the evolution of mind in animals. Of the fact of this there can be just as little doubt as there is of organic evolution. If we have evidence to convince us of the gradual and derivative origin of their bodies, it is obvious that we accept the derivative origin of their mental faculties. The processes of derivation are quite beyond us. We understand neither the inheritance of instinct nor the inheritance of form : the variations of ability are as unintelligible as the variations of stature or colour, yet instinct and ability are inherited : the law of selection of the fittest must hold. We accept the theory of mental evolution even though we cannot form any conception of the processes of mind or their transmission.

In brief, then, the study of Natural History leads of necessity to some general theory of connection between all forms of life, vegetable and animal. The theory which attributes this connection to descent with modification, gradual or sudden, is the theory of Evolution applied to Zoology. The *processes* of Evolution, it must be remembered, may be mainly undiscovered even while we have a reasonable certainty of the theory. There are still unsolved questions in the evolution of the earth, and of the solar system, which depend purely on physical laws; how much more shall there be unsolved problems in the infinitely more complicated and newer problem of the evolution of life and mental faculties? Darwinism is by many persons confounded with Evolution. Darwinism is a reference to known causes of one of the processes in one sphere of Evolution. Darwin's clear grasp of the consequences of the struggle for existence revealed to naturalists a true *modus operandi* of nature in giving origin to new species. It was a splendid discovery—the greatest in this great century, and it has given to naturalists a fresh aim and method. But there are problems of life wholly untouched by Darwin. We are far enough yet from mastering the laws of Evolution, when we know nothing as yet of the causes of permanence of species, or of heredity, or of slow variation, or of sudden sports. And behind all these stand the great questions as to the nature of life itself, whether cell life or aggregate life, and the realms of instinct, habit, and reason. Darwinism is but one single step in the onward march of knowledge; but we cannot doubt that further steps will but verify and complete the theory of Evolution,—the theory, that is, that the cosmos which we see, organic and inorganic, physical and mental, has become what it is by successive stages of orderly development.

But the doctrine of Evolution does not stop here. On the one hand it asks the further question whether the organic world is not by some means evolved out of the inorganic. There are forms of animal and vegetable life so simple, so elementary, that it is impossible to pronounce whether they are animal or vegetable; and even far up on the twin branches of animal and vegetable life traces of the characteristics of the other branch of life occur. Here, indeed, is one of the extraordinary interests attaching to the study of botany in some of its recent developments, for example, carnivorous plants, and plant instincts and sensibilities. But this common stock of life from which animals and vegetables came to diverge, the question arises inevitably—Is it an exception to the otherwise universal law? or is it too evolved in some way from some yet simpler inorganic form? No one can say. No living organism has been manufactured. Life is invariably connected with protoplasm, but the synthesis of protoplasm and the origin of life from non-living matter has not been witnessed, and not been effected. This is one direction in which Evolutionists are stopped.

In another region the doctrine of Evolution has profoundly affected the study of all sciences that group round man ; not only his physical origin, but the study of races, language, laws, philosophy, ethics, customs, art, religion. In a word, history. Every historian and student now writes with the consciousness that he is describing a stage in an evolutionary process. The study of origins is becoming a necessity in all branches of study. Whatever study we take up, it runs back ultimately into the study of origins. Psychology itself becomes not merely the classification, but the study of the origin of the mental powers. Even ethics have to be studied as evolutionary. "A zoological factor," says H. Sidgwick, "enters into the history of the moral sentiments." Take man as he is with his instincts, his passions, his intellect, his spiritual faculties. Was he created with these full-grown? This is the question. We see them developed from the germ to the infant, from the infant to the boy, from the boy to the man—an "ontogeny," to use Häckel's phrase, of mental powers. And further, we see family, and social, and racial characteristics, the heredity of intellect, of moral qualities of character, and we see progress and development in all human activities. We all admit Evolution up to a certain point in the race, as we admit it wholly in the individual. The thorough-paced Evolutionist admits it wholly in the race. The unity and completeness of the theory charms him. No chasms in the demonstration appal him. The theory is so simple, so complete, that it must be true. Life, functions, instincts, will, intellect, conscience, religion, are to the thorough-paced Evolutionist all gradually evolved products proceeding along a single chain of causation ; the human soul as well as the human body is the product of evolution : the riddle of the world is read ! Only a few details to fill up !

Such is the complete theory of Evolution simply stated.

And now the question arises, How far is this complete theory proved or probable?

It may certainly be said that of general inorganic and Zoological Evolution, organic and mental, there is no reasonable doubt. The only alternative to it is that of sudden creation, and this admits of neither proof nor refutation. But of two of the great extensions of the theory of Evolution that I have just indicated,—one to the origin of life from inorganic matter and force, and the other to the development of all human faculties, from the conditions of animal life alone,—the same cannot be said.

As regards the first of these, the origin of life from inorganic matter, it may seem a small step from a drop of water to the transparent and formless organism in it that is just visible as it darts across the field of the microscope. But that it seems a small step is due simply to our want of eyes to see. If we could see a drop of water as it really is, the sight would be far more astonishing than that of the starry heavens themselves. If we could magnify a drop of water to the size of the earth, it would then be on a scale large enough for our eyes to see what its nature is. Shall I briefly describe it to you? We should see it consist of nearly a million million million million of molecules, each in itself a triplet, on that scale about as large as cricket balls, darting hither and thither with their actual velocities of twenty miles a minute magnified in like proportion to something inconceivable, dancing like gnats in a summer swarm, colliding and rebounding thousands of millions of times a second; dissolving partnership and re-combining —a scene of infinite activity, an endless play of intensely active forces. That is a drop of water! But if this is a drop of water, what would a speck of protoplasm, the simplest form of matter which lives, be like? The constitution of protoplasm, whether dead or alive, infinitely surpasses that of water in complexity. Here are elements not combined in triplets, but in groups of such intricacy and in motions so complicated as to defy totally our mode of expression and our imagination alike. The difference to the eye is small: the difference to the imagination trained by knowledge is enormous. How did protoplasm come into being? What is the difference between living protoplasm and dead? No one has even attempted to answer the latter question ; and the only attempt to answer the first is to suggest, as W. K. Clifford suggested, that it happened "by coincidences," by chance. That among all the possible combinations of combinations of molecules this one did occur once ; that it was a stable combination ; that it had the power of forming similar combinations in adjacent inorganic matter, also by a coincidence ; and hence by a series of coincidences the stately tree of life grew upon the earth. It is not unfair to compare this theory to the suggestion that if a bag of letters were shaken about a line of *Paradise Lost* might by a coincidence be formed ; and have by a coincidence the power of com- pelling adjacent letters to form metrical lines related to the former, and that so the whole poem grew up. This is not an unfair comparison. Try to conceive the complexity of protoplasm, and the molecular activities of living proto- plasm ; the formation of a cell ; the cell producing other cells, and then differentiating them into their various highly-specialised functions, so as to compose the body, that marvellous cosmos, with its nerves and veins, and brains and bone ; and then conceive these cells developing consciousness, and will, and personality, and the sense of right and wrong. It is only by fixing the mind on this chain of supposed evolution that we become conscious how far it is from being proven or even conceivable.

It is only the fascination which a complete theory has always exercised on men that can account for its being accepted by any one as established or even probable in its present form. The history of science is written in vain unless we lay to heart its lessons that a theory like this needs many modifications, even reversals, before it takes its final shape. It seems as if every form of error must be exhausted before truth can be found. Geocentric theories must precede heliocentric ; "theories of the earth" precede geology. Take the theory of light. How do we see one another in this room? "Our eyes," was the first reply, "put forth invisible feelers and thus we touch one another;" explaining sight by the sense of touch. " No," was the second reply; " the objects dart out little imponderable molecules, and they affect our eyes, and produce sight." " No," is the third reply; " the objects are in incessant molecular motion, and produce vibrations which an omnipresent imaginary ether transmits to our eyes." And who shall say that this at last is *fact*. This imaginary ether— what physicist quite believes in it? A new theory of light may replace all these before the century is closed, if some man's intellect and imagination are powerful enough to grapple with the problem. Or take Chemistry. Are chemists really satisfied with their theories? Of course not. It is plain that the vast complexity of modern Chemistry demands a simplification, as much as the epicycles of Ptolemaic Astronomy demanded the ellipse. But the Kepler of Chemistry has not yet come.

It is only such as do not fully realise the imperfection and the transitional evolutionary character of our scientific theories that can suppose that the processes of the grand central doctrine of Evolution are as yet even outlined in their final form. The history of science is written in vain unless it teaches us modesty in affirmation, and makes us cherish a high, almost a mathematical, standard of proof,— unless it convinces us that many a reversal, many a modification, must be submitted to before the theory emerges into its final form. And these modifications will come not by ignoring—which is such a temptation to the young and enthusiastic student—but by steadily facing and exploring those " residual phenomena " which refuse to be included in the present theory. And of such there are plenty.

So far, then, the theory of Evolution is not proven, nor can it be said to be even slightly probable in the extreme form that life and mind are the unguided development of matter and inorganic forces alone.

Let us now turn to the other great extension of the theory of Evolution,—to the development of all human faculties, from the conditions of animal life.

I do not enter here on the question of the physical

connection between men and animals. It is not one of
the highest importance : it is more and more plain that
the connection is very remote in time, because the mental
evolution in man has advanced so immeasurably in front
of that in animals. And it is the mental evolution rather
than the physical which is of interest. On the possibility
of this it is well known that the leading naturalists differ.
I do not, therefore, touch this question, but speak only
of the mental evolution of man regarded as a solitary
species.

I have said some time ago that the study of origins was
becoming a necessity in all branches of study. And it
may be necessary to expand this a little before it can be
quite intelligible. Take language. No one .could be said
to have a thorough and scientific knowledge of any
language—English, French, or Greek, for example—without knowing something of the way in which its inflexions
and forms have grown up. As Max Müller says, we want
to know why the addition of the single letter *d* should
make the pathetic difference between I love and I loved.
We want to know why and how *j'aime* came to mean I
love, and *j'aimerai* I shall love. At first we come across
these facts, and regard them as ultimate facts ; but the
study of language and languages compels us to notice the
connection among such facts, shows us the derivative
origin of much that was once regarded as ultimate, and
compels us, in a word, to regard all language, as we see it,
as derivative from earlier forms. Languages fall into
families and groups ; traces of connection occur even
among distant groups ; and the origin of language becomes
a recognised problem for the reason of man to face. We
can watch the processes by which languages change, by
which children learn, by which savages communicate, by
which a written alphabet is formed. It is plainly a
problem of evolution, from the study of the causes now in
operation, from the living languages of the present, the
fossil languages of the past, to trace the origin and the
development of language on the earth.

So it is a similar problem to trace the development of

an art such as architecture; and no treatment of architecture, which was not more or less historical, would be regarded as scientific. In this evolution, as in biological evolution, we should find curious verifications from the abortive and useless organs surviving in debased architecture; massive cornices, internal and external, retained in stone with no meaning except in wood; senseless parapets and ornamentations; sham buttresses supported on corbels. We cannot doubt that the history of architecture is an evolutionary history, in the sense that its present condition has sprung from previous conditions. And this is so obviously the case with every art and every applied science, that no more time need be spent on this part of our subject. It is quite intelligible, indeed almost inevitable, to speak of the "evolution" of the steam-engine or the telegraph as a short way of expressing the development of their present forms by successive improvement out of foregoing forms, and even germs.

So again there is an evolution of customs and law. The study of the customs of primitive tribes, and of extinct systems of legislature, is to the study of modern law what the study of the comparatively undeveloped living forms and of fossils is to the Zoologist.

There remains another subject to the growth of which the term Evolution is sometimes applied, and which will offer a very valuable illustration of an ambiguity in the word Evolution, and will be important when we proceed into still further and more difficult questions. I mean the evolution of knowledge. And as a typical branch of knowledge I shall take mathematics.   ·

The so-called evolution of mathematics may at first sight seem to be precisely analogous to the evolution of architecture or of a steam-engine, the obvious point of resemblance being that each new discovery seems a step for some further discovery. Nevertheless, the difference between the evolution in practical science or art and the evolution in mathematics is so great, that unless we take great care we shall fall into confusion by using the same word. We must keep in mind that there are necessary

and certain truths in mathematics which exist quite independently of our knowledge of them. This is not the
case in inventions, whether in art or science. The one
is an evolution of knowledge of truths, which are true
everywhere and depend on reason alone to discover, and
not on any properties of matter. That the three angles
of a triangle are equal to two right angles is a truth independent not only of man's discovery of it, but also of
man's existence, or even the existence of matter. The
same cannot be said of the existence of a Gothic
cathedral, or the telephone, or a language.

In fact, in the study of mathematics, and perhaps in
that of the primary laws of matter, we find ourselves dealing with necessary and absolute truths; and any attempt
to trace the evolution of mathematics without the recognition of this fact could only end in confusion and disaster.
In mathematics, however, this is so obvious that no one
would be likely to attempt it. We therefore recognise
that there exists one science, at least, the evolution of
which, if we must use the same word for the progressive
discovery of truths in it, is essentially different in nature
from that of the experimental sciences. There is an
element of absolute truth in mathematics, there are truths
of pure reason, to which discovery is perpetually approxi-
mating. It is not mathematics which are undergoing an
evolution, but our knowledge of them is progressing in an
orderly way.

These few remarks on the nature of evolution in mathematics will enable us to turn to the question of the
evolution of ethics or morality with at least a clear
understanding what the nature of the question is. The
question of the so-called evolution of ethics is one of the
very highest philosophical importance. The ultimate question, of course, is why right is right and wrong is wrong.
Now it is obvious that among the various systems of ethics
that have been or can be proposed there is one broad and
deep division. And it turns on this. Has right grown
to be right, and wrong grown to be wrong, by convention,
by experiences of utility or the reverse ? of happiness or

the reverse? Or is the distinction of right and wrong, like the truths of mathematics, absolute, necessary, whether we know it or not? In a word, is the evolution of ethics comparable to that of experimental science or to that of mathematics? Is it morality that progresses, or man's knowledge of it?

Now, at the close of a lecture, already I fear too long, you will not expect me to enter on so great a question. I will tell you something only of two great books on ethics in which you will find attempts at the solution of this question. One is by Henry Sidgwick, on methods of Ethics, in which he examines all the ordinary solutions of the question, and finds that all alike — hedonism, utilitarianism, and intuitionism—fail to furnish a scientific basis of ethics as they actually exist. There exists no system of ethics on the purely experimental basis; another element must come in. It does not enter into Mr. Sidgwick's scope to discuss what that is. But with the impartiality of a rarely judicial mind he finds that his data are insufficient to construct a system of ethics, and he frankly says so. The evolution of ethics is not parallel to that of law or science or language or art.

There is another famous work by a man better known, but of a less judicial mind, Herbert Spencer, entitled *Data of Ethics*, which is an elaborate attempt to construct a system of evolutionary ethics on selected data. And an examination of this work will convince most people who are competent to examine it, and are not convinced beforehand that ethics must be evolutionary in the same sense that law is evolutionary, that the data he assumes are not adequate to the solution. He does not find this out. I understand him to say that truthfulness, for example, *has become right* because it has in the past conduced to happiness. The theory compels us to regard morality as provisional and traditional, based on ancestral experiences rather than on our own. It leaves out some of the most obvious facts of human nature; it gives no reason why only certain acts of utility should receive the stamp of righteousness from our conscience; and is only

made consistent with itself by resolutely or blindly not
seeing all that conflicts with it.

Hence I wish you to infer that my own opinion is that
the extension of the evolutionary method to ethics is
analogous to that in the case of mathematics, and not to
that of scientific inventions or language : it is a progressive
discovery, by revelation or otherwise, of absolute truths
which would be true here and everywhere in all past and
all future time, as much as it is true that the angles
at the base of an isosceles triangle are equal, and were
equal before there was a human being in existence.

Lastly, there remains the so-called evolution of religion ;
and you will at once anticipate what I have to say on this
subject.   In form it is evolutionary, in essence it is like
mathematics and ethics, and contains an element of
absolute truth to which religion tends to approximate.
That it is evolutionary in form is obvious.   The study of
the bygone religious cosmogonies of Assyria and Egypt
explains some of the characteristic forms and beliefs of
Judaism ; and we can find even still more rudimentary
forms of religion among savage tribes.   The evolution,
that is the progressive change of Judaism, from the time
of Moses to that of the prophets, and from that of the
prophets to the age of our Lord, is obvious to all students
of the Bible : in the New Testament the stride is vast, but
even here too the teaching of Christ is based on Judaism ;
and the fact of the development of the Christian Church
in its forms of worship and doctrine from the Apostolic
age to the present is also perfectly obvious.   The present
forms of Christianity are not and cannot be identical with
those in which the surroundings were different.   They
adapt themselves to their environment, and have, it would
seem, an unlimited power of such adaptation.   The
antiquarianism which would limit our forms to those of
far distant ages,—forms of worship or forms of speculation,
—is a resistance to the universal law of Evolution.   The
happy mean has to be preserved.   " It hath ever been
the wisdom of the Church of England to keep the mean
between the two extremes, of too much stiffness in refusing

and of too much easiness in permitting any variation from our Liturgy." We acknowledge an evolution of religious thought and expression.

But while the forms of religion are evolved, religion itself is evolutionary, not in the sense in which science or art is evolutionary, growing without a defined goal, but in the sense in which mathematics are evolutionary; the progressive advance is towards the knowledge of absolute truth. This distinction may be difficult to a beginner to grasp, but it is a fundamental difference; and I commend it to your careful attention.

You will see that by placing the evolution of ethics and religion in the same class with mathematics, as the sciences which investigate absolute truth, the acceptance of Evolution is directly opposed to determinism and even materialism. These give us no aim. But there is always the absolute truth as the inspiring goal alike of Mathematics, Ethics, and Religion. The methods differ; for the essential and unique characteristic of religion is the fact that truths have always been believed to come to man in the form of a revelation. From the nature of the truths this has always been the case; the discovery has always been regarded as an inspiration and a revelation. And the humble student, if he approaches this subject without a prejudice, will, I think, confirm the verdict of man's spirit that it is an inspiration, that it is a revelation, from the ultimate source of Reason and of Right.

What a magnificent addition to our conception of the greatness and unity of the cosmos is made by this great doctrine of Evolution! It was a great step in human thought to conceive the size of this great globe we inhabit; it was another great step, it must have strained men's minds to the utmost, to learn that the Earth is but a pebble compared to our vast and distant and central Sun. That thought reduced the Earth almost to nothingness. A still greater step, one that surpasses our utmost imagination, was taken when it was shown that our central Sun is but a single star among an infinity of stars. And reflect what have been the corresponding extensions in our conceptions

of the duration of past time, and of our ideas of creation.
From the few thousand years through which men once
thought the earth had existed, we have to pass to un-
numbered myriads of years and even centuries, and the
six days' drama of Creation is seen to be but the image of
a creation of matter and life and mind infinitely more
wonderful, extending from the farthest verge of time down
to the present hour.

And in our religious conception the gain is as vast
when we once steadily contemplate the extended outlook.
We may look back on man's past history and accept the
overwhelming probability of the view that connects him
physically with other animals in a far distant age: we may
accept as proved the development of his reasoning faculties,
his instincts, his affections ; and we may therefore connect
them remotely with the reasoning faculties, the instincts,
the affections of animals.   But besides these two elements,
there is the third, the independent consciousness of right
and wrong, the reference to an external and absolute moral
law as independent of man as are the truths of mathematics.
Of this law there is no evolution, though there is a progressive knowledge of it on the part of man.   It is absolute.
It is the perception of this which lies at the foundation of
all religions ; and so far from being obscured by the theory
of Evolution, I think it is made clearer ; so far from being
itself evolved, its absolute character shines out the more
clearly.   Hence, speaking for myself, I find in this doctrine
of Evolution fresh grounds for responsibility, for faith, for
hope.   For it isolates and exhibits to the reason the
absolute moral law, the imperative of duty.

The facts, then, on which the principle of Evolution
throws no light are these : (1) The origin of matter ; of
those marvellous molecules with their fierce and restless
forces of which I spoke just now, and their initial distribu-
tion and motion.   (2) The origin of life, with its myriad
manifestations of organism and instinct and mind.   (3)
The origin of spirit, *i.e.* of man's distinctive spiritual faculties and convictions of absolute truth.

It remains, however, that I should add a few words on

the relation of the theory of Evolution to the Christian faith.   At the close of a long lecture such words must be very few, and take the form not of reasoning so much as of the conclusions at which I have arrived.

In the first place, Christian theology is in no way connected either with the theory of Evolution or its denial. Of course the literal interpretation of the Mosaic account of creation is a thing of the past.   We do not now interpret it literally.   And when we come to study the underlying truths we see that it, and all the spirit of the Bible, is as consistent with an evolution in creation,—a creation proceeding according to law,—as it is with any other theory that can be imagined.

But, in the second place, the conception of creation as an evolution still going on, is far more in accordance with the highest Biblical teaching, and with the most philosophic theology both of past ages and the present.   The difficulty which the popular mind has felt in Evolution has, as is well known, not been shared to any very large extent by the clergy, and scarcely at all by the better theologians among the clergy.   And this remarkable result arises from a plain cause.   The popular conception of God is that of a Transcendent Being existing and operating somewhere and somewhen in space and time.   All the phraseology of prayers and hymns is *primâ facie* based on this ancient and Biblical conception and presentation of the Deity.   The necessities of language, and the finite nature of our minds, make some such semi-materialistic conception necessary, and this is the natural and popular conception.   Now unquestionably to those by whom Creation was attributed to the operation of this Transcendent Creator, dwelling apart from matter and mind alike, it was a shock to be told that Creation had now to be regarded as an evolution, requiring no external interference in the past any more than in the present.   But theologians knew that their conception of the Transcendent God was but a metaphor and a form of speech : and they knew that the highest teaching of our Lord, as preserved in the Gospel of St. John, and the teaching of St. Paul in his most philosophic Epistles, and the teaching of the great Fathers of the Greek Church, all presented to our minds God as indwelling and immanent rather than as external and transcendent ; and to minds familiar with this conception, not only does Evolution present nothing antagonistic to their conceptions of Creation, but it is hailed as an advance in science that has brought science somewhat more nearly up to the level of theology. It cannot be too often said that the aim of theology is the *absorption*, not only the reconciliation of science. Theology "knows of no principle which compels it to arrest the advance of human knowledge at a particular point, lest some outwork of dogma should be overthrown or need reconstruction."

We therefore do much more than admit Evolution, we welcome it. It is true that to teach the evolutionary theory of Creation in scriptural language requires some degree of transformation of the language of theology ; but this is equally true of most, if not all, of the other doctrines of theology. In their ordinary form they lend themselves rather to the one theory than the other, because the transcendent conception has been always current in the Western Church ; but theologians—to repeat what I have said before—do not find the difficulty as great as others do, because their studies necessarily compel them to form in their own minds the more philosophic and less popular conception of the immanent God.

And now time compels me to conclude, not without a hope that I may have helped some of you to see in Evolution a view of Creation which may satisfy at once the demands of Reason and of Faith.

FUNDAMENTAL CHURCH PRINCIPLES[1]

THE origin of this paper is to be found in my belief that the fundamental principles of the Church of Christ are the best justification of the existence of the Church of England, and that a clear perception and statement of those principles are among the best measures both for reforming and for defending it.

There are two preliminary remarks I wish to make, to define what I am *not* going to speak about.

(1) I am not speaking about Christian Principles, but about Church Principles. And the difference is this: the universal Church—that is, the whole body of faithful men and women—is the organ through which Christ, who is in the heavens, works still on the earth. Each individual Church is an organisation for the spread of Christianity, and we are discussing the principles, not of Christianity, but of the organisation. My paper is therefore an essay, and not a sermon.

And (2) I am dealing, not with applications or details, but with principles. It would be out of place to go into historical or antiquarian questions; to touch on the relations of the Anglican to the Roman Catholic Church; still more, to talk about the Public Worship Regulation Act,

---

[1] This address was given on 9th November 1885 in the New Schools, Oxford, to the St. Matthew's Guild, consisting of members of the University. I had been, in the first instance, requested to speak on Church Defence or Church Reform.

or the Courts of Final Appeal. I am not going to speak
about Ritualists or Evangelicals, or indeed about Ritual or
Doctrine. I am not going to speak about Establishment
or Disestablishment; about Acts of Uniformity or terms
of Subscription; I am, in fact, going to speak on the subject of the paper, which is—Principles. The paper will
very likely be thought dull. I fear that is inevitable; but
it will not be controversial or political.

Fundamental Church Principles.—Let us define our
words; and let me advise you always to be ready to define
your words. There was once a great controversy which
almost rent the Church of England in two; and the great
Bishop Thirlwall remarked, after it was all over, that it had
never happened to occur to either side to define the terms
in dispute. Had they done so, the dispute would have
ceased at once. And definitions are not easy things.
They are very easy until you try to make them, and get
them criticised. Also, I would ask you to remember that,
strictly speaking, a definition comes at the end, not at the
beginning of a study. You are going to study Logic or
Political Economy, and you want a definition of them.
Very well; but you must have some notion of Logic before
you can understand its limits. You must know something
of Political Economy and its kindred sciences before you
can appreciate the boundaries that separate the one from
the other. Would you all understand me if I gave you a
definition of Partial Differential Equations?

So, in fact, we ought to know the Church first before
we can define it. But we do all know, in a rough, general
way, by the experience of our life, something about the
Church, and so, perhaps, it is clearer to work in the reverse
order in a short paper like this; to take a definition first,
and to test it and explain it, maybe to add to it or subtract
from it, but, at any rate, to see whether it does not throw
real light on Fundamental Church Principles. And this
will demand your best attention.

All lines of thought on which I have attempted to think
out this question appear to me to converge towards one
definition of the Church of Christ,—a definition which

states the fundamental principles that we are in search of.
Let us try this definition.

*The Church of Christ is a Divine, self-organising associa-
tion of which Christ is the Head, knit together by a common
faith and sacraments, whose aim is the spiritual education of
mankind in the spirit and faith of Christ.*

This is the fundamental, original, and permanent principle; and it is from sometimes losing sight of this that
Churches have been led into error and weakness and
suffering, on the one side or the other.

Before proceeding to examine this definition in detail,
let me make one or two general remarks on it, by way of
indicating its significance.   It follows from this definition
that the Church of Christ rests on no human charter.   Its
charter is the Divine command, "As My Father has sent
Me, even so send I you."   Its bond of union is its common faith and common sacraments, and allegiance to a
common Head, with no other necessary unity.   It is a
society, moreover, not to enforce control, or exercise
domination over men's conduct or intellects, but to influence and educate the world; it is as leaven hid in meal;
it works slowly till the whole is leavened; and inasmuch as
it educates its members and others in the faith and spirit
of Christ, it is one whose work and aim is primarily spiritual;
it helps men, that is to say, to live in the presence of the
Unseen and Eternal; to recognise the true nature of man,
as revealed by the incarnation of God in Christ; to keep
His image and memory in our hearts, acting almost like a
second conscience; to live in a spirit of trust in God and
love to man; to realise God's fatherhood and man's
brotherhood; to lead the life of purity and kindness; to
lay hold on eternal life;—the especial revelations of the
teaching and life of Christ.

Seeing the close relation of spiritual and moral progress
with intellectual and physical conditions, it is impossible
but that the Church should be deeply, even ardently,
interested in all that concerns the intellectual education
of mankind; all that bears on increasing man's power
of judging rightly, and on his self-control; and in all

that concerns the external conditions of life.   Progress
in these is essential; but to the Church they are the
means, not the end.

The Church is knit together by a common Creed and
Sacraments.   All experience shows that this bond is
essential.   Without it the Church would become a loosely-
held-together philanthropic association.   We should be
grains of sand.   Experience also shows that those religious
communities whose faith is defined still more closely acquire
a momentum and intensity which a broader creed fails to
supply.   There is room inside a Church for such bodies
bound together by these closer ties, as well as relations of
alliance with others outside who dispense with those ties.
But we cannot to the whole Church give much narrower
or wider limits than these, the acceptance of the substance
of our common Creeds, Apostolic and Nicene, and the
observance of the two Christian Sacraments.

You will begin, then, to see what are the Fundamental
Church Principles as contained in this definition; but
before I proceed to develop them more at length, perhaps
it will help you still more clearly to understand what are
fundamental Church principles if I proceed to mention
some principles which, though of high importance, are not
fundamental.

I have said, you will remember, that the Church is an
association of which Christ is the Head.   This implies an
organic unity, a *life* in the Church, and an altogether peculiar relation to Christ.

No conception or definition of the Church of Christ
would be satisfactory, or even tolerable, if it did not include
the influence and spiritual presence of Christ among its
members.   This presence it is as impossible to define as
it is to define life itself.   Our spiritual life and experiences,
the inter-communion between man's spirit and God, tran-
scend definition.   But they are facts, and they are the
foundation of the life and continuity of the Church.   It is
the deep conviction of this real life of the Church in Christ,
and of Christ in the Church; a mystical conception, but
not an imaginary one ; a conception true, and experiment-

ally verifiable and verified—it is this that is fundamental. It has taken many forms, which, to one generation, one race, one type of mind or another, have appeared least inadequate to express that conviction. But these forms are not fundamental. And it is to this I wish to call your attention. They are, so to say, of private interpretation, and cannot command universal assent. For example, we may well believe that there is, historically, an unbroken line of succession in laying on of hands from the Apostolic Church to the present time; we may well hold with Lightfoot that the threefold ministry is "the historical backbone of the Church," and that the Episcopal form of government certainly, "if any event in Church History can be trusted," dates from the time of St. John; but to say that the grace of ordination and power to administer Sacraments depend for their spiritual efficiency to others on this unbroken succession is a belief or theory which, however, does but express in a concrete, material, and, so to say, portable form the profound truth of the continuity of Christ's spiritual presence in the Church. And therefore, if we care to think accurately, we shall not consider the form of the expression of this truth of Christ's presence in the Church as in itself fundamental and universal; what is fundamental is the truth of which it is an expression, the spiritual presence of Christ in the Church—that is, in the whole association of faithful men and women—a presence which men can hardly fail to represent to themselves in different ways.

So, too, all theories relating to the efficacy of the Sacraments, Baptismal Regeneration, the Spiritual Presence of Christ in the Holy Communion, all questions of ritual, all questions of the powers of the clergy, even all questions of prayer and worship, arise, if you will reflect on the matter, from the conviction, which is absolutely fundamental, that the inter-communion of Spirit between Christ and the members of His Church on earth is continuous, and has many channels and manifestations. All methods of expressing that inter-communion and reciprocal influence are utterly inadequate, and there neither is, nor will be, any

formula which the wit of man can devise, which contains
the whole truth about it; and therefore no formula of
belief on these points is in itself fundamental. As soon
as we attempt to embody the spiritual truth in intellectual
forms, we pass out of the region of unity in spirit into the
region of diversity of opinion. And this we must recognise, and cling to the faith for us all, and to the formulæ
for such as they help. These formulæ, however, are commonly regarded as Church principles, but they are not
fundamental principles; it may be difficult for us to recognise that such points as these, which we believe to be
sacred, and know to be valuable, in our own Church
teaching, must yet be regarded as superstructure, and liable
to change and development and variety of opinion. But
nevertheless it is so. All such theories are imperfect,
inadequate, and largely erroneous. Each conveys to some
mind a great truth, but it cannot be forced on another as
in itself the truth of which it may be in some cases a
channel. There is in the theory, to use the common
phrase, a subjective element. What is fundamental—to
repeat once more—is the continuous spiritual presence of
Christ among men, a veritable life of the Church, however
we express this fact.

I will now, after these general remarks on the definition
as a whole, and especially on that part of it which defines
the Church as an association of which Christ is the Head,
proceed to develop, with such detail as time will permit,
some of the other terms of the definition.

We call the Church a *Divine* association. We mean by
that phrase that it goes back to Christ Himself. In Him
is its origin. We look on it, therefore, as a part of the
Divine purpose and plan for the education of the world.
It is with the deepest humility and consciousness of human
limitations that we can venture to use any such phrase as
" Divine purpose and plan." The more we think of such
words, the more we shall shrink from using them lightly.
Still, if there is any Divine plan to be traced in history, if
all religion is not a dream, the work of the Church of Christ
is a part of the Divine plan for the education of the world.

We call the Church, moreover, a *self-organising* association. It is not enough that men should combine into an association for a common purpose; they must also have a regular organisation in order to secure efficiency. But the world is too large, and the difficulty of inter-communication in ancient times was too great, and the diversity of the religious and intellectual tendencies of nations is too pronounced, for a single organisation to hold throughout the Church, although there may be unity of faith. Divergences in forms and philosophies between the Eastern and Western Churches soon began to show themselves, and later on Teutonic and Roman divergences began; and, as all the world knows, national and other Church organisations exist, all being branches of the Universal or Catholic Church of Christ. They may be one in faith, in sacraments, and in allegiance to Christ, and yet differ in organisation. In each such branch, as, for example, in our own branch, the Church of England, organisation is necessary to deal with such various subjects as its finance, its laws, its customs, its ritual, its doctrine, its extension.

But there exists no universal organisation for the Church; its unity consists in spirit alone, nor is there any necessary type of organisation. Any one who studies ecclesiastical history impartially will be impressed by the gradual and, so to speak, casual growth or modification of most of its institutions and organisations; he will notice how they followed the laws of growth and quasi-evolution of all things human, altering by the perpetual process of self-adjustment and adaptation to circumstances. This is their origin, and this is equally their sanction or their condemnation. The sacredness is not in the institution, but in the truth to which it witnesses; not in the organisation, but in the purpose it was intended to effect, and the spirit that animates it. No one, on the one hand, can study ecclesiastical history and fail to be impressed with the vast importance to Church life of the institution of Episcopacy. It has given continuity, coherency, strength. It enabled the Church to do the work it had to do. It is still, both at home and in our colonies, to all appearance, essential

to Church work.   It is the framework·on which the
organisation rests.   But, on the other hand, no one who
quietly contrasts what may be regarded as the minor
characteristics of our present Church of England with
those of the Church of Christ in its first age—our permanent separation of ministers from secular pursuits, our
setting apart places and buildings for sacred purposes, the
inequalities of rank and money-payment associated with
offices in the Church of England, our parochial system,
our tithes and endowments, our relation to the State, our
prelates in the House of Lords, our *congés d'élire*, our order
of administration of the Sacraments of Baptism and the
Lord's Supper, and other similar points,—no one, I say,
with adequate knowledge, can quietly contrast these
developments with what they have sprung from, and trace
even in outline the processes by which they have sprung
up, and yet doubt that the Church of Christ has had, and
that the Church of England at home and in the colonies
still has, the capacity for self-organisation and growth and
adaptation.   The claim of the existing customs for our
reverence rests on no claim to separate Divine origin.   No
one can doubt that, in their present form, they are human
in the sense that anything that the spirit of man devises
and executes is human, and, therefore, that they are both
capable of, and may demand, further growth, adaptation,
and alteration ; that these minor points of organisation,
whether we regard them as merits or defects, are in themselves indifferent, and to be judged by their efficiency for
their purpose, and that purpose is the spiritual education
of men in the spirit and faith of Christ.

The clear recognition of these points—that there must
be organisation, and that the society always has been and
is self-organising, according to the law, not of revolution,
but of life and free continuous growth and expansion, and
that its organisation is to be judged, not by antiquarian
standards, but by its efficiency in the present, in which continuity is a *very* important factor—may greatly help us.   They
are elementary truths, but they are sometimes forgotten.

In the first place, they may teach us a willingness to

submit to organisation and law. The spirit of self-will, of
insistence on our own views, which views we have probably
never really "bottomed," or traced to principles, and the
spirit of ἐρίθεια and faction, is still rife among Churchmen,
as it was in the time of St. Paul, and still deserves his stern
rebukes. It would be useful to remember that where men
have differed there must be ground for differing, and where
good men have for ages differed, there must be solid and
good ground for difference. It would teach us to be
modest. It would teach us to look for principles on which
we agree, not formulæ on which we differ. It would prevent the schismatic spirit within the Church, and the
possible ripening of such spirit into actual disunion. To
tell another that this or that way of doing things, this or
that attitude or mode of expression, is alone the right one,
provokes contradiction and schism; to tell him that this
or that way is old, and works pretty well, and that if we
can improve it we will, is an invitation to co-operate. It
furnishes the best possible inducement to make our system
work well. It makes men calm.

In the next place, these elementary truths would teach
us to face the great defects in our Church organisation
with the united resolve to grapple with them, which we can
never do till we feel that our hands are absolutely free,
that we are not destroying what is Divine, but promoting
the growth of what is human, in the same spirit of service
of God in which it has hitherto grown. If we regard
either the minor difficulties and defects in our organisation, such as the inefficiency of our cathedral system, the
uncertainty and difficulty of ecclesiastical legislation, the
need of reform of patronage, and the difficulty of removing
of inefficient ministers; or the incomparably greater
defects, that though the Church is theoretically national,
and though Parliament and the Crown have supreme control, yet in effect the laity have at present so little power
and active interest in the Church; and hence that we have
so little hold on national enthusiasm, so little power of
rapid adaptation to the needs of special classes, so few
great forces at our command in dealing with the festering

evils and the degraded types of life in our great cities;
that, being the Church which has witnessed the "Extension of England," we should have done so little for that
extended Empire; that the Church in all our colonies, in
spite of the devoted work of individuals, is our weakness
and not our glory—not a specimen of young and vigorous
Church life, planted in new soil by an experienced and
careful Mother-Church, or spontaneously springing up
wherever Englishmen are found, but an ever-present warn
ing of what our Church of England may become; that,
being the Church of the greatest commercial country in
the world, our efficiency as a Christianising agent should
have been so small—if we regard these considerations
steadily, they will, it may be hoped, at last create that
public opinion in our Church which will urge on and
support our rulers in far stronger dealing with questions of
Church reform than has hitherto been tolerated,—a reform
which should enlist on the side of the Church those great
forces of true, deep Christian love and feeling which hang
so loosely to the skirts of the Church at present, or, indeed,
are even alienated from her, distrustful of the possibility of
reformation.   Our rulers must wait for the tide of true
Church feeling that shall carry them on.   Reform must
come from within; from without will come something
different from reform.   Reform must be the outcome of
the whole Church of England.   It is public opinion here,
as everywhere, that forces on legislative progress.

You will now have realised what stress must be laid in
our definition on the word *self-organising*.   The Church of
England is at once a Divine and a *self-organising* association
—Divine in origin, as we reverently believe; human in
detail, as we see.   All things are lawful to us—we must
willingly abridge our liberty, in order to work with others
—we must grow.   Such are some of the immediate consequences of this part of our definition, or, rather, for you
must always look at it in this way, such are the obvious
conditions of our society, which lead up to and necessitate
such a definition.

Next, let us consider what is involved in the word

Q

association. It implies that the work which Christ has given man to do is one which men cannot do by themselves, and for themselves alone ; that individual salvation is not our sole aim ; we do not join an association to get ourselves to heaven. No ; it implies that we are essentially a brotherhood, a communion, the foundation of it being our common sonship to God, influenced by one life and one Spirit, owning allegiance to one Master, having one aim, and that not an exclusive individual aim. Our nature is such that individual holiness is, in general, unattainable without such association, for holiness is incomplete without brotherhood. We associate for the good of others as well as of ourselves : this is our aim ; but the immediate effect is a blessing on ourselves. There is no one who does not get more than he gives ; and the more he gives the more he gets. It is the holiest and saintliest who get most from our Church, because they give most.

The mere fact of an association, moreover, that is, of a Church, by its corporate existence, its universality, its antiquity, its permanence, the immense variety of characters it embraces, bears incessant witness to the world of the Divine origin and spiritual nature of *all* men, and not only of an elect few. It is true, perhaps, that the effect of this silent witness is small, and that we must trust far more to the living voice ; but yet who can say how deeply the religious sentiment, the sense of God's presence, the quiet consciousness of God in our daily life, has penetrated into the fibre of our English hearts, by the centuries of quiet parochial ministrations, the unceasing witness borne to the reality of the life of the Spirit by the outward and visible signs of Baptism and the Lord's Supper, by the sight of village spire and the sound of the church-going bell, by the mere visibility of the machinery of the association which we call the Church.

The definition also teaches us that the Church is a net which gathers of every kind. It is an educational association, not a club for enjoying Christian fellowship. It admits the weak, the unformed, the doubtful, the sinful, in order that it may educate them. There is no attempt to shut out from the school of Christ those who most need His teaching; no attempt by human tact or discernment to separate tares from wheat, and give special privileges to a few. The conception is *Catholic*, rather than *Puritan*, to express the point in a single epithet. It is inclusive, not exclusive. It imposes tests on its teachers more than on its members.

Again, an *association* for a purpose implies that there is work for all. It reminds us that the aim of this association is not one that can be discharged by paid ministers in stated duties; that its members cannot commute their obligations for a money payment. It does not consist merely of teachers and learners. No; all may and must contribute to the spiritual education of mankind in the spirit and faith of Christ. It suggests to us, it impresses on us, the necessity for fuller co-operation in this work, fuller sympathy among the members and ministers of a congregation. Those are the best parishes in which the aim of the clergyman to foster the spirit of association is most realised. All members of our Churches should, in some way, be made to feel this membership; that their relation to the body is not that of passive recipients of teaching or other means of grace, but that of active co-operation in the multiform work, spiritual, intellectual, moral, physical, that devolves on a Church. I have read of an American congregation in which the first question on admission is, What are you ready to *do*? Every member of a congregation should feel that he has joined an association whose object is to *do* something—something for their neighbours, for their country, for the heathen. You young men who are members of the Church of England are members of an association. What are you doing to carry out its purpose? What are you ready to do?

By calling it an association, again, we recognise the rights of those that are without. All disqualification or persecution of those who voluntarily stand aloof from a Church is absolutely out of place. Religious equality follows as a matter of course. The Church is not identical with the nation. Inasmuch as we are a Church, we have duties to others; but the duties are the duties of gentleness, of persuasion, of attraction. Inasmuch as we, the Church of England, are professedly a National Church, all the nation have their rights in us. We have no rights over them; we have only duties. We cannot fail to see that the Church of Christ, in the past, often mistook its origin and purpose, and hence arose fearful evils: they claimed rights; they ignored duties; we must resolve to remove all traces and survivals of such a spirit in the present. The notion of "compelling them to come in," or cursing them if they stand without, of making any exclusive claims, is at length seen to be absolutely incongruous with the fundamental ideas of a Church, even of a National Church.

And further, by calling it an association, we bring before our minds the duty of merging our own individual hobbies and interests in the interests of the community: the duty of great loyalty to our Church. A hard lesson to learn, but one most necessary.

We are thus compelled to reflect on our relations to other associations, such as the foreign and Nonconformist Churches. It might have been thought that a single association, under uniform organisation throughout the whole world, would have been best adapted for its great purpose of educating mankind in the spirit and faith of Christ; but it has not been God's will that it should be so; and it seems more reverent to inquire whether such diversities as we see of Greek and Latin Churches, of National Churches, of Reformed Churches, of Nonconformist Churches, are not carrying out, or may not carry out, the purposes of the Church of Christ more efficiently than any imagined unity of organisation would do. For it is not diversity of organisation or administration which is wrong, inasmuch as there is no one type of organisation or administration which is exclusively right; nor is diversity of opinion on speculative points wrong; neither is establishment wrong, nor disestablishment, *per se;* the only thing that is wrong is an un-Christlike spirit, the abandonment of the faith and allegiance to Christ, and failure to attain the end for which organisation exists—viz. the spiritual education of man in the spirit and faith of Christ. If the Church of England, and in so far as that Church, ever lost sight of that great end, and was narrow, or unjust, or incapable of growth; and if Nonconformity arose in a spirit which was not of love, then there were faults, because the temper of both retarded the attainment of their common end. But just so far as that spirit of exclusiveness or bitterness survives, so far only is the fault hereditary. The fault does not lie in the want of unity of organisation—for the unity of the Church does not lie in unity of organisation, but in unity of faith and purpose—the fault lies in the mutual temper of the diverse organisations. For there may be an association of associations, as there may be an association of individuals; and just as Congregationalism is an association of congregations, each an independent and self-organised unit, so the Divine idea of the Church Catholic may be, and apparently is, an association of many associations of diverse types, each independent and self-organising, and gradually learning to co-operate for a common end. Among us one, the historic, Episcopalian, must necessarily be universal and inclusive; others will be partial and exclusive; but they may work together, and waste no energies in mutual disparagement.

It is not irreverent to suppose that it may be God's will to meet the diverse needs of our countrymen, as we see that He partially does meet them, by such diverse associations; and that what we should aim at is such a unity of spirit as will lead us to bind together these associations, by conferences, by communion, by united prayer and worship, cordially recognising our essential community of aim. That one of these should be territorial or parochial, so that none in the nation can be neglected, would seem to be highly desirable; and on this the main responsibilities *must* rest; but that allied organisations, to suit the vast diversity of type in a nation, should exist wherever there is a demand for them, not in a spirit of rivalry, but as co-operating in different parts of the field, would not seem open to objection. When we once regard as the fundamental principle of the Catholic Church of Christ, which includes all such bodies, that it is an association, with Christ as its Head, having a common faith and sacraments, for the spiritual education of man in the spirit and faith of Christ, I cannot see why one organisation should be jealous of another, why Nonconformists should wish to interfere with the Church of England, or why the Church of England should not welcome as allies the Nonconformist bodies that are working with the same end and the same faith, but under systems and formulæ different from our own.   The existence of such bodies is a sign of varied intellectual and spiritual activity; a sign of life; often the result of a living protest against deadness or error in the National Church. They too are members of the body of Christ, and all the members have not the same office.   Rivalry, as between the Churches of Macedonia and Achaia, may stimulate all to fresh efforts.   Vigorous life in one congregation often provokes another to good works.   But our rivalry must be in the attainment of our common end, and our end is service; not monopoly, not rule, but the service of man, the education of mankind, of our own congregations, of our poor and neglected population, our colonies, of the heathen world, in the faith and spirit of Christ.   Here is a sphere for noble rivalry.   Who will be the most devoted, the most self-sacrificing?

This is the spirit of co-operation, of association of bodies, as well as of individuals, in a common work; and this is the growing spirit of our time.   If you, young men, wish to be in the front, and not in the rear, in movements of spiritual activity, grasp this principle, and regard Nonconformists in this light.   Be as staunch churchmen as you please; you cannot, I believe, be stauncher than I am; but remember that the age of exclusiveness and bitterness is past, and the age of co-operation is begun.   We have begun to stand shoulder to shoulder in face of the tremendous problems which the Church of Christ has to meet in the present age.

Finally, to speak of the Catholic Church as an association will recall to us the qualification for membership, and

the sacrament of admission. That is, of course, the profession of faith in God the Father, God the Son, and God
the Holy Ghost, and in the historic basis of Christianity as
contained in the Apostolic Creed, and the rite of baptism
—baptism which places the child or the adult within the
association, there to be educated in the faith and spirit of
Christ, and there to share the duties of the members.
Every baptism of an infant imposes on the association a
new duty, for it is a pledge and promise that the child
shall be brought up to live as a child of God and member
of the kingdom of heaven. Every adult baptism or confirmation is the enrolment of a new acting member of the
great association. It will recall to us also the sacrament
of membership, the Holy Communion, in which we constantly renew our spiritual life, and exhibit our union with
one another in those sacred memories it perpetuates.

These seem to me to be among the immediate and
practical inferences from what I have stated as fundamental principles of the Church of Christ, viz. that it is a
Divine, self-organising association; or rather, to repeat
what I said before, these are the fundamental principles of
the Church of Christ, and we see that they are included
in the definition. We must now go on to consider, and
much more briefly, the rest of the principle,—that which
defines the aim of the Church. It is the spiritual
education of mankind in the spirit and faith of Christ.

And note, first, that by regarding it in this way, we
exclude some other ways of regarding the Church. For
example, it is not what the Jewish nation considered themselves to be, a body with exclusive privileges, within which
is safety, and without which, *sine dubio in æternum peribunt*,
"no doubt they shall perish everlastingly." Privilege
there is none, except the privilege of working with this
association for God, and the actual membership of the
kingdom of heaven on earth, in so far as we are worthy
workers, and the blessing and happiness and hopes that
come from working for the love of Christ. It is an
association which has blessings and privileges common to
all who belong to it. To be living in the faith and spirit

of Christ is, we hold, the highest actual blessing and
happiness that man is capable of; it is eternal life to
know the true God, and Jesus Christ, whom He hath sent;
it is a blessing which we cannot but wish to give to others.
It is a blessing which we do not believe terminates with
our earthly life.   But this is all.   This way of regarding
the Church of Christ cuts at the root of many a controversy and doubt; many a selfish way of regarding our
Church as an ark of salvation for ourselves.

Nor, again, is the Church of Christ the mere depository
of traditional and unalterable truth on speculative subjects.
The limit of what the Church has to teach is the spirit and
faith of Christ; and the faith of Christ is not identical
with the body of inferential theology which is the growth
of later ages, and the outcome and expression of their
piety and reverence.   The spirit of Christ is the spirit of
His life and words and thoughts; it is the mind to be like
Him, taking Him as the standard of perfect manhood, the
goal of the human race, the Divine ideal of humanity.
The faith of Christ is the belief that He is this, and that
He is Himself Divine; and that, by the self-sacrifice of
His life and of His death, He has truly redeemed man
from the death of sin; that His promise is being even now
fulfilled; that He is ever spiritually present in His Church,
and will be so to the end of the world.   It is the belief in
what He taught us of the fatherhood of God.   It is not a
system of philosophy, it is a disposition of mind and heart,
it is goodness and brotherhood, that it is the aim of the
Church of Christ to propagate in the world.   To spread
and deepen in our own selves, and in our society, by word
and by example and by prayer, the spirit and faith of
Christ, and consciousness of God's presence, and love to
our brethren, to subdue the sins of the flesh and the
spirit—these are the aims of the Church of Christ.

That an examination both of our Lord's teaching and
of St. Paul's will convince us that these practical aims will
not be attained only by aiming at practice, I need scarcely
suggest.   The work of the Church is not merely to extol
goodness, and to display Christ as a pattern of goodness.

It is not this that convinces and converts sinful men, and overcomes in them the power of sin. It is the awakening of their spiritual nature by the presentation to them of Christ as He was, human and yet Divine; it is the new sympathy and power that stirs in them. And hence the Church, as the guardian of the faith and spirit of Christ, is specially bound to protect and fence, from age to age, the modes of presentation, to our finite minds, of the person and work of Christ, and of the Holy Spirit in the Church. Such presentations are the Apostles' and Nicene Creeds, historic definitions of the faith, which prevent the work of the Church from degenerating into mere philanthropy, and, by being cut off from its springs, losing itself in desert sands. Hence the fundamental position assigned to them in the definition of the Church.

A subject like this must be looked at from many sides, and I think it may be useful to some of you if I try to examine and test this definition in a different way, and to show how the failure of individual churchmen in general to keep this idea of the Church clearly before them is the source of some of our present greatest difficulties. The two great problems now before the Church are to recover its lost hold on the intellectual classes, and to get a hold on the lowest and most uneducated classes. It is with these two classes it has most failed.

First, as to the intellectual classes. Every one knows that there is a widespread, tacit, and not wholly tacit, disbelief of much of the ordinary teaching of the Church of England, as it is popularly supposed to be. What is the meaning of it? How has it arisen? Shall we repeat the words of St. Paul, wholly misapplying them, and say "not many wise are called." He was stating a fact respecting the constitution of the Corinthian Church. There is no reason that education should make the reception of truth more difficult; it has not been proved, though we have made it a commonplace, that it does so.

The meaning is this: it is a reaction against the error of the Church in past ages, in pressing too exclusively Theoretic Truth; in regarding doctrine, instead of the spirit and faith of Christ, as the end and aim and test and foundation of the Church of Christ, instead of its means, its method, and the expression of its piety. For it is not the spirit and faith of Christ that men hate and disbelieve; it is a very different thing; it is the claim that the teaching members of the Church have so long made, that the interpretations and guesses and science of the past are the limit of the thought of the present. Men do not hate Christ; the spirit of that life is a vast power among those whom many churchmen thoughtlessly call unbelievers or schismatics; but men do hate and distrust and disbelieve some unwarrantable customs, inferences, and systems that have grown up in the Church, or have been extracted from the words of that Bible in which we see Christ. It is only by abating mistaken pretensions to limit thought and expression, and by seeing her true aim, that the Church of Christ and of England can win, as she ought to win, and might win, the hearty co-operation of the intellectual classes. I mean by the intellectual classes those who are more or less penetrated with the scientific spirit. This spirit compels them to regard man himself, and all that concerns him, as a subject of scientific investigation; but while it is not too much to say that the results of observation and investigation are inconsistent with much that has passed for theology, they are not in the least inconsistent with Christianity, or with the true aims and methods of the Church of Christ. The scientific spirit is the development of man's God-given faculties, and must be in itself good. It is only when unbalanced by higher faculties of the soul that it seems an evil. In itself it is a gift of God. Nothing which is uncertain and disputable can be the foundation of a church. It must rest on what is certain. And hence as knowledge grows the Church must widen itself to welcome and honour its most thoughtful sons.

And next as to the working classes, and specially those in our great cities. It is not true that the working man is averse to religion or to Christianity; it is a blunder and a slander to talk of the infidelity of the working man. Nothing can be more false, thank God for it; and yet the

working man does not altogether love the Church of
England or its clergy, as a rule.   How *should* he love the
Church of the eighteenth century?   And there is still
something left of the old eighteenth-century spirit.   It is
altogether too far from him.   It is because of the distance
from him of those who profess to be his teachers, and
because of their belonging to a class with which he has
little sympathy, and often also their dulness, their opinion-
ativeness, their doggedness, their unworthiness.   It is
because of the indifference of the professing Christians
of the upper and middle classes to the spiritual interests
of the poor.   How little there has been of the real spiritual
education of them—taking them as they are—in the spirit
and faith of Christ, apart from all other ends.   Though
something has been done, more must be done.   It is
necessary to live for their sake, to sacrifice all other aims,
to live among them, to work for them, humbly, loyally, for
Christ's sake.   Thus did Franciscans and Dominicans once
revive the motives and true aim of the Church by living in
brotherhoods among the poorest ; and this and similar
work has to be done again.   It is the plain obedience to
the most solemn of our Lord's sacramental commands :
"If I have washed your feet, ye ought also to wash one
another's feet."   There is no service so menial but that it
ought to be done in the name of Christ.   That is the
work of the Church, and that will win love and respect
wherever it is seen.

And now I would add that this definition and view of
the fundamental principles of the Church of Christ explains
to us the present movements of opinion, and shows us how
exceedingly hopeful they are.   For, first, it removes to their
proper plane all those questions which at various periods of
our life agitate us ; questions which belong to speculation,
not to faith ; to detail, not to principle.   We have been
perplexed about the authority of the Church, the inspiration of the Bible, the powers of the clergy, the nature of
the Sacraments, the nature of the future life, the explanation of the Atonement, the relation of faith and works, or
other points of speculative theology, and it may be even

about the mystery of Christ's incarnation and resurrection. We had thought that all these were, *in some defined form*, a part of faith, and that membership of a Church required our assent to certain definite but disputed opinions on these points.   But it is not so.   The essence of Church membership is the effort to live, and to help others to live, in the spirit and faith of Christ.   That alone is primary, and we can relegate many a perplexing question to a plane on which it ceases to distress us.   It is a great thing to put these questions on the second plane, the intellectual, instead of the first, the spiritual.   Now this is what is actually taking place; it is impossible not to notice this change in the importance attributed to life compared to views.   And it is a right and hopeful change.   It is a truer perspective of the Christian life.

Again, it teaches us the true position of the clergy. Service, and not rule, is the ideal of the Christian minister. He is not to exercise lordship over God's heritage, but to be amongst them as one that serveth.   Service is the Christian ideal for all men—to be the *servi servorum Dei;* the rich are but stewards of their wealth, the young of their strength, the talented of their ability, all to be used in the service of man, to establish and cement a brotherhood in the spirit and faith of Christ.   And if this is true of all, it is pre-eminently true of the clergy, that service is their ideal.

And once more, if this principle were grasped, it would guide us in the process of putting our Church on a much more national and popular basis than it now possesses. This transformation I hold to be absolutely necessary, if we are to remain the true National Church, and not become merely an Episcopalian and perhaps somewhat exclusive branch of the Church.   I believe that the people have lost the sense of ownership and of responsibility in the National Church, and that this can only be restored by giving the laity more defined rights by means of national and parochial as well as ruri-decanal, diocesan, and provincial councils.   A nation will not destroy what is truly its own.   You will see that this deduction follows immediately from our definition of the Church.

To turn to another and very important consequence of this definition. It will remind us of our sole primitive source of knowledge of the faith and spirit of Christ in the Bible. It is, therefore, for ever the duty of the Church to guard the Bible; and it is especially the duty of the clergy to do what the clergy promise to do at ordination, "to be diligent in reading the Holy Scripture, and in such studies as help to the knowledge of the same." No one who has read the service for the ordination of priests is likely to forget what stress is laid on being studious in reading and learning the Scriptures. It is not needful to enforce this now. You will readily understand that the study of the Bible is implied in the definition of the Church. And besides the Bible, we of the Church of England have another heirloom and treasure to guard, itself the product of eighteen Christian centuries. Even before the canon of the New Testament was closed, thoughts and aspirations and praise were assuming defined forms of expression, and establishing themselves in the liturgies of the Church. Perpetual additions and perpetual selection and revision made the liturgies of the mediæval Church, and have finally made our own Prayer-book, a treasure-house and record of the inspiration of the Church of Christ. It is not too much to say that as the Old Testament is the record and selection of the inspiration of the Jews in the ages before Christ, and the New Testament that of the age of Christ and the apostles, so the Prayer-book embodies the inspiration of prayer and praise and worship of the Christian centuries; it counteracts the influence of mere passing phases of opinion; it resists the partisan tendencies of individuals in every age.

Again, the perception of the true aim of the Church is freeing us from an unintelligent use of the Bible. For if we wish primarily to learn what is in very truth the faith and spirit of Christ, we cannot but welcome those critical and scientific researches, which are enabling us to see more clearly the real and historic Christ, among and through the mists that have gathered round Him. Our religion is not the Bible, but the God that is gradually

revealed in the Old Testament, the Christ that is revealed
and is the revealer in the New; and our one desire must
be and is increasingly to know that Christ as He truly
spoke and lived.   Now it is one of the happy results of
critical research that men's minds have been concentrated
by it on Christ; and it is undeniable that at this moment
that great Personality towers more above His disciples,
His biographers, His exponents, His Church, than ever
before, since the days of St. Paul and St. John.   Science
and criticism have not destroyed one outline of the figure
of the Divine Son of man nor made our faith vain, but
they have dissolved much that stood between us and
Him; they have enabled us to realise His Headship of
the Church, His relation to God and man.

And, lastly, the recognition of the true aim of the
Church throws a flood of light on all her methods; on her
services, and their inadequacy to meet all the needs of the
nation; on her ministers; her organisation; the use of her
wealth.   All is intended for one purpose only.   Especially
does this clear conception of the aims of a Christian Church
throw light on the nature of the Holy Communion.   There,
in memory of our Master, we offer and present ourselves,
our souls and bodies, to be a reasonable, holy, and lively
sacrifice to God; there we are assured that we are very
members incorporate in the mystical body of Christ, which
is the blessed company of all faithful people; there we
renew and draw closer our bonds of union with one another
and with Christ, and so get new strength for our arduous
and ceaseless work.

I do not doubt that this way of regarding the Church
will not at once approve itself to all minds.   To some it
will seem too mystical; the ideas of continuous life, of
Christ's presence, of the Holy Spirit's influence, will seem
indirect, imaginative, and, in a certain sense, false ways of
describing the ordinary continuity of motives of a mere
philanthropic or philosophic association.   With these
persons it would avail nothing to argue.   I can but say
that these images seem to me the truest representations of
the spiritual truths, and there we must leave it.   The

difference is not vital; in fact, it may be little more than verbal, if we could fully sound one another to the bottom, and speak—but that it is impossible to speak—without metaphor.

But to others the objection is of a different kind. The view will seem too earthly and practical, and their objection will perhaps take this shape: "Your definition and your remarks," they may say, "destroy my whole conception of the Church. The Church is as important a spiritual factor in the education of the world as the coming of Christ. Christ is the head, but the Church is the body. You resolve it into I know not what. The Church has absolute authority: your 'association' has only moral weight. The Church has had continuous Divine guidance; her councils, the consent of the Fathers, the long tradition of usage and belief, give a supernatural sanction to her dogma. All history," they say, "concurs in this view. The Church during all the centuries was no mere 'association'; it was a great, visible, embodied, supernatural power. Nonconformity is schism. This whole aspect of the Church is wanting in your view. The Sacraments are the channels of Divine grace: dogma is the divinely authorised expression of the Church's teaching. To treat it as an open question in any point is displeasing to God. You ignore all ecclesiastical history from the first century to the nineteenth." This is, of course, to exaggerate and misrepresent what I have said; but it points to a real difference of view. I hold that the view of the Church here put forward is largely unhistoric, imaginative, and unbalanced. But with one who has adopted this view it may be possible to reason exactly as St. Paul reasoned with the Galatians about the promise to Abraham and the law. No shock could be greater to the Jew than to learn that the law which he had regarded as primary, authoritative, everlasting, "as the one divinely inspired, perfect, and eternal thing on earth," was, in fact, secondary, educational, and temporary; that it came in as an after-thought; was given by the ministry of men; and could not disannul the direct revelation of God that came before. No shock could be greater than this.

Yet this, you will remember, is St. Paul's reasoning; and all the fifteen centuries of the law passed away, as the discipline of immaturity, to make way for the freedom of the Gospel, which he saw heralded to Abraham, and clearly announced in Christ. After that faith is come, we are no longer under a schoolmaster.

The parallelism is very striking. This is not the place to expound it; but I would suggest to any such thoughtful reader of this paper to weigh it well. He may find reason to think that, just as St. Paul had to go, as it were, behind the law which had trained the nation and preserved the religion for so many centuries, to find in the promise given to Abraham the true principle by which Judaism could be enlarged to embrace the new light of Christianity, and thus to treat the law as parenthetical, and not permanently authoritative, so we may gradually have to go *behind the Church* to find Christ Himself, who is greater and wider even than His Church.

And now I will conclude. There is nothing new in what I have been saying. But I do not think that it is sufficiently brought before young men that this is the absolute fundamental Church principle, and that all else is development, and is secondary, or erroneous, or matter of speculation. What I have said may give you, if you are thoughtful—and I do not care to speak to any who are not thoughtful—a logical and firm position, from which you can see your life and duty and conduct as Christian men. It will, I trust, help you to rise to a more adequate conception of what Christianity is and ought to be; it will help you to grow in grace and knowledge and faith and enthusiasm; help you to realise what we mean when we say that "the Church is the body of Christ." It will help you to realise what we mean when we say that our Church is essentially a supernatural society; that the aims of its association, the bonds and principles that unite it, the Holy Spirit that should animate every member of it, are not things of time, but ideas in the eternal and spiritual world.

It will help you to avoid being carried away by tem-

porary movements and phases of thought, even while you
sympathise with them.   The tendency of man towards a
legal and ritual and materialistic conception of religion and
the relation between God and man is very strong, and is
always reappearing in one form or another.   You will
remember how the Galatians went back to the law, unable
to maintain the spiritual level of the Gospel.   So it is now.
We find it difficult to maintain, even if by glimpses we see,
the high level of the revelation of Christ.   We seem compelled to bring it down from that sublime level, and formulate it in a thousand ways, in Churches and articles and
channels of grace; and we are very apt to mistake our
formula for the thing formulated.   Hence our disputes;
hence the difficulties of growth and of conciliation.   Who
will be the first to say—I have but fragments of the truth;
and I welcome those who have different fragments, if only
they love our Lord Jesus Christ, and try to live in His
faith and Spirit?

It will help us to assist in the new Reformation—a
reformation in which spiritual truths will be more precious,
while we shall feel that our expressions of them are less
adequate; and in which conduct and charity and heavenly
grace will be thought the truest evidence of the possession
by the soul of those spiritual truths, independently of the
selection of the intellectual form in which those truths may
be deemed least inadequately expressed.

It will give you, moreover, the soundest possible justification for a defence of the Church of England—viz. its
approximate realisation of this idea; and the surest possible method for defending it—viz. securing its greater
efficiency for the purpose of all Churches, the spiritual
education of the nation in the spirit and faith of Christ.
The thoughtful consideration of what I have said will give
you a new point from which things will be seen in truer
perspective.   And such a point is, I believe, much needed.

But history tells us how slowly changes of opinions are
worked out; and these currents of thought, which we can
clearly see among us, and which seem so completely justi-
fied in principle, will run side by side, with other currents

gradually modifying them, for many a long year, before they transform, as by a new reformation, the existing currents of opinion. Therefore, young friends, patience : patience and toleration. Patience with this old world of ours, which mostly comes right at last; patience with the narrow-minded, the positive, the noisy; toleration even of the intolerant, the one-sided, the silly. Work with men of all opinions—opinions are not the real test by which to judge men—work with men of all opinions if in their hearts they are striving to lead men to the spirit and faith of Christ, even if it be in ways you do not like. The work to be done is vast, almost appalling, of infinite importance to England and to Christendom. Courage, therefore, and patience and modesty and toleration and strenuous work, and an undying faith in the ever-presence of our Master.

ROMAN STOICISM AS A RELIGION [1]

I PROPOSE to say a few words this evening on Stoicism under the Empire, especially in its religious aspect, and its relation to modern thought. It is a very large subject, and touches on all sides on still larger subjects, and all I can give will·be but a sketch. Doubtless there are some here who are well acquainted with the period and writers I shall refer to. I hope they will recognise that I deal fairly with them. I do not doubt, however, that to many this period is almost a blank, and the writers little more than names. The only compliment they can pay me is to resolve, as they leave this room, that they will follow up my slight sketch by a study at first hand of some of the great Stoic writers of this age, or at any rate of some of the best books written about them.

The history of Rome in the first and second centuries of our era lies just outside the ordinary range of study. We read a little about the first few emperors and then we stop. The history seems to lose its dramatic unity and completeness: it becomes a confused mass of detail. Its literature, too, becomes crabbed or tawdry, artificial and uninteresting; originality and the sense of style are perishing; the only forms of literature that flourish are the two worst forms of it, rhetoric and satire—the two forms that mark loss of respect, first for others, and then for oneself. The revival of Greek literature in Rome fails to interest us. It is but an imitation. It dealt either in commonplaces or

[1] A lecture given at the Bristol Museum and Library, 2nd February 1886.

in fantastic and puerile subjects.   It had no root in realities.   The man that can read the literature of that period
must have an omnivorous appetite.   The period is therefore a blank in our ordinary education, and the writers are
known to us only by the first syllables of their names in
dictionaries and lexicons.

Yet in truth this period throws much light on our times.
Roman Stoicism was a religion.   I do not propose to trace
the growth of Stoicism, or point out the sources from which
Roman Stoicism was derived.   It had by this time absorbed
much that was characteristic of Platonism ; the thought of
God, and of likeness to Him being the aim of man, is
Platonic rather than Stoic in its origin, and this must be
remembered in what follows.   Roman Stoicism was by this
time more than a school of philosophy ; it was a religion.
It was not the rival of Christianity, and not its opponent.
It was a parallel to Christianity.   Stoicism was the religion
of the educated and philosophical classes ; and Christianity
was the religion of the lower and less philosophical.   Both
were alike militant.   The name of Stoicism as a religion
has perished ; it was not conquered ; it was absorbed as
Christianity grew upwards.   But the origins of Stoicism lie
deep in human nature and in circumstances, and Stoicism
has never perished.   It will not be difficult to detect Stoic
principles, and the circumstances from which they rise, by
looking round us in the England of this century ; it will
not be necessary to point the parallelism.   I am sure we
shall understand ourselves and our age the better for spend-
ing an hour with these great Stoics of the Empire, in that
marvellous period in which Rome, and Greece, and the
East were fused together ; for out of the law, the philosophy,
and the religion which they contributed arose Western
Christendom and Latin Christianity.   What Horace says
of the supremacy of Greek art and philosophy in Rome,
Græcia capta ferum victorem cepit, is not more true than what
Seneca says of the influence of Eastern religion, *victi vic-
toribus leges dedere*.

Stoicism was the real Roman religion at that time.   The
old mythological deities were totally discredited.   The old

Roman religion had ended in superstition among the
ignorant, and entire unbelief among the wise.   Silently
there grew up a faith and principle that became a religion,
although it was not called by that name.   The priests of
the old religion still celebrated mysteries and offered sacrifices on the altars ; processions of robed worshippers were
still seen in their temples, and a sort of traditional respect
was still paid to them and to their ritual; but the whole
region of conduct and thought lay outside the sphere of
the priests.   Perhaps it was for this very reason that it did
not interfere with conduct or thought, that men tolerated
it so long : it was not till an attempt was made to revive
its authority and its dogma that it was swept away in ridicule.   But men need guidance in conduct and thought ;
and those who can give it, and those only, become, whether
they are so called or not, the teachers of religion.   These
teachers were at that time the Stoics.

The decay of Paganism, and its subsidence into mere
superstition and ritual, was then one cause of the rise of
this new religion ; the turning inward of men's thoughts
was another.   The empire destroyed politics as a field
for human energies; the energies that found scope
under a republic were crushed by Cæsarism ; men turned
to philosophy ; and the Greek philosophy was now accessible to all, with its engrossing speculations on man and on
matter, on life and conduct, on the present and future of
the soul.   The great political crimes, the avarice, the dis-
sipation, the recklessness of life had the same effect.   The
Roman Stoicism, it must be remembered, that we are considering was that of the Rome of a Tiberius, a Caligula, a
Claudius, and a Nero ; the Rome which Tacitus, Suetonius,
and St. Paul have described ; "when virtue," as Tacitus
tells us, "was a sentence of death."   The unrest without
drove men in on themselves and on philosophy ; and of
all the sects of philosophy that sprang from the school of
Socrates, the one that had been formulated by Zeno and
Chrysippus was the most Roman in its nobleness.   Duty
was to be the lodestar of life, not pleasure.   That might
or might not be added : *non dux, sed comes, voluptas.*

It was by this time a religion; and a noble religion: and a few of the Christian fathers recognised it as a parallel religion to their own. It is true, as Justin Martyr says, that the Stoics could teach little or nothing about God, but in so far as a religion is separable from a theology, it cannot be denied that some of the fathers claimed the Stoic writers as allies. Jerome speaks of *our* Seneca— *Seneca noster;* and he claims them not in conduct and purity of life only, but in their positive teaching—*Stoici in plerisque nostro dogmati concordant,* he says. Seneca was quoted, as a Christian father might have been quoted, at the Council of Trent. Philosophers were freely and frankly compared with prophets. It is a 'comparatively modern thought to draw a broad line of separation between their inspiration and that of prophets or apostles. We have thus high authority for speaking of Stoicism as a religion.

But what do we mean by religion? I reply, that whether we describe it as morality tinged with emotion, or give it the higher definition of a sense of the presence of God who speaks in our conscience, and can be approached through prayer; whether we test it by its possessing a philosophical system and authorised dogmas and visible cultus; or by its giving rules of conduct and moulding the character; by its giving guidance in life and consolation in death; or if we judge it by its saints and missionaries and martyrs; its preachers or its literature; or by its organisa-tion as a Church; or if, on the other hand, we judge it by its failures, its base imitations, its overstrained dogmas, its hypocritical professors, and self-seeking ministers; in what-ever way we judge it, we shall satisfy ourselves that Roman Stoicism was a religion. It is this religion of Stoicism in which so much of our modern way of regarding life was anticipated to which I wish to direct you.

I have said that Roman Stoicism contained the element of morality tinged with emotion. The most systematic of all the Stoics of the Empire was Epictetus. This is no place to tell you of his life or works. He was, as his epitaph tells us, "a lame slave whom God loved." He was a contemporary of St. Paul. He left no writings, but

his friends treasured his conversation. You can get all
that remains of him, and learn all that is known about
him, in Bohn's invaluable series for a few shillings. You
will see that the morality he taught sprang from a deep
but suppressed fountain of emotion, a passion for virtue.
No isolated passages can prove this. It is the atmosphere
of the book. "He turned Theism from a speculative
dogma," says Conington, "into an operative principle, bid-
ding his disciples follow the Divine service, imitate the
Divine life, implore the Divine aid, and rest on the Divine
Providence." But I must give you one or two specimens.
"Those who would be Stoic tutors," he says, "must themselves be examples of what they teach, remembering that
their work is a ministry of God, a διακονία τοῦ θεοῦ. They
must possess neither house nor wealth, nor slaves, nor wife.
Have they not all they need? earth and sky and a cloak."
Or take this, "As most men are blind, ought not some
one to sing on their behalf a hymn of praise to God?
What can I do, old and lame as I am, except praise God?
This is my task: here I take my stand. This will I do
while I live, and I charge you all to do the same."

But if one can say this of Epictetus, who is usually so
unimpassioned, what shall we say of the Emperor Marcus
Aurelius? His whole life, and not his writings only, is
itself morality inspired by emotion. "The only thing
worth living for," he says—and he lived in the light of the
saying—"the only thing worth living for is to keep one's
soul pure and holy, and to do deeds that are useful to the
world. We ought to be like the vine that gives its crop
willingly, and then immediately prepares for another crop."
Again, in these meditations with his conscience, meant for
no mortal eye, and absolutely free from all trace of auto-
biographical vanity, he says to himself, "You do not yet
love men: it is not enough to pardon them; you must
love those who injure you. Against injury and ingratitude
God has given you the power of sweetness." It is of
course true that Stoicism taught men to suppress emotion,
or the manifestation of it. But it was none the less a
passion, an emotional passion, for duty and for the supremacy

of reason, that drove them to the suppression of all other emotions. That emotion must indeed have been at a white heat, however suppressed, which made men sacrifice all to their stern idea of duty, without fanaticism, and without hope of reward or immortality. The enthusiasm of brotherhood, "a reasoned and passionless philanthropy," as Lecky calls it, an enthusiasm which allowed of no emotional expression, took the place of all other emotions.

But it is not necessary to prove that Stoicism has this element of exalted and emotional morality. Let us see how it is also pervaded by a sense of God's presence. The passage I have already quoted from Epictetus illustrates how profoundly Epictetus felt the beauty of nature, and the necessity laid on us to recognise a Divine Presence in nature. But the Stoics felt still more deeply the presence of God in the human heart, and in human affairs. "No heart is good unless God be there," *nulla mens sine Deo bona est*, is one of Seneca's sayings. "When you have shut your door and darkened your room," says another Stoic, "say not to yourself you are alone. God is in your room." And we find Marcus Aurelius expressing the necessity for solitude, for self-examination, for standing face to face with God, for living close to Him, for banishing books and imaginations and passions, and entering into the secret chamber of his soul, and seeking to meet God. "What is it to me," he says, "to live in a universe devoid of God?" No words can convey the impression left by his writings. The God of the Stoics was one who could worthily be honoured by moral worship alone; sacrifices were a mere bribing of the gods: unworthy prayers were an insult to them: the gods knew best what to give: the most worthy prayer was, Juvenal tells us, for the *mens sana in corpore sano*, a sound mind in a sound body. "Ask," says Seneca, "for a good mind, for good health both of mind and body." "Ask," says Persius, "for

> Compositum jus fasque animi, sanctosque recessus
> Mentis, et incoctum generoso pectus honesto—

a mind set on duty to God and man, purity in the secret

soul, and a heart steeped in nobleness and virtue : I know
no worthier prayer of man—

> Be thine a mind that's equable and whole,
> A shrine of purity within the soul ;
> Truth, reverence, justice, learn to exercise ;
> Fill thy whole heart with human sympathies ;
> Offer no gold, no liturgies prepare ;
> A pious heart alone commends to heaven thy prayer."

But, perhaps, the most truly Stoic utterance on prayer is
due not to a Roman Stoic but to Emerson.   "Not
thanks," he says, "nor prayer seem quite the highest or
truest name for our communication with the infinite, but
glad and conspiring reception.   It is God in us which
checks the language of petition by grander thoughts."

Stoicism had also a philosophical basis and a dogmatic
system.   God was to a Stoic the name of that Universal
Reason of which our minds are a fragment ; Nature, in its
harmony and wisdom and order, was a revelation of God.
Stoicism thus tended to become an abstract Theism.   The
duty of man consisted in conforming to this revelation of
God which is contained in our reason and in nature ;
impiety consisted in the forsaking that law.   And so there
sprang up in the highest Stoic mind a passionate and
enthusiastic love of the order of the world, which we
should call God—a love for goodness and virtue.   It does
not appear that the problems of free will and fatalism, of
prayer and providence, agitated them much : they seem to
have been lost in the sublimity of the thought of the
Divine order.   A good Stoic was almost necessarily an
optimist.   For the propagation and firm grasp of their
faith they saw the need, as we do, of clear definition and
positive dogma.   But their dogmas were few, and were
rather what we should call broad principles than articles
of faith.   They may almost be reduced to a belief in the
providence of God, and the duty of trusting to Him ; that a
man's happiness is in himself, and in virtue, and not in
circumstances ; and in the brotherhood and equality of
men.   These, soundly taught, would inspire men with the

love of the good. They would guide them, they said, as the stars guide the sailors.

But round these principles there grew up metaphysical and materialistic dogmas, an elaborate system of what we should call casuistry, which hampered the teachers. Take such a dogma as this, "that the wise man is always rich and always happy." It sounds sublime; but what could they reply when pressed. "Never poor?" say you, "but you admit he may have neither food nor clothing. Always happy? and yet he may be tortured to death." The Stoics were hard pressed to maintain the literal truth of their exaggerated dogma. Seneca was constantly embarrassed by the dogmas of his school. His whole writings are a struggle between his good sense and the fetters he had imposed on it: and to this is attributable in part their unattractiveness. There are quibbles and distinctions which remind us of scholastic philosophy and theological works, vain and wearying questions which occupy a part of his teaching. He is a professed teacher, and therefore he cannot evade them. But it is his good sense and good principles, the human nature below his in dogmatic system, which makes his letters so valuable; and as for these quibbles, he declares he takes no pleasure them. *Illud toties testor hoc me argumentorum genere non delectari*—nay, he is bold enough to laugh at them—*libet ridere ineptias Graecas.* They are useless, they do not make men better, but only more learned. *Quid ista res me juvat? fortiorem facit? justiorem? temperatiorem? non faciunt bonos ista sed doctos.* True wisdom is open to all, not hidden in scholastic phrases. *Aperta res est sapere.*

Hence dogma and system are not the strong side of Stoicism; and it was not the side that attracted the Romans. It was the Greeks who made a theology and a system. The Romans looked for organisation and a working basis for conduct. This was the strong side of Stoicism. "Life is a rough business," *non delicata res est vivere*, is the thought at the bottom of the Stoicism of Rome. What men needed was to be taught how to live

well, and how to die well. "Up to the time of old age,"
says Seneca, "I studied the first ; in old age the second : "
*ante senectutem curavi ut bene viverem, in senectute ut bene
moriar.* To help men to this they felt that more than
dogmas were necessary ; men needed examples, authority,
help, special guidance. Men must have a guide. *Sit ergo
aliquis custos,* and especially the advice of men who are
sympathetic, experienced, wise. All teaching was to be
turned immediately into practice ; turn words into deeds :
quæ fuerunt verba, sint opera : let all which you read react
on character ; *quidquid legeris ad mores statim referas.*

Hence the Stoic teachers were constantly consulted in
cases of conscience. Seneca had a correspondence like
that of Pusey or Kingsley. The young sceptic, the sensitive doubter, the hardened sinner (the *veteranus*), the
young guardsman, the Roman official, such men as you
meet every day, consulted him as to their sorrows, their
doubts, their sins. Where was the cure for the fierce
unrest of the soul, the unhappiness of life ? There was no
question of morals or casuistry that did not come before
these Stoic teachers. And we can see how wise were for
the most part their replies.

There is as subtle a dissection of human motive, as
great a care against self-deception, as you could find in
the writings of any priest. Take the warnings given by
Seneca against ostentatious retirement, itself a sort of
vanity, chosen that people might talk of you : *Jactandi
genus est nimis latere,* he says : it is only a way to feed
vanity. *Absconde te in otio,* he says ; *sed et otium tuum
absconde.* Let there be no affectation : differ from others
in greater devotion to duty : *eadem sed non eodem modo
facere :* enjoy society without yielding to luxurious habits,
sine luxuriâ agere festum diem. Or take the question of the
right use of wealth : Ought a man to give it up ? "No,"
they reply, "it is a weakness to be unable to use wealth ;
use it rightly." "Possess riches, but let them not possess
you." "Frugality of soul does not exclude elegance. It
is excellent to use silver as though it were earthenware."
"Hold riches so loosely that you will not mind if they

take wings and fly away." Marcus Aurelius was at once emperor and Stoic, and no man ever so shrewdly watched his own heart to prevent its being corrupted by power and wealth. His religion was the service of man: not in a spirit of Stoic austerity, but of Stoic piety and goodness. In his meditations are no petty scrupulosities, no reveries. They are always the thoughts of a man, and a great man, and a man who controlled great affairs. He was the emperor more even than the philosopher. There was nothing in his reign to justify the saying of Frederick the Great—"If I had a country to punish I would hand it over to philosophers." His one principle was to do his duty where God had placed him; to be like a soldier at his post. Perhaps the principles of the man are best expressed in this sentence: "It is not for himself that the gods make a man a king, but only that he may be the people's man. To them he owes all his toil and his love, and he is worthy of royalty in so far only as he forgets himself to sacrifice himself to the public good." These are noble words, the very embodiment of Roman Stoicism : but they are not the words of Marcus Aurelius; they are the words of Fénélon in his *Télémaque*, and the words which Louis XIV. never forgave, because he felt that they were aimed at him.

The Stoic religion was as sincere in death as in life. Religion usually occupied the thoughts of the dying. It was mentioned as a sort of shock to the feelings of society, when Petronius, as Tacitus tells us, died without such thoughts or conversation. *Nihil de immortalitate animæ, et sapientium placitis.* The hope of an after-life was rather an aspiration than a dogma; and the tone in which it was spoken of varies. Sometimes it is the longing of despair. "How can it be," says Marcus Aurelius, "that the gods who have ordered things so well should have neglected this one point, that men of virtue who have lived with God during their life, and have been loved by God for their piety, should have no hope after death, but perish for ever?" At other times it was a great hope; and they dwelt on the purifying and ennobling effect of the hope. *Dabam me spei tantæ*, writes Seneca, *nihil sordidum animæ subsidere sinit.*

Their teaching about suicide is well known. They held it to be within a man's right to retire from life when he chose. But it was not to be from cowardice, but from principle. A man must not run away from life; he must withdraw from it. *Non fugere debet e vitâ sed exire.* There are few more touching scenes in history than the voluntary death of Stoic men, and even Stoic women, who preferred death to dishonour. Arria, to encourage her husband, who shrank from death, stabbed herself mortally before his eyes, and handed him the dagger with the words, "See, it does not hurt!" Her daughter, wife of Thraseas, died with him voluntarily in that reign of terror; and the grand-daughter Fannia, wife of Helvidius, fell not less nobly by her own hand. There might be made a long list of such Stoic heroes and heroines. That religion must have had some power, even if we deem it mistaken, that could nerve them to that last deed. But others, again, thought it nobler not to forsake the post at which God had placed them, and repeated the well-known words of Socrates. Such was the Stoic emperor, who only permitted himself to pray, "Come quickly, Death, lest I forget myself at the last."

Judged, then, by its effect on conduct and character, by its giving guidance in life and consolation in death, you will see that Stoicism cannot be spoken of as other than a religion. It was also a discipline, a religious training of youth. The best families in Rome had Stoic tutors for their sons. The tutor was attached to the house, as a chaplain might be. A Roman nobleman writes of "his philosopher," *philosophus suus*, exactly as he might write of "his doctor" or "his secretary." Seneca had the unenviable post of being tutor to Nero. The most beautiful and the typical example of the Stoic education of youth is that of the poet Persius. May I venture to hope that some of you will read this in some detail for yourselves: the Clarendon Press edition, by Conington and Nettleship, contains all that is wanted,—introduction, text, translation, and notes. Here I can but indicate its outlines. He was of a noble and religious family, carefully brought up by his mother till he was twelve; and then taught by a grammarian and scholar till he was sixteen. At sixteen he was placed under Cornutus, one of the leading Stoic tutors of the time. To him Persius, in his 5th Satire, pays the most graceful and the most sincere compliment ever paid by pupil to master. It was a devoted and reverential attachment. Every care was taken to surround the young Stoic noble with generous and worthy friends, and with men of genius. Among his friends we find Cæsius Bassus, the lyric poet, who edited the poems of Persius on his too early death; Lucan, the young Spaniard, the poet of Stoicism; Seneca; and noblest by far, Thraseas, the finest example of reasonable Stoicism, of whom Tacitus says that he was "virtue itself: gentle, modest, considerate; fearing, as he said, to hate vice too much lest he should hate men:" holding so unique a position in the senate that his silence was as much commented on, and carried as much weight as his words. There too was Helvidius, obstinately upright as he is pictured to us, *recti pervicax*, inaccessible to fear; the only fault that could be imputed to him was the love of honour, that last infirmity of noble minds, *quæ etiam sapientibus novissima exuitur*. In the same society were Stoic women also, noblest of women, who seem to have been raised up for the honour of their sex, just at the time that the Messalinas and Agrippinas were disgracing it. Pliny writes of one of them, the mother of the wife of Thraseas, as one might write of some sweet, motherly lady now. "How pleasant she was, how agreeable! We venerated her, but we loved her too, and this cannot be said of many: mother and daughter, I cannot tell which I loved most." Such was the education provided for a young Stoic noble: and Persius was worthy of it. We have only his youthful poems, harsh in style, but full of noble thoughts and true religion. He is described as most winning and gentle in manner, as modest as a girl, and as beautiful, *morum lenissimorum, verecundiæ virginalis, formæ pulcræ.* The only parallel I can find for him is one who, like

Persius, died young, loved for his genius and his sanctity alike by young and old, rich and poor, Arnold Toynbee.

But did Stoicism inspire men with an enthusiasm to propagate its creed? Did it send out preachers and missionaries? Had it any gospel to preach to the poor? Yes, to some extent, though this is the weakest side of Stoicism, and one of the reasons why it failed to establish itself as a universal religion. Stoic preachers tried persistently to reform men. Seneca bids them never despair of a man, in the tone of a bishop writing to a young clergyman: persevere even when it seems hopeless, he says, *in ipsâ desperatione extrema remedia tentes.* Nothing more excites his wrath than Stoic preachers who care more for their own reputation for eloquence than for the moral reform of their congregations. "What!" he says, "try to be admired when sick people come to be cured? offer words to people who want help? Give us light: advise us how to face life: speak to me of piety and justice and temperance: give me none of your rhetorical tricks: help me to some pure resolution: teach me some lesson: reform me, or at any rate make reformation possible: *aut sanior domum redeam aut sanabilior.*" Unquestionably there was a moral propagandism that emanated from the Stoic school; they popularised philosophy and the preaching of virtue. One of the Christian fathers, Lactantius, urging the duty of preaching to all, quotes as an example the Stoics who taught philosophy, he says, even to slaves and women,— *qui etiam servis et mulieribus philosophandum esse dicebant.* "Strange and shocking would it be," said Musonius Rufus, "if the tillers of the ground were incapacitated from philosophy, which is really a business of few words, not of many theories."

There were Stoics in the latest age of Stoicism, when Stoicism, however, had lost some of its characteristics, who went about like mendicant monks and preached from village to village, like Wesley. Dio Chrysostom was an eclectic, with a leaning to Stoicism. He preached on the confines of the Roman empire in Scythia, in Asia, Egypt,

Rome, and Greece. He was as famous a preacher as Whitefield. When he went to see the Olympic festival at Greece, he was recognised by the crowd and compelled to preach to them, just as Spurgeon might be invited to preach at the Derby. He took for his text Phidias's statue of Jupiter, as St. Paul took the altar dedicated to the Unknown God, and dilated on the excellences of the Divine qualities. Stoic preaching was the forerunner of Christian preaching. They took texts from Homer and other poets as we take texts from the Bible. Stoicism became a religion, not a philosophy. It is obvious, I may remark, how this preaching prepared the way for Christianity. It accustomed people to listen. An apostle of religion was not an unfamiliar sight.

And as there was the reality, so also there were plenty of shams among Stoic and Cynic preachers. There were scandals among the professed Stoic preachers, men who professed indifference to wealth, and yet courted the rich, and accumulated money; men who professed virtue and lived gross lives. There were popular preachers, too, who assumed a peculiar dress and manner, who were toadied and half-worshipped by Roman ladies, and who were pronounced by men to be untrustworthy, arrogant, and even voluptuous. For want of matter they studied the art of rhetoric, and could speak by the hour, with the loud applause of admiring audiences; and yet shrewd men asked in vain what it was that they had said. No one could remember, except that they were beautiful words, *pulchra verba*. And before long fresh abuses grew up, such as Juvenal tells of—sham priests of Cybele, with long white locks, imposing penances, getting into houses and leading away silly women, who could not distinguish the man from the charlatan. No preparation or learning was required. As Lucian says, the cost of the outfit of a preacher was small; a gown, a beard, a good deal of dirt, and a book under the arm, formed the stock-in-trade of these impostors, who drove a thriving trade; for religion had become a business which those who failed in anything else might take up.

You cannot fail to have been struck by the parallelisms

between Stoicism and Christianity, not in one respect only, but in many. I have not pointed the parallelisms, and shall not do so now. It will be more profitable to consider two or three questions that are suggested by this parallelism, and which bear on our modern problems of society and religion.

It is plain that the Stoic religion contained not only much that was fine, but also much that seems fundamental in religion. It was the final protest of the best Romans, at the time of a general tendency downward, in favour of a pure and positive faith in God : the very essence of Stoicism is the intimate relation of man to that which is "not ourselves." God is close to you, with you, in you, *tecum est*, *intus est*, writes Seneca. It almost startles us to see him writing that the Holy Spirit is in our hearts, *Sacer intra nos Spiritus sedet*, and watches all we do. Stoicism aimed, moreover, at a lofty disinterested morality and virtue, and it aimed at realising the brotherhood of man. These are indeed fundamental teachings. They constitute human duty. The detailed comparison made by Bishop Lightfoot between St. Paul and Seneca in an appendix to his edition of the Epistle to the Philippians will amply justify this statement.

It is plain that Stoicism was a most valuable reaction against the vices and superstitions of the time, and therefore a most valuable ally of Christianity. The question is, Why did it fail? Why did so noble a religion, enthusiastically held and propagated by the best men in Rome, fail; and Christianity, which was then working chiefly, if not entirely, among the poor and ignorant, succeed?

It did not fail with the noblest. It is difficult to see that Marcus Aurelius could have been a better man had he been a Christian. "If there is anywhere," says Niebuhr, "an expression of virtue, it is in the heavenly features of Marcus Aurelius." He would have been far happier had he been a Christian, far more hopeful, far more creative, far more spiritual ; the permanent gloom and isolation in which he strove cheerfully to do his duty would have been

dispelled by the revelation of a Father in heaven; but
better, in the sense of more moral, more unselfish, more
nobly principled, he could scarcely have been.   It is a
character so perfect that one involuntarily speaks of him
as one speaks of a saint.   There is nothing in him of Stoic
harshness; there is perfect gentleness, humility, charity,
consideration for others; nothing of affectation, or of
posing before the world or himself, even in his most
private meditations; instead of this sham humility, there
is the most entire simplicity.   He was a philosopher, without the least trace of the pedant or the doctrinaire; he
never tried to make men good by imperial edicts, but was
content "to push matters forward a little in the direction
of virtue and humanity"; he is on his guard, as he tells
us, against "those wretched politicians who affect to treat
affairs like philosophers"; he never gives way to weariness,
or misanthropy, or contempt for his fellow-men.   He is
the most even-minded of men; his thoughts are always
those of a man of affairs, always practical, and always with
the sense of being at his post, discharging a service under
an ever-present Divine influence.   And it was a Stoic education and the Stoic religion, ennobled as Stoicism then
was by its Platonism, that made him what he was.   It
taught him to do right simply because it was right.   It
cannot then be said that it failed with the noblest, and yet
it failed on the whole.

There are many secondary and co-operating causes of
this failure; and we will look at them first.   Stoicism set
before men an unlovable ideal, which was, in fact, a
monster that did not and could not exist; it served for
discussion, but not for imitation; it was a lay figure, not a
man.   A consistent Stoic was unlovable, and even odious.
Cato the elder was conspicuous and consistent in his
inhumanity to slaves.   Brutus was equally consistent, and
starved some of his debtors to death.   And, in fact, the
Stoics were attractive and influential in proportion as they
varied from their ideal.   Some of them were aware of this
weakness.   Seneca writes that he continues to try and
persuade himself that the Stoic ideal is admirable, but that

he has not succeeded. *Suadeo adhuc mihi ista quæ laudo, nondum persuadeo.*

Stoicism could not help the weak, the fallen, the sinful, and broken-spirited. At best it was only the religion of the strong. It gave no happiness. The most touching characteristic of the meditations of Marcus Aurelius is the proof they everywhere give that he found no happiness. It lacked sweetness, the chief element in attracting men to a better life; it made little appeal to imagination, to love; it was a school for heroes only. It mistook hardness for courage; and it regarded with a sort of fatalism the benighted and suffering and sunken millions. They lay outside its area. It had no message for them. They must first of all rise, somehow, out of their degraded condition, and then perhaps Stoicism might do something for them. Of undying hopefulness and self-sacrifice, even for the most degraded of human creatures, Stoicism knew nothing. For ordinary human nature there was no deliverance from evil and the power of sin in Stoicism.

Another element in its failure was its want of popular dogma. A clear and defined nucleus of principles, of what is to be believed—a creed, in fact—is essential to the vitality of a religion. The Stoics had principles, but they were too abstract for the mass of men; they needed a concrete shape, and this the philosophers could not give them. A religion that is to command the masses must rise among the masses and adopt their modes of thought. I do not say their thoughts, but their *modes* of thought. It must express the loftiest and most divinely inspired thoughts of man, but in a language and mode that the unphilosophic majority can grasp. And in this Stoicism failed and Christianity succeeded.

And again it failed in organisation. The organisation of a religion is not an unimportant part of it. There was no authority to restrain unlicensed and ignorant professors of Stoicism. No learning, no philosophy were necessary. Morality was all; and anybody with a glib tongue, and nothing better to do, could talk about morality; and so the teaching of Stoicism fell into the hands of Greek rhetoricians, in an age when to be a Greek was synonymous with being a liar.

Still I believe these are all secondary causes of failure, important and very instructive to us, but still secondary. Christianity has also often been presented in very unlovable forms; it too has often lacked sweetness, and often failed from disorganisation, and from the ignorance and unworthiness of its ministers; and yet Christianity has won, and is winning, its victories in spite of these disadvantages which it shares with Stoicism. We must look farther yet.

The causes seem to me to be three. One was that Stoicism took a low and imperfect view of evil. This arose from its materialistic and pantheistic conception of God. Although Stoics thought that man's spirit was Divine in nature, they did not feel deeply that evil was a breach of the Divine law. Vice was a mistake that lowered the dignity of man, not a sin that incurred the wrath of God. Now there may be a philosophical point of view, from which these two statements may be regarded as identical, as the same truth looked at from the human or the Divine side; but there can be no question at all but that they will seem different to all but a few philosophers, and that the motive power is carried by the Christian way of stating the truth. But not only is the thought of sin so vastly more moving, and so much truer to human conscience in general than the thought of mistake, but it also involves its great correlative thought of forgiveness and redemption springing from the *love* of God. This is indeed "deep answering to deep"; and here in the thought of the love of God for the weak and sinful is an inspiring truth which, however expressed, is never present in Stoicism and never absent from Christianity.

Another cause is the absence from Stoicism of any sure and certain hope of an after life. The difference has been expressed by saying that the Stoic had fortitude, but the Christian had faith. The exceptional Stoic could face death with unaverted eye, but even the ordinary Christian could welcome it with joy. It was this thought which filled the Christian missionaries with a different spirit from their

Stoic parallels: they had verily good tidings which they burned to impart to all the world, and which enabled them to face all dangers in so imparting it. It was not a mere aspiration, which, as Seneca said, while it was entertained, would not allow any sordid thought to rest in the soul, but it was an absolute conviction; and there is all the difference in the world between an aspiration and a conviction.

But the greatest cause lay in the personality of Jesus Christ. To this Stoicism had no parallel. It would be out of place to speak here in any other way than I am now doing; I have only now to point out that, however inadequate was the conception of Christianity entertained by the uneducated dwellers in Rome, however much Christians exposed themselves to satire for credulity and superstition, they had a power here, in that ideal and Divine life, which no other religion even professed to have. It was "the Galilean who conquered," as one of the Roman emperors confessed. All else, the new motive given for duty, the new power of love in the world, the making brotherhood not a sentiment but a reality, the replacement of selfishness by self-devotion, the replacing of egotism by humility, independence by trust, and fate by providence—all this is involved in the personality and revelation of Jesus Christ. This was the fundamental difference, and gave the victory to Christianity.

And now it is time to conclude. I will do so without attempting to draw inferences from the past and to apply them to the present. I have shown you, I trust, in how many points Roman Stoicism touches modern thought. And I will express my conviction that if we would rightly understand the Stoic element, no inconsiderable or valueless element, in our modern semi-religious, semi-philosophical way of regarding life, we shall do well to study what a noble religion Stoicism was at its best under the Empire, and to study why, nevertheless, it perished.

We shall see how closely a religion of Stoicism is akin to a religion of humanity, in its weakness as well as in its strength; and how both tend to pass into Cynicism. I am sure that the study will be a help to all thoughtful persons, and will send them back with fresh appreciation and conviction to the study of the records of Christianity and its essential principles; and with fresh faith and enthusiasm to the effort to purify Christianity from its superstitious accretions, and realise it in something of the sublime simplicity in which it existed in the mind of its Founder as the kingdom of God. We shall see that Christianity has absorbed most of what is best in Stoicism; and that it contains what Stoicism, ancient and modern, does not contain, an impulse, a hope, a power which has made it prevail over all the great opposing movements of the human mind in the past, and will assuredly prevail over all similar movements in the present. *Vicisti Galilæe.*

THE END

Printed by R. & R. CLARK, *Edinburgh*